Numbers and Narratives in Bangladesh's Economic Development

Rashed Al Mahmud Titumir

Numbers and Narratives in Bangladesh's Economic Development

palgrave
macmillan

Rashed Al Mahmud Titumir
Department of Development Studies
University of Dhaka
Dhaka, Bangladesh

ISBN 978-981-16-0657-1 ISBN 978-981-16-0658-8 (eBook)
https://doi.org/10.1007/978-981-16-0658-8

This Palgrave Macmillan imprint is published by the registered company Springer Nature Singapore Pte Ltd.
The registered company address is: 152 Beach Road, #21-01/04 Gateway East, Singapore 189721, Singapore

To my son
Muharrir Munir Arshad Titumir
wishing you a life in a happy Bangladesh

Preface and Acknowledgements

This is a book of evidence: throughout the chapters, the numbers are put to prove causal relationships. The variables and indicators, shown in frameworks, construct narratives. This allows to offer a reality check on the current state of Bangladesh's economy in the light of its stability, transformability and sustainability conditions.

The book is also aspirational. In assessing Bangladesh's development trajectory as the country envisions to reach the status of a developed country by 2041, the book delves into the parameters of these three conditions. The stability condition measures whether Bangladesh's economy meets the minimum standards to be on the rungs of the middle-income group countries as per the agreed international criteria. The transformative condition, articulated in terms of attaining the yardsticks of East Asia, reveals that the economy has a longer path to travel. Finally, the sustainability condition, assessed in terms of the OECD benchmarks, divulges the indices of progress that Bangladesh has to beat to attain the status of a developed country.

It is crucial to consider the conditions for sustainability of the growth and improvement of performance in real sectors, an expanding financial sector, and reductions in poverty and inequality, in order to ensure that the gains are long-standing. The path to sustainability starts with making the advances in economic indicators balanced and coordinated, leading to conditions for stability. Simultaneously, the COVID-19 context in particular has shed light on the risks and fragilities facing the economy, which may hinder the capacity to create a new system when ecological, social or economic structures render the current system unsound, hence requiring corrections for transformability.

In Bangladesh, there is a lack of endeavours that explores development by drawing variables of politics and economics to investigate a causal relationship. The absence has caught somewhat misplaced lamentations. This is often termed as a "development surprise", "development paradox" or "development conundrum", given the absence of good governance. Pointing out the "high" rate of growth in Bangladesh's Gross Domestic Product (GDP), on the contrary, a section is disseminating a belief of the precedence of economic growth even without functioning institutions. They often assert that economic development is more important than an inclusive political system. The foundation of the project lies on the comprehension that such illusory propositions are backed neither by solid theoretical footing nor by empirical validation. It is therefore, imperative to undertake a critical scrutiny and debunk these claims by examining the political economic dynamics and focus on the patterns of growth in the last decade, which has been validated further and not restricted by the COVID-19 context.

The book, thus, investigates the numbers and narratives through analysing the necessary and sufficient conditions for development. The necessary conditions imply an incisive inquiry into the factors of economic growth—land, labour, capital and technology while the sufficient condition is captured in terms of political settlement. The project interjects these variables on themes such as growth, agriculture, the manufacturing industry, the financial sector, health, education, poverty and inequality.

The book, therefore, presents an understanding of the state of Bangladesh's economy that demystifies the myths on Bangladesh, helps international and national policymakers grasp the ground reality to set its course for appropriate action, and equips the academia and the policymakers with much-needed rigorous independent analysis on Bangladesh's contemporary development.

I am grateful to the Palgrave Macmillan's two anonymous referees for their incisive comments for the development of the book.

I wish to express my gratitude to my "never saying no" team at the Unnayan Onneshan—Md. Shah Paran, Mostafa Walid Pasha, Wahid Haider, Fahim Shahriar and Adrina Ibnat Jamilee Adiba—who provided brilliant research assistance. Parbon Khan from Toronto deserves special mention for the pre-review copy-editing assistance.

Two women - mother, Rawshan Ara Begum and wife, Munira Nasreen Khan – both teachers – are my sources of inspiration and have been standing by my side, in sickness and health, in joy and in sorrow. My father—Prof. Dr. M Arshad Ali—has never missed the chance of reading my manuscript at first. I am grateful to my youngest brother, Rashed Al Ahmad Tarique, who made the book accessible through painstaking copy-editing, despite his busy life in Melbourne. With my three brothers and one sister and their families—I have been laughing, crying and growing with you in mind and spirit.

I am alone responsible for any errors, inadequacies and omissions still remaining in the book.

Dhaka, Bangladesh
December 2020

Rashed Al Mahmud Titumir

Introduction

As this book is taking shape, a global crisis facing the entirety of the world's population has been brought on by the contagion of the coronavirus pandemic which grapples the world economy by enforcing nearly 90 per cent of it under some form of lock-down, disrupting global and national supply chains, curtailing consumer expenditure and putting millions out of employment.

The Bangladesh economy has been witnessing signs of distress well before the strike of the pandemic as jobless growth, slowdown in poverty reduction, decline in export–import and unfulfilled targets of tax revenue collection were rampant, despite having higher economic growth. Economic growth in recent periods has largely resulted from labour migration from rural areas to urban cities and abroad. Migration of labour has increased the consumption expenditure. Investment and real wage growth remain stagnant. Remittances, constituting the core of rural consumption expenditure, though, had been declining prior to the pandemic, and is expected to plummet after cohorts of migrant workers have returned home from countries in Europe and the Middle East. The agriculture sector has been lagging behind in terms of technological advancements and increased agricultural input prices. The disruption in supply chains of agricultural produce, due to the shutdown of transportation, will dampen future production incentives for farmers. Simultaneously, the manufacturing sector has transformed into a one-sector industry tainted by low productivity, diminishing competitive advantage and a lack of product diversification, and an eventual fall in export volume. This may in turn worsen economic inequality that had been escalating. The pandemic has thus exposed the frailties in the building blocks of an unstable and unsustainable economy.

At the onset of the COVID-19 crisis, the economic aftermath stretched far and wide, impacting both the rural and urban economies, disproportionately the marginalised communities—households vulnerable to poverty, returnee migrant workers, the informal sector, women, children and the elderly population. Fiscal support provided to cope with the systemic shock induced by the pandemic is likely to favour larger industries than small businesses, and more integrated communities at the core than at the periphery due to faults in documentation. In an economy where every group copes differently with the same systemic shock, inequality will worsen and well-being levels may take a hit for prolonged periods of time. Unemployment is likely to increase, particularly in the informal sector because of a lack of targeted stimulus packages and also legally binding employment contracts. Altogether the COVID-19 crisis will exacerbate the existing fractures in the economic and social structures, feeding into the norms and values, established by institutions and political settlements, of rapid accumulation of resources.

Introducing the Framework

Remarkable strides in economic growth in the Bangladesh economy, often dubbed as the "fastest growing", has been a widely celebrated achievement in recent years. For a country marred with climate vulnerabilities, weak governance, permeating inequality and ubiquitous disregard for the social contract, Bangladesh may, in fact, be culturing an imbalance in its macroeconomic indicators that poses doubts in the quality and durability of this growth. In this decade, export earnings have been on the decline, the apparel industry has been losing its competitive edge in the global market, agriculture continues to employ most of the labour force despite being a less productive sector, private investment remains inadequate for capital formation, and the education sector is yet to resolve skill mismatch and foster innovation.

This book therefore addresses the numbers and narratives that help analyse the necessary and sufficient conditions of the development of Bangladesh's economy. The necessary conditions imply the factors of economic growth—land, labour, capital and technology—while sufficient conditions include class, power, political settlement, formal and informal institutions. Exploring these conditions as well as the numbers and narratives, this book attempts to expose the reality of a "perfectly" growing economy.

In addition, it is crucial to also consider the conditions for sustainability of the growth and improvement of performance in real sectors, an expanding financial sector, and reductions in poverty and inequality, for the gains to be long-standing. Sustainability conditions focus on living in harmony with nature—supporting large-scale green initiatives in industry, addressing climate vulnerabilities and enabling the capacity for self-insurance against systemic shocks.

The path to sustainability starts with making the advances in economic indicators balanced and coordinated, leading to conditions for stability. Stability conditions ensure that advances made in one indicator is supported and stabilised by similar strides of progress in related variables.

Simultaneously, the COVID-19 context in particular has shed light on the risks and fragilities facing the economy, which may hinder the capacity to create a new system when ecological, social or economic structures render the current system unsound, hence requiring conditions for transformability. Transformability will require structures and institutions to be strengthened for growth to be stable and also withstand unforeseen risks.

The spurt in economic growth of Bangladesh, despite the lack of good governance, is often considered a "surprise", "paradox" or "conundrum". In fact, a section of the society now believes that economic growth is possible and can be secured even without inclusive institutions, asserting that economic development is more important than an inclusive political system. However, this illusory proposition is not backed by solid theoretical underpinnings or empirical validation. It is, therefore, imperative to undergo critical scrutiny.

The interrelations and intersectionality between politics and the economy require further investigation. It is, nevertheless, more important to analyse the causality between the two. The difficulty, however, lies in determining the compatible variables that represent politics. As a discipline of study, both politics and economics have evolved in their own distinctive way. It is therefore difficult to establish causality between political variables and economic factors. Again, it can be challenging to examine the causality by exerting an equal weight upon each of the provisions. Although there are numerous studies including different views and discussions on Bangladesh's politics and economy, there is a lack of endeavours that explore the political and economic spheres simultaneously.

Moreover, there is no universally recognised theoretical framework to analyse the effects of politics and economy on one another. As a result, the analysis surges in complication. Different schools of thought attempt to explain the relationship of politics and economics from different points of view. It is, thus, neither possible nor appropriate to provide an analysis following a particular narrative.

The analysis ventures to understand the necessary and sufficient conditions of development by examining and comparing the state of the economy of Bangladesh with the economy of other relevant countries in terms of growth, the real sector, the financial sector, health, education, poverty and inequality. The stability conditions are ascertained by inquiring whether the economy of Bangladesh meets the minimum standard to be in the lower rungs of the middle-income group countries. As opposed to this, transformability conditions are envisaged in terms of attaining the level of East Asian countries. Sustainability conditions, however, involve achieving the potential capacity of OECD economies.

Scope of the Book

The following chapter explores the growth scenario of Bangladesh's economy. This chapter mainly asks two questions: Firstly, do GDP figures of Bangladesh corroborate with national income accounting? Secondly, is the growth transformative and environmentally sustainable, given the factors on which the growth is reliant? It also analyses the state of growth in different decades. The statistics ushers that income has reduced for most of the people and hence they cannot save. As a result, investment does not increase, rather stagnating over the years. The estimation also shows a negative trend both in public and private consumption. Moreover, due to the increase in import costs in comparison to the export earnings, there is a deficit in the overall balance of payments since fiscal year 2017–18. The analysis, therefore, cannot avoid suggesting that the official figure of GDP growth rate is overestimated, and hardly substantiated by the available evidence. Governments in many developing countries tend to engineer growth statistics to inflate the performance of the economy. For example, a recent study in India depicts that the country's actual GDP growth rate is 2.5 percent lower than the official estimation (Subramaniam 2019).

The third chapter investigates the declining trend of productivity in agriculture. It explores whether the agricultural production is sustainable as well as whether the structural transition is realised in the economy. It is observed that Bangladesh has experienced little technological advancement post-green revolution. On the other hand, the poor and marginal tenants, comprising most of the total farm population, cannot afford the high cost of using high technology inputs. Primary producers do not get the larger share of the profit; instead, it goes to the middlemen. Bangladesh has achieved food adequacy, even though large swathes of the population still suffers from severe hunger. The role of institutional variables in agriculture is studied in this chapter. Despite higher cropping intensity, the declining trend in the availability of arable land causes the growth in the agricultural sector to fall. Crop production has become centralised. Moreover, the so-called green revolution has been adversely affecting the sustainability of both the environment and nature.

The fourth chapter explores the question of whether the manufacturing industry can create productive expansion, realise technological deepening and reach a stage of maturity where high mass consumption is assured. It explores the stability, transformation and sustainability conditions compared to international standards and delineates that the manufacturing sector is not performing to the required standard either. The number of productive manufacturing sectors is limited, and diversification is not taking place. The entire manufacturing sector is reliant upon one sector—readymade garments (RMG). There also exists a lack of product and market diversification in the RMG sector. Besides, there have been notable cases of shutting down of RMG industries in recent periods. The fundamental reasons behind such a fiasco include the uncertain political environment, fragility of the institutions, a clear lack in business confidence and widespread capital flight. The productive expansion of the economy, therefore, remains constricted, resulting in low job creation.

The fifth chapter analyses the financial sector of the economy and examines whether the banking sector and the capital market can facilitate capital for growth. It underscores that the exacerbation of default loans in the banking sector and the frequent scams in the capital market exhibit a vicious cycle in the financial sector. Instead of taking legal steps against the defaulters, the government is offering a plethora of facilities in favour of the defaulters. Besides, the excessive borrowing by the government from domestic sources to finance the mega-projects and repay the loans has pushed the banking sector to a liquidity crisis. The prevalent regulatory discrepancies have emerged as the malediction in the financial sector's volatility.

The sixth and seventh chapters deal with the state of education and health. It investigates whether education and health outcomes are realised in forming human capital and citizenship. The chapter argues that the outcome of education has failed to achieve its desired results in terms of creating a skilled workforce, fostering innovation and forming citizenship despite an increase in enrolment rates and literacy rates. On the other hand, although out of pocket expenditure (OOP) in healthcare has increased wildly (the highest among the SAARC countries), the quality of the services is not satisfactory. The poor quality of health and education is reflected in the low skill and productivity of the labour force.

The penultimate chapter examines the state of poverty and inequality in Bangladesh's economy. It explores whether the outcome of economic growth is positively affecting the standard of life of people irrespective of caste, creed and class. The analysis suggests that the poverty reduction rate has declined recently, making it incompatible with the story of high GDP growth of the country. At the same time, inequality is expanding at an alarming rate, the highest ever recorded. Resources are being concentrated in the pockets of a few at the expense of many. There runs widespread primitive accumulation of capital through using the monopoly power of the state resulting in the centralisation of resources to clientelist networks, which are then minimally invested in the productive sector.

The final chapter identifies the effectiveness and efficiency of institutions—understood through norms, values customs, power and political settlement—as the sufficient conditions. Compared with the other countries in terms of stability, transformability and sustainability conditions, the statistics further underscores that, if sufficient conditions are not met, the quality of growth and development cannot be achieved. Such growth and development, therefore, fails to transform and sustain.

Most importantly, in all chapters, a conscious effort is made to lay out conditions that could transform the sectors from the identified fragilities and risks. These chapters also contain an exercise of visioning as a part of outlining the sustainability conditions, with the expectation that such a roadmap of transformability and sustainability would help realise the potential of the country. The book, thus, embarks upon a dual role of identifying the challenges as well as of charting out of breaking the barriers, a much-needed endeavour as the country embraces its 50th

anniversary of independence. The present book, in its entirety, is based upon the aspiration of the war of liberation—equality, human dignity and social justice—which are enshrined as the fundamental pillars in the proclamation of independence.

Contents

Abbreviations

ADB	Asian Development Bank
AML	Anti-Money Laundering
APSC	Annual Primary School Census
ASTI	Agricultural Science and Technology Indicators
BADC	Bangladesh Agricultural Development Corporation
BANBEIS	Bangladesh Bureau of Educational Information and Statistics
BARD	Bangladesh Academy for Rural Development
BARI	Bangladesh Agricultural Research Institute
BB	Bangladesh Bank
BBS	Bangladesh Bureau of Statistics
BDT	Bangladeshi Taka
BGMEA	Bangladesh Garment Manufacturers & Exporters Association
BMET	Bureau of Manpower, Employment and Training
BRRI	Bangladesh Rice Research Institute
CCB	Capital Conservation Buffer
CIP	Competitive Industrial Performance
CMSME	Cottage, Micro, Small and Micro Enterprise
CPD	Centre for Policy Dialogue
CRAR	Capital to Risk (Weighted) Assets Ratio
DFI	Development Finance Institutions
DP	Annual Rate of Poverty Decline
DSE	Dhaka Stock Exchange
DSEX	Dhaka Stock Exchange Index
EPI	Environmental Performance Index
EPS	Earnings Per Share
ESCAP	Economic and Social Commission for Asia and the Pacific

EU	European Union
FAO	Food and Agriculture Organisation
FDI	Foreign Direct Investment
FSI	Financial Stability Index
FYP	Five Year Plan
GDP	Gross Domestic Product
GED	General Economic Division
GFI	Global Financial Integrity
GY	Annual Growth Rate of GDP per capita
HHI	Herfindahl-Hirschman Index
HIES	Household Income and Expenditure Surveys
HSC	Higher School Certificate
HYV	High Yielding Variety
IFA	International Fertiliser Association
IFPRI	International Food Policy Research Institute
ILO	International Labour Organisation
IMF	International Monetary Fund
IPCC	Intergovernmental Panel on Climate Change
LDC	Least Developed Countries
LFS	Labour Force Survey
MDG	Millennium Development Goals
MFA	Multi-Fibre Arrangement
MHT	Medium and High Tecch
MNC	Multi-National Corporations
MoF	Ministry of Finance
MoP	Muriate of Potash
MoPME	Ministry of Primary and Mass Education
MVA	Manufacturing Value Added
NBR	National Board of Revenue
NEET	Not in Employment, Education or Training
NGO	Non-Governmental Organisation
NIM	Net Interest Margin
NPA	Non-Performing Assets
NPL	Non-Performing Loan
NSC	National Savings Certificate
OECD	Organisation for Economic Co-operation and Development
OOP	Out of Pocket Expenditure
PCB	Private Commercial Banks
R&D	Research and Development
RADP	Revised Annual Development Programme
RBCA	Risk-Based Capital Adequacy
RMG	Ready Made Garments
RoA	Return on Assets

RoE	Return on Equity
SAARC	South Asian Association for Regional Co-operation
SBTC	Skill-Biased Technical Progress
SDG	Sustainable Development Goals
SFYP	Seventh Five Year Plan
SMI	Survey of Manufacturing Industries
SOCB	State-Owned Commercial Banks
SSC	Secondary School Certificate
STEM	Science, Technology, Engineering and Mathematics
TFP	Total Factor Productivity
TIN	Tax Identification Number
TSP	Triple Super Phosphate
UGC	University Grant Commission
UNCTAD	United Nations Conference on Trade and Development
UNDP	United Nations Development Programme
UNCTAD	United Nations Conference on Trade and Development
UNESCO	United Nations Educational, Scientific and Cultural Organisation
UNICEF	United Nations Children's Fund
UNIDO	United Nations Industrial Development Organisation
UPE	Universal Primary Education
USA	United States of America
VAT	Value-Added Tax
WHO	World Health Organisation

List of Figures

List of Tables

CHAPTER 1

Economic Growth in Bangladesh

Introduction

This chapter attempts to examine the current state of economic growth of Bangladesh in terms of stability and analyse the conditions for transformability by looking at power, political settlement and institutions. It further scrutinises the conditions for environmentally sustainable growth that ascertains good quality of life of both humans and nature. In addition, it analyses whether the claimed high rate of growth is commensurate with related variables.

Rapid economic growth of Bangladesh has become a much-discussed topic in the recent times. Once touted as the 'basket case', economic growth along with the improvement in the social indicators has rekindled attention (Asadullah et al. 2014; Barai 2020).

The growth path has largely followed the conventional drivers, despite many interpretations including lamentations such as "surprise" or "paradox." This was made possible in large part by migration of the underemployed from the countryside to urban cities and flowing out to the world over, mostly concentrating in West Asia. The continual greater-than-before participation of women in the labour market, particularly in the RMG sector, as well as women's entrepreneurship and demonstrated resilience of farmers who have continued to work tirelessly in their green croplands, exhibiting innovation and intensity, have been responsible for new and inspired changes. Remittance from home and abroad

R. A. M. Titumir, *Numbers and Narratives in Bangladesh's Economic Development*,
https://doi.org/10.1007/978-981-16-0658-8_1

has fuelled largely consumption-led economic growth. Consumption is one of the four elements of Gross Domestic Product (GDP) and the others are—investment, government expenditure and net of export and import. The introduction of consumption-based tax, value added tax (VAT) has resulted in a higher capacity of the government to undertake public investment. Nevertheless, public investment in the social sector has remained lower than the countries that have witnessed transformational change, with the quality of education and health particularly remaining in question. Yet the people at large have endured one of the highest out of pocket expenditure in South Asia and comparable countries in education and health to achieve progress in the social sector. This consumption expenditure has reached such a high level that ordinary people's ability to save has remained at extremely low. As a result, investment have not increased; rather, stagnating over several years. The lack of productive expansion has left a major portion of the labour force unemployed or underemployed, resulting in jobless growth.

Besides the conventional economic drivers of growth, political settlement plays an important role in directing policies. The prevalence of extractive institutions as well as little room for competitive and representational political systems have been the major bottlenecks in transforming growth, thus leaving various impedances to realising the full potential of the economy. The current growth process has been identified as environmentally unsustainable, and therefore threatening to harmonious living between human beings and Mother Earth.

Authoritarian and military rules finally ended in 1990 and the country moved to an era of competitive clientelism. This era was characterised by higher real wages from higher return on factors of production. Investments and savings were higher than during the authoritarian regimes as the real wages grew.

During the authoritarian clientelism, elections were sporadic and elite groups and the members of the ruling regime captured rents. As a result, the return on capital was much higher and accrued only by the ruling regime. A rentier class was born and nurtured by the authoritarian regime. Primitive accumulation by this class resulted in capital flight and money laundering, which denied the nation much needed investment. The Government tended to control the political process and the factors of production. Return on labour on the other hand was lower during this period.

Bangladesh has already been facing a plethora of challenges, which have been exposed and further entrenched by the onset of the global pandemic

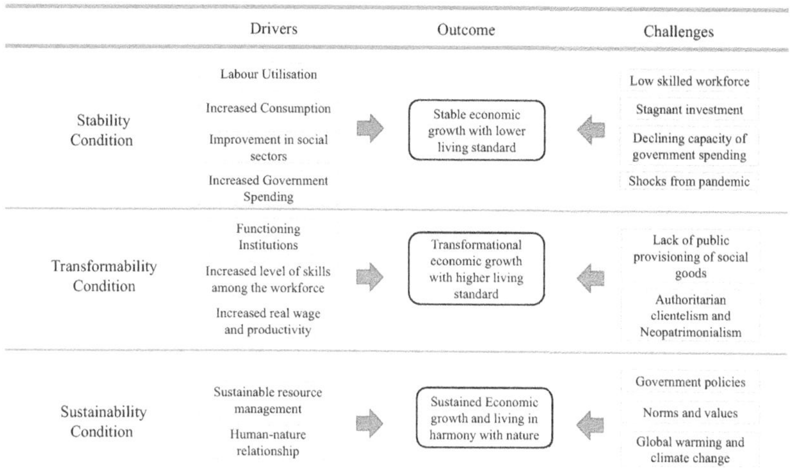

Fig. 1.1 Framework for growth (*Source* Author)

and the economic slowdown that followed. The downturn will be intensified by income reduction, diminished savings and hence dwindling investment which has been hovering around 23% in the last few years. Loss of jobs and reduction of remittance earnings from migrant workers who have been sent back because of the crisis, will dampen consumption spending, in turn constricting the GDP, 70% of which is private consumption (Unnayan Onneshan 2020). Simultaneously, it has the potential to affect different sectors of the economy differently, discriminating between physically interactive and physically disjointed sectors—simply put, not all organisations can make use of a 'work-from-home' approach because of the nature of their work.

The stupendous economic growth of Bangladesh relies on real economic sectors as well as the achievements in the social sector. The following chart illustrates the outline of the chapter. The stability condition of economic growth is driven by factors which ensure a stable economic growth over a long period of time without significantly changing the quality of life. Such growth cannot be sustained without the transformability conditions to sustain the economic growth for a longer period and bring a transformational change in the living standard. Such transformational growth in the long run will create a balance between the economy and the environment as mankind is confronted by the global warming crisis (Fig. 1.1).

Stability Conditions

Stability conditions are characterised through the factors of production and government intervention. Productivity of the factors of production determines economic growth. Government intervention in the form of public goods can enhance productivity. Further discussion will delve into examining the national accounts of the country, condition of the factors of production and spending capacity of the government. Scrutinising different elements of the national account will provide a clearer picture of the economy.

Economic progress requires harmonisation between major economic factors like households, firms, and government. Households, firms, and factor markets are interrelated with each other where government plays a pivotal role to stimulate growth. Households supply labour to factor markets, which further facilitate the movement of labour to firms. Firms and factor markets provide innovation to each other. Naturally, wages go to households from factor markets. Households store their savings in the capital markets and partake consumption spending in the consumer markets. Apart from household savings, business savings enter the capital markets. Next, investments arising from savings and consumer markets supply receipts from goods to the firms. To keep this multidimensional relationship active, government contributes public expenditure on human capital, which are then received by households. Government also formulates policy, enforces regulations, and provides incentives for firms. Government acquires tax revenue from firms and households. Here, technology is an exogenous factor. Government bears public spending for knowledge creation, benefitting both the factor market and households through knowledge and better services. It becomes unequivocal that when incidents like more labour supply to factor markets and firms take place, it leads to greater innovation with simultaneous provision of high savings in the capital market, more investment in the firms, high wages, high government spending on human capital, high revenue, and high technological creation (Fig. 1.2).

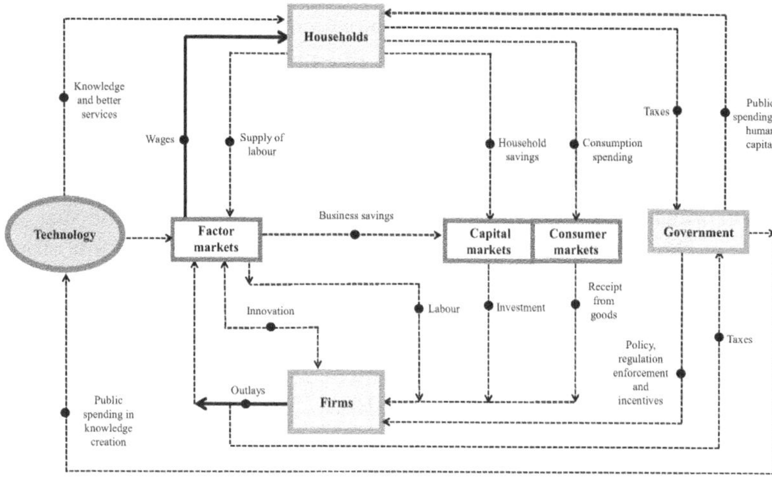

Fig. 1.2 Stability of growth (*Source* Author)

Labour Utilisation and Migration

The rapid growth of Bangladesh has largely been possible due to utilisation of the labour force. Historically, agriculture had been the dominant sector in the economy and employed well over 70% of the working population after the independence. Two events were particularly important in shifting the labour dynamics in the country. First, the readymade garments sector sprung up in the 1980s and was built upon the abundance of labour. The sector did not require high level of skills and hence tapped into the unskilled and semi-skilled labour force. Second, overseas employment opportunities in the Middle Eastern countries opened at the same time. This sector also relied on unskilled and semi-skilled workers. This worked in favour of the large number of unskilled workers in the agricultural sector in rural areas who migrated to urban areas and abroad for employment. The structural transformation in the economy began at that stage and only accelerated in the following decades. Readymade garments sector also had a long-lasting impact on female employment. This sector also caused migration of unemployed females from rural areas to cities. The shift from the low waged agricultural sector to the higher waged industries and the overseas employment resulted in an increase of private consumption. The outcome of this increased consumption was a sharp reduction in poverty, especially in rural parts of the country.

Consumption-Led Growth from Shifts in the Labour Force

International migration to the Middle East was fuelled by the first oil shock in the 70s. In 2017, the number of international migrants stood at 7.5 million and represented 4.5% of the country's population or more than 11% of its labour force (United Nations 2017). The flow of remittances increased with the ever-increasing rate of migration. Starting from a modest USD 23 million of remittances in 1976, the flow of remittances reached USD 13.5 billion in 2017. The Gulf countries are the main sources for remittances. Saudi Arabia and the UAE lead the pack and accounted for more than USD 2 billion in 2017. Amongst the East Asian countries, Malaysia is the leader with more than USD 1 billion of remittances in 2017 (BMET 2018).

The monthly income, consumption, and savings in remittance-receiving households were higher on average by 82%, 38%, and 107% respectively compared to those without remittances (BBS 2011). In 2010, about 13% of the remittance-receiving households were below the poverty line, compared to about 34% of non-receiving households. At this time, the poverty incidence rate was about 32% nationally (World Bank 2011).

The unemployment rate has increased, which has made the situation even worse, leaving 27.4% of youth not in education, employment or training (Table 1.1). The total unemployment rate is reported as 4.4% in 2017 (Table 1.1), albeit with most people working in the informal sector, getting paid lower wages and lacking basic rights (Fig. 1.3). A large

Table 1.1 Employment situation in 2017

	Labour force participation rate (%)			*Youth labour force participation rate (%)*			*NEET (%)*			*Unemployment rate (%)*		
	M	*F*	*Total*	*M*	*F*	*Total*	*M*	*F*	*Total*	*M*	*F*	*Total*
2017	80.7	36.4	58.3	54.9	26.4	40.5	9.8	44.6	27.4	3.3	6.7	4.4

Source ILO (2020a)

swathe of people is thus losing their income leading to a reduced standard of living. In the onset of the covid-19 pandemic, unemployment has risen more due to a countrywide shutdown. A returning migrant workforce will also add to the numbers.

The number of people constituting the economically active population above the age of 15 year is 63.5 million (BBS 2017), out of whom 43.5 million are male and 20 million are female. Around 60.8 million are working in various professions. Among the broad sectors of the economy, agriculture has the highest share and employs 40.6%, followed by 39% in the service sector and only 20.4% in industries. Around 44.3% are self-employed, followed by 39.1% as employees and 11.5% as contributing family workers. Between the sexes by largest share, there were more males in all categories except among contributing family workers, where the number of employed females (5.3 million) was thrice that of employed males (1.7 million).

Incongruent Improvements in the Social Sector

Bangladesh has made significant achievements in social indices including health and education. Such achievements have put Bangladesh forward as a role model for developing countries. Much of the debate on Bangladesh's surprise case relies on the achievements in social indices. Life expectancy has increased to 72 years in 2017 from 48 years in 1975. Female life expectancy exceeds the male life expectancy, showing a significant change in the living standard of females in the country. Literacy rate now stands at 79% in the country which was just above 29% in 1981. Mortality rate per thousand births aged under five years has reduced to 30 in 2018 from 217 in 1975. Improvements in these indices show that economic growth has brought a change in the living standard of the population. Many suggest government initiatives for the stunning achievements in the social sector. While Bangladesh made inroads towards higher living standard, much of it has been achieved through out-of-pocket expenditure which stands at a whopping 71% (World Bank 2019). Skill level among the labour force remains low due to a lack of investment by the government in skill enhancing education.

Jobless Growth

Given that the largest proportion of the labour force is employed in the least productive sector, the nature of growth in Bangladesh may well be jobless growth, shown by the inability to create new jobs in manufacturing industries despite higher growth rates. The structural transformation in Bangladesh is directed from agriculture to the service sectors. Manufacturing employment has rather reduced in the last 5 years, while in service-oriented sectors, the share is rising. A lack of increase in private investment is one of the key reasons behind the decline in job creation in the productive sectors, which in turn could be a result of the deficit financing undertaken by the government through the banking sector, which might have led to crowding out of private investment over the years (Table 1.2).

Higher Concentration in Informal Employment

Bangladesh still has the highest employment in informal sectors with around 85.1% of the labour force involved in low skilled informal sectors (Fig. 1.3). Informal employees are prone to job losses and income erosion. Employment in the informal sector was 35.1% in 2002–2003 which increased constantly and rose to 50.1% in 2013. During this period, the employment of female workers has almost doubled in the informal sector (15.2% in 2013 from 7.9% in 2002–2003) and the employment of male workers increased to 35.6% in 2013 from 27.2% in 2002–2003.

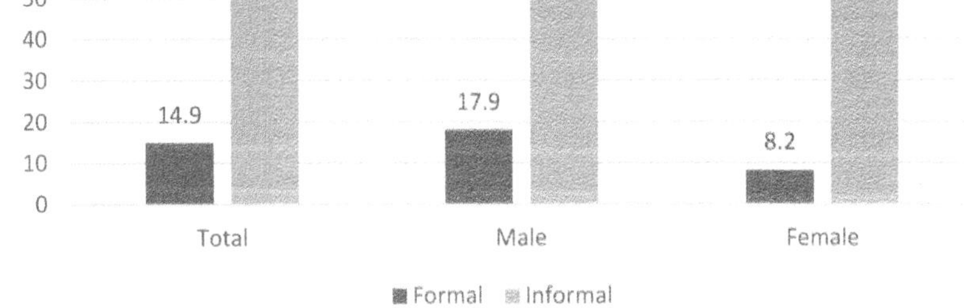

Fig. 1.3 Percentage distribution of informal employment by broad economic sector (*Source* BBS 2019)

Table 1.2 Share of employment

Sector	*LFS 1995–1996*	*LFS 1999–2000*	*LFS 2002–2003*	*LFS 2005–2006*	*LFS 2010*	*LFS 2013*	*LFS 2015–2016*	*LFS 2016–2017*
Agriculture, forestry and fishery	48.85	50.77	51.69	48.10	47.33	45.10	42.70	40.62
Mining and quarrying	–	0.51	0.23	0.21	0.18	0.40	0.20	0.20
Manufacturing	10.06	9.49	9.71	10.97	12.34	16.40	14.40	14.43
Power Gas and Water	0.29	0.26	0.23	0.21	0.18	0.20	0.30	0.20
Construction	2.87	2.82	3.39	3.16	4.79	3.70	5.60	5.58
Trade, hotel and restaurant	17.24	15.64	15.34	16.45	15.47	14.50	13.40	14.34
Transport, maintenance and communication	6.32	6.41	6.77	8.44	7.37	6.40	9.40	10.50
Finance, business and services	0.57	1.03	0.68	1.48	1.84	1.30	1.60	1.97
Commodities and personal services	13.80	13.07	5.64	5.49	6.26	6.20	6.20	6.08
Public administration and defense	–	–	6.32	5.49	4.24	5.80	6.20	6.08
Total	100.00	100.00	100.00	100.00	100.00	100.00	100.00	100.00

Source Based on several Labour Force Surveys of BBS

Share of informal sector employment in total employment has increased to 87.4% in 2013 from 79.23% in 2002–2003 (ADB 2016).

Stagnant Investment and Savings

Scrutinising different elements of the national accounts provide a clear picture of the economy. In comparison with fiscal year 2016–2017, both domestic savings and national savings rates declined in 2018–2019. In fiscal year 2012–2013, national savings was 30.53% of total GDP and further decreased to 28.41% in 2018–2019. The statistics usher that either income has reduced for most people or consumption expenditure has reached such a high level that they cannot save. As a result, investment did not increase; rather, it stagnated over the years or decreased (Table 1.3).

The ratio of private investment to GDP has remained stagnant for the last few years, hovering around 23%. This is primarily due to the lack of business confidence owing to political uncertainty as well as inadequate availability of infrastructure, driven by reduced public investment. This is mainly due the government diverting resources to service non-development expenditure, including payment to employees and debt servicing (See details in following sections). The rate of growth in investments, however, does not commensurate with the GDP growth rate and is a more miniscule figure in contrast to it. Therefore, it is evident that the total savings are not being converted into investments, indicating the growing gap between savings and investment over the years. This situation might have occurred because of the siphoning of capital or a clear lack of security in capital leading to either reduced savings, less investment or both. The Global Financial Integrity (GFI) estimates that 5.9 billion US dollar was siphoned off from Bangladesh during the period of 2006 to 2015 (GFI 2019). Foreign Direct Investment (FDI) declined to USD 1.6 billion in 2019 from USD 3.5 billion in 2018 (UNCTAD 2020).

National income and consumption expenditure are intertwined with each other. Expansion in consumption expenditure is necessary in order to boost national incomes at the rate claimed by the government. The consumption in both public and private sector has increased slightly during fiscal year 2017–2018 compared to 2016–2017. In the fiscal year 2016–2017, the share of consumption in public and private sector to total GDP were 6.0% and 68.67% respectively. This share has increased

Table 1.3 Savings, investment and consumption as percent of GDP*

Fiscal Year	*2012–2013*	*2013–2014*	*2014–2015*	*2015–2016*	*2016–2017*	*2017–2018*	*2018–2019*
Domestic savings	22.04	22.09	22.16	24.98	25.33	22.83	23.93
National savings	30.53	29.23	29.02	30.77	29.64	27.42	28.41
Private investment	21.75	22.03	22.07	22.99	23.10	23.26	23.40
Public investment	6.64	6.55	6.82	6.66	7.41	7.97	8.17
Private consumption	72.85	72.57	72.44	69.13	68.67	70.81	69.77
Public consumption	5.12	5.34	5.40	5.89	6	6.36	6.30

Source Ministry of Finance (2019) (*2018–2019: provisional data)

to 6.36% and 70.81% respectively in the 2017–2018. The temporary estimation for fiscal year 2018–2019, however, shows a declining trend both in public and private consumption (Table 1.1).

There is also a deficit in the overall balance of payments since fiscal year 2017–2018 (Table 1.4) due to the increase in import costs in comparison to export earnings. The export-GDP ratio has decreased to 13.2% in fiscal year 2017–2018. The deficit between trade balance and current account balance is increasing. Despite being currently non-negative, the financial balance shows a stellar increase in loans. This situation of overall balance will worsen with the commencement of loan repayments. This picture of the balance of payments fails to align with the narrative of increasing national income.

Average household consumption is the lowest in the present decade. Average gross savings have increased but the average investment in the same period increased only marginally, meaning that a large portion of the savings are left idle. The agricultural share in the GDP went down drastically but the industrial share in the same period only increased by a few points. The service industry's contribution to the GDP has also slightly increased.

Table 1.4 Decadal average of some macroeconomic indicators

Indicators (% of GDP)	*Period*			
	1981–1990	*1991–2000*	*2001–2010*	*2011–2018*
GDP growth rate (Annual %)	4.02	4.68	5.58	6.74
Consumption	86.27	84.21	79.36	77.34
Investment	14.04	11.21	10.78	13.82
Gross savings	21.85	23.78	34.01	37.31
FDI net inflows	0.0075	0.1670	0.7323	1.2097
Employment to population ratio		55.40	54.72	54.65
Agriculture (Value Added)	31.95	25.80	18.76	14.89
Industry (Value Added)	20.23	22.36	23.76	26.68
Services (Value Added)	45.45	47.68	52.56	53.38
Export	5.16	9.92	14.67	17.80
Import	13.22	15.18	20.18	24.68
Current account balance	−2.25	−0.38	0.89	0.023
Population growth (Annual %)	2.58	2.12	1.45	1.12

Source Author's calculation based on World Bank (2020)

Since the lion's share of public expenditure goes towards unproductive sectors, such as recurrent expenditures (Fig. 1.4), productive expansions of the economy and job creation are withheld.

Declining Capacity of Public Spending

Public expenditure has remained constant over the years. A detailed analysis of government expenditure shows that recurrent expenditures still supersedes development expenditure. The expansion of the economy requires government spending in projects which can generate employment and stimulate growth. This process is handicapped by low development expenditure.

Deficit financing by the government only becomes viable when excess funding is used in expansionary activities. Public expenditure in development projects creates and boosts new businesses, which result in higher revenue collection. Increasing recurrent expenditure through deficit financing will only raise the public debt.

Weak Revenue Collection

The amount of income tax collection is not increasing at the desired rate. The ratio of income tax with the expansion of GDP does not align; neither has the tax coverage increased. Of the total population in

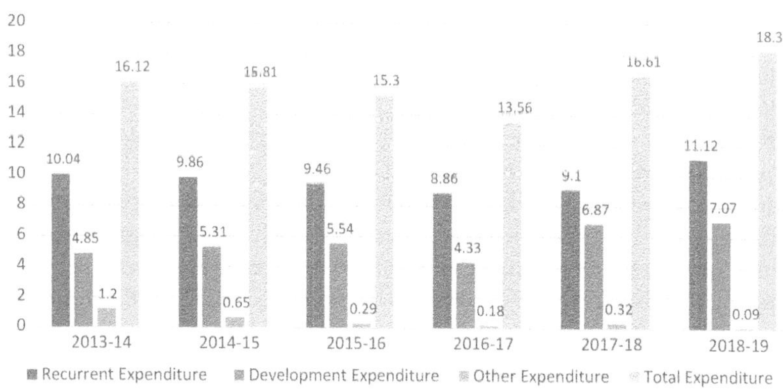

Fig. 1.4 Public expenditure composition as percent of GDP* (*Source* Ministry of Finance 2019 [*2018–2019 data are based on revised budget])

Bangladesh, only 2.1 million pay income taxes. In neighbouring countries, even though the amount is not high, the collection of tax revenue is about 18%. On the other hand, estimates suggest that 68% of capable individuals are out of tax coverage in Bangladesh. The tax-GDP ratio is also low compared to other developing countries manifesting an incompatibility with the growth of national income. On the one hand, tax is not collected properly and on the other, money laundering is stirring rampantly. Attempts to accommodate loan defaulters, instead of punishing them, are also markedly visible. Lower tax revenues result in the government borrowing money from alternative resources as well as acting as an impediment its expenditure in the social sectors.

The slow pace of tax mobilisation is hindering the overall performance of the economy and the capacity for government spending. Tax collection amounted to nearly BDT 651 billion during the July-October period of fiscal year 2019–2020, which represents 4.3% growth. This growth was 6.74% during the same period of 2018–2019. The target for revenue collection was BDT 3256 billion for the fiscal year (FY) of 2019–2020. The target until October of the same fiscal year was BDT 853.17 billion. However, this target was missed by around BDT 200 billion. The targets for all types of National Board of Revenue (NBR) revenue—duties from import and export, consumption tax and income tax—have also not been met (Fig. 1.5).

Regressive Tax Structure

The tax structure is heavily dependent on VAT. The incidence of this indirect tax falls heavily on the general public (see details how policies induce inequality in Chapter 9). The lower- and middle-class people are burdened with a greater incidence of this tax. On the contrary, tax exemption and tax evasion for the upper classes have become the norm. The ordinary taxpayers are working as the main sources of debt repayment and development. Though it is proclaimed repeatedly by successive governments, income tax is not made the primary source of tax revenue. In the implemented budget of FY 2009–2010, VAT was BDT 238.78 billion. In FY 2018–2019, VAT has been estimated to be BDT 1105.55 billion; which implies that VAT has increased by 380% in 9 years. Overall, it is succinctly clear that the tax structure has become severely regressive.

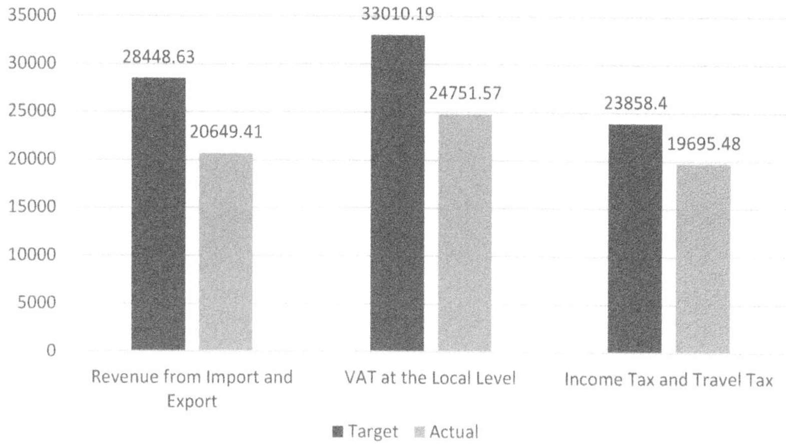

Fig. 1.5 NBR revenue in October, 2019 of 2019–2020 (in crores BDT) (*Source* National Board of Revenue 2019)

Institutional Weakness in Public Spending
Infrastructure cost in Bangladesh is also relatively higher than neighbouring and East Asian countries. A large portion of the development expenditure is lost and wasted due to mismanagement and poor governance. Bangladesh ranks 100 among 160 countries in the Logistics Performance Index with a score of 2.58. The cost of constructing one kilometre (km) road is between 2.5 to 11.9 million US dollars whereas the cost of constructing the same road in India is between 35,900 to 45,600 US dollars, 63,100 US dollars in Nepal, 59,500 US dollars in Thailand and 85,400 US dollars in Vietnam (World Bank 2017).

Discrepancies in Accounting Methodology

GDP is considered the most basic indicator for measuring the economy, despite its many limitations. There is no better indicator to demonstrate the growth of an economy with a single number than the GDP. The growth rate is calculated from the national accounting estimates. The reliability of these estimations though has been questioned in many fronts. Governments in many developing countries tend to engineer growth statistics to inflate the performance of the economy. This has political

Table 1.5 Summary of major indicators of growth

Indicators	*State of Bangladesh*
Investment	Investment as percentage of GDP has declined during 2011–2018 period
Consumption	Consumption as share of GDP has declined throughout the years
Employment	Employment to population ratio has fallen down after 2000
Real wage	Growth of real wage has declined
Share of informal employment	Share of informal employment to total employment has increased to 87.4% from 79.23% in 2002–2003
Remittance inflow	Growth of remittance inflow became trivial during 2011–2018 period. Growth rate of number of expatriates has declined during the last decade
State of RMG sector	Growth rate of export share of RMG as percent of GDP has decreased during 2011–2018
FDI net inflows	Growth rate of FDI net inflows has declined after 2010
Current account balance	Current account balance decreased during 2011–2018
Public expenditure	Recurrent expenditure as share of GDP remain greater than the development expenditure
Governance resiliency	Bangladesh is on the negative margin in terms of the governance indicators
Environmental sustainability	Air pollution has increased and several coal-based power plants are being set up in ecologically critical areas

implications as a deteriorating state of the economy has in many cases led to the fall of the ruling regime. Weak accounting institutions and methodology may also lead to misrepresentations of national accounting statistics. A recent study in the case of India has that the country's actual GDP growth rate is 2.5% lower than the official estimation (Subramanian 2019).

The estimates of GDP in Bangladesh have been under scrutiny for the past several years due to its apparent dissociation with several other key macroeconomic and development correlates including private sector credit, revenue mobilisation, import payments for capital machineries, energy consumption, export receipts, employment and others. Rapid increments in the growth rate in the last decade were largely led by sectors such as manufacturing exports and remittances. The combination of these indicators, however, generally does not forecast a high-growth economy; yet the growth rate of GDP reflects an accelerating trend (Salma et al. 2020).

A study on the growth experience and GDP estimation in Bangladesh sets out to verify whether discrepancies exist in the accounting methodology, and whether official growth figures corroborate the pace of economic growth experienced in the country. The paper tests if GDP figures are entirely congruent using an econometric exercise concerning time series data on the real sectors of the economy. Real sectors are assumed to have a direct impact on the aggregate production in the economy. Regressions attempt to establish whether proxy indicators for the manufacturing and service sector have any real impact on the official national statistics of the value-added indicators for each sector (Titumir et al., unpublished paper).

The mentioned paper finds no long-run relationship between the independent, proxy indicators and the national statistics for the performance of the real sectors. The findings are further buttressed using several tests for cointegration and causality, which exhibit no cointegration or causality between the variables. As a result, it concludes that data discrepancies may be responsible for the gap in causality between variables that are expected to have a long-run relationship. Myriad discrepancies may be found in the survey, data and accounting methodology for each of the real sectors—agriculture, manufacturing and services. For instance, there is no systematic method of survey in measuring horticultural output in the agriculture sector, the base year for the small-scale sector remained unchanged at 1995–1996 in the manufacturing sector, despite the change in base year for large industries, and the recorded value of sales and receipts for services of public sector transport rendered does not reflect the true value of output because of what is euphemistically called 'system losses'(Titumir et al. unpublished paper). The analysis therefore suggests that the official figures of GDP growth rate are grossly overestimated, and the government's narrative is hardly supported by available evidence.

Covid-19 and Risks

The covid-19 pandemic and resulting shutdown has worsened economic conditions all around the globe. The three-month shutdown of economic activities has adversely affected the livelihoods of people. In view of this, the Government projected a growth rate of 5.2% instead of 8.1%. As the economy restarts, the Government projects a V-shaped growth pattern with a growth rate of 8.2% in the year. A 3% increase in the growth rate in a year is unrealistic, as the pandemic has widened the fractures within the economy. The fundamental institutions in the country remain weak. RMG sector that contributed to the rapid growth, has suffered heavy losses during the pandemic. Garments remained closed during the shutdown. International buyers of garment products cancelled orders worth three billion US dollars and withheld payments. Export earnings fell by 83% in April of 2020 compared to last year (EPB 2020). Export in the first 8 month of 2020 fell by 4.8% whereas the RMG export saw a decline of 5.5%. In 2019, RMG export saw a staggering 14.2% growth (ADB 2020). This led to massive job cuts in the sector. Informal sector employees have lost earnings during the shutdown. The poverty rate, for the first time, will increase from the loss of livelihoods of many.

Consumption expenditure comprises more than 75% of the GDP. Consumption will decrease sharply in the face of widespread job losses and income erosion. Investment and savings are set to nose-dive as well. Foreign Direct Investment in the country hovers around 1% and is about 4% of private investment (Ministry of Finance 2019). Import of capital machineries, export payments and investments saw a decline even before the pandemic hit the nation. In this circumstance, the Government's projected growth rate appears unrealistic.

Revenue collection was already dawdling before the covid-19 pandemic. Collections will decrease even further due to income erosion. The shock absorption capacity of the Government will reduce further owing to its dependence on a single industry and a paucity of diversification strategies. Recovering from this shock depends on the coping mechanisms built into the economy. These conditions will be discussed in the next section.

Transformability Conditions

The transformability of growth depends on the functioning and strength of institutions. Institutions are understood as power, political settlement, rules, laws, policies as well as informal ones such as norms, values and customs. There is a positive relation between institutions and growth meaning that if institutions function well, create inclusive and competitive political environment and ensure checks and balance, continued growth can be achieved. Economic institutions encouraging economic growth emerge when political institutions allocate power to groups with interests in broad-based property rights enforcement, create effective constraints on powerholders, and have relatively few rents to be captured by power-holders (Acemoglu et al. 2001). Economic institutions influence the structure of economic incentives in society and help allocate resources to their most efficient uses, determining who gets the profits, the revenues, and the residual rights of control. Moreover, institutions are responsible for creating, regulating, stabilising and legitimising markets. In the case of India after the reforms in the 1980s, economic growth spiralled upwards. This was possible due to the existence of its strong institutions. Even a small trigger, such as modest reforms, could lead to a large spurt in growth as the productive potential engendered by the quality of institutions was previously left underutilised (Subramanian 2009).

Political Settlement

Bangladesh, after its independence saw rise of intermediate classes, with a hunger for primitive accumulation. Intermediate classes are formed of classes that occupies an intermediate position and plays a key role in the political process, but not as dominant as the capitalist class. Broadly, the intermediate classes comprise of rich and middle farmers, urban petty-bourgeoisies and educated middle classes, having a greater degree of organisational ability resulting from their better education and greater wealth. These classes are different from workers, poor peasants and the illiterate unemployed.

The drive to primitive accumulation of resources has formed a clientelist networks in the country that exercises power and coercion. The ever-increasing hunger for accretion of economic rents warrants an exclusive political system to spread all over the horizontal and vertical levels, creating a culture of occupying a position—from member of parliament down to the chairman of the Union Parishad—uncontested or without any competition from opposition political parties.

The authoritarian clientelism in Bangladesh spanned from 1975 to 1990 when the military directly or indirectly controlled the state apparatus. One significant event during this regime was the beginning of the readymade garments industry in the country. When the Multi Fibre Agreement (MFA) forced developed countries to shift production to developing countries, a rentier class born out of the authoritarian regime utilised the opportunity. To take advantage of the transferred technology alongside the abundance of labour, investors built new factories and invited or poached outside workers and managers with the expertise to operate them (Sonobe et al. 2018). Hence, the RMG sector emerged in the country because of the nature of the authoritarian regime. Owners of the RMG sectors were thus mostly retired civil bureaucrats and military officers (Quddus and Rashid 2000; Islam 2003; Khan 2013).

Under the competitive clientelism, which spanned from 1990 to 2007, the RMG sector saw an astonishing growth. The sector could work without many regulations from the Government and at times the Government promoted this sector by providing subsidies and tax holidays. The growth of the RMG sector during the competitive clientelism allowed the country to become the second largest exporter of RMGs in the world after China. In 2017, the industry's contribution to exports exceeded USD 28 billion and employed more than 4 million workers, 80% of whom are women (BGMEA 2018).

Democracy in Bangladesh came into question again in 2006 when the country fell into semi-military rule. The two-year regime of the caretaker government ended in 2009. Constitutional amendments by the ruling party again brought upon a crisis when opposition parties refused to take part in the election. The polity score reflects the democratic nature of a regime (Table 1.6). The index is measured by a scale of −10 to +10 with a positive score indicating a democratic nature and a negative score indicating an autocratic nature of the regime. The authoritarian regime pre-1990 had an average polity index of −6. The following era of competitive clientelism saw a moderate score of +6, a ten-point change in the index. The score again changes its sign during 2007–2008, thus ending

Table 1.6 Polity index in different regime

	Polity Index
1972–1973	8
1974–1975	−4.5
1976–1990	−6
1991–2006	6
2007–2008	−6
2009–2013	5
2014–2018	−4

Source Polity Project, Center for Systemic Peace 2020

a stretch of almost 15 years of democracy (Marshall et al. 2020). Elections held in 2008 brought the country back into the democratic band of the index only to change in the next election. The competitive clientelist nature of the state thus spiralled into an authoritarian nature in 2014.

The process of fear and exclusivity has created a sense of low business confidence, which has resulted in depressed investment demand which has led to lower job creation. The economic rents also fly out from the country as exhibited through increased capital flight from Bangladesh. The absence of an inclusive political system has also exerted pressure on the institutions, which has resulted in their disintegration. Authoritarian clientelism leads to a syndicate, which accumulates power and resources. With the absence of strong institutions, this elite group grows and helps the government stay in power. The mutual benefits of both the groups prolong this relationship in the state. The outcome of such a relationship is capital flight and tax evasion in the country.

In 2018, Bangladesh ranked in the 27.59 percentile in voice and accountability, which was as high as in the 50 percentile in 1996. During the same period, political stability and absence of violence ranking worsened from 26.6 to 13.81 percentile, government effectiveness declined from 27.32 to 21.63 percentile and control of corruption worsened from 17.74 to 16.83 percentile. The overall downward trend over time in the governance indicator ranks provides the evidence of weakening administrative institutions in the country (Kaufmann et al. 2020).

Competitive Clientelism

Achievements and progress made during 1990 to 2006 again reversed. For example, in Bangladesh, investment rose to a level and then was caught up in inertia, remaining stagnant (Table 1.3). The rate of reduction in poverty incidence declined significantly (Table 1.7). In the cases of upper poverty and lower poverty incidence, the rate of reduction was

Table 1.7 Rate of reduction in poverty incidence

	2000–2005	*2005–2010*	*2010–2016*
Upper poverty	1.8	1.7	1.2
Lower poverty	1.8	1.5	0.8

Source BBS (2019)

Table 1.8 Real wage growth and productivity growth (percent per annum)

	Nominal wage	*Food CPI*	*Real wage*	*GDP per worker*
1981–1989	12.43	9.52	2.91	0.25
1989–2000	5.44	5.31	0.13	2.34
2000–2010	8.94	8.17	0.77	3.18

Source Osmani (2015)

1.8% during the period of 2000–2005 and stood 1.2 and 0.8% respectively during 2010–2016.

There was an improving trend of real wage growth during the 2000s, with the rate of about 0.8% per annum even though the productivity growth was higher. This implies that return to labour was miniscule compared to return to non-labour factors. The rising inequality since this period supports this contention. The increasing trend of real wage growth during 2000s, however, ceased and has further deteriorated since 2013 (Table 1.8). Bangladesh witnessed the sharpest fall in their real wages among their peers in Asia and the Pacific in the last decade. The country witnessed a 5.9% decrease between 2010 and 2019. The only country in Asia and the Pacific whose minimum wage does not reach even the lowest international poverty line is Bangladesh (ILO 2020b).

Besides, the leap in growth of RMG exports started in the 1990s and continued in the 2000s. However, in recent years, RMG export growth is showing a decline trend. Growth of export will decline even more in this decade because of the covid-19 pandemic (Table 1.9).

The volume of export has increased, but with a declining growth rate over time in Bangladesh. The average growth of exports was 15.73% between 1990 and 1999. The average growth rate of export since then has been declining. RMG sector dominates the export volume and the growth rate of the share of RMG has also shrunk significantly in the

Table 1.9 State of export sector

Growth rate	*1980–1989*	*1990–1999*	*2000–2009*	*2010–2017*
Export growth	9.38	15.73	12.75	10.40

Source World Development Indicator

Table 1.10 State of remittance

Growth Rate (%)	*1980–1989*	*1990–1999*	*2000–2009*	*2010–2017*
Remittance inflow	19.65	11.09	18.60	6.01
Number of expatriates	10.15	5.39	6.63	5.34

Source World Bank, Bangladesh Bank 2019

recent times. Several factories have closed their operations and the average change in the number of operating factories shows a negative trend in the current decade.

Remittance volumes may have increased over the years, but the rate of this increase is the slowest in the present decade. The average growth rate of remittances in the current decade stands at only 6.01% whereas the remittances grew faster in the previous decades. The number of expatriates has shown a declining trend due to existing tensions and restrictions from the Middle Eastern countries, the primary market. The skill level of the workforce is another issue impacting the remittance sector as most of the expatriates have low level of skills (Table 1.10).

The economy of Bangladesh has long benefited from the high level of remittances. However, recent changes in the global migration sphere that cultivates the 'anti-immigrant sentiment' may imply that this may not continue in the future. The number of overseas employments decreased to 604,060 during January and November of 2019 from 684,962 during the corresponding periods in the previous year (BMET 2019). Some Bangladeshi workers have often encountered occasional bans in the Gulf countries as well as Southeast Asian economies and such restrictions may become increasingly stringent in the future. Some countries are persistently taking up indigenisation programs, such as the Saudi Nitaqat programme, that give preferential treatment to the locals over immigrant workers.

Another example is the case of the banking sector and the capital market where the plundering and the breakdown of discipline have led to perpetual fragility (see details in Chapter 6). Of late, crisis in the banking sector has made the financial sector in Bangladesh the worst among the emerging Asian countries, reflecting the poor risk management ability of the central bank, the Bangladesh Bank (BB). A recent heist has again shattered confidence in the financial system and the economy. The ongoing crisis in the banking sector, mainly due to increased default loans, reflects the institutional weakness of the financial system and leads to increased cost of funds and shortfalls in capital for the banks.

Investment in Human Capital

The world is experiencing a rapid technological revolution in robotics and artificial intelligence, a revolution that has been heralded as the fourth Industrial Revolution—or Industry 4.0. The potential for automation seems to be higher in manufacturing than service sector jobs, which typically require creative thinking or face-to-face interactions. Most manufacturing activities, which are routine, repetitive, and codifiable, are in the bull's eye of the automation revolution. This poses a concern for developing countries, such as Bangladesh, that have large pools of low-skilled workers in labour-intensive manufacturing. The local RMG sector has adopted to involve the most labour-intensive processes such as cutting, sewing and knitting because of the nature of their functions. Recent advances in technology and a shift to capital-intensive replacement methods may lead to structural unemployment in the sector. With a lack of plans for diversification in manufacturing, the abrupt takeover of capital-intensive production methods in the global RMG industries will lead to downscaling of the manufacturing sector. A probable case for developing countries facing this could be to expand their global trade on services by shifting labour into the service sector, often leading to a situation of premature deindustrialisation (Rodrik 2013). Currently, many developing countries are experiencing a decline in manufacturing at levels of income that are a fraction of those at which the advanced economies started to de-industrialise. This deindustrialisation is more pronounced concerning employment than output. However, the question remains as to whether the labour in Bangladesh is skilled enough to take on this major shift to the service sector, given the lack of investment in human capital.

In addition, Bangladesh is experiencing its period of the demographic dividend, which needs to be capitalised on through adopting both public and private provisions for continued growth. The demographic dividend is experienced when there is an increase in the working age population and a decrease in the dependency ratio, which is the intermediate or productive phase (Titumir and Rahman 2017). The dependency ratio of Bangladesh was at its highest at 93 in 1975, which declined by 45% to 51 in 2015, and is expected to drop further; reaching its lowest during the 2030s. The key challenges at this stage are ensuring adequate investment and employment opportunities, expanding the productive capacity and adopting 'job-rich' growth enhancing policies.

Productive Expansion

The transfer of technology and knowledge were the main factors that led to the emergence of the dominant garments sector. Some discrepancies, however, can be observed in the sector today that holds back the growth of this sector, or may do so in the future. Garment-producing firms in Bangladesh have specialised in various processes such as cutting, sewing, and knitting, which are more labour-intensive than weaving and spinning. Instead, they use imported made-up fabric and yarn as their basic materials.

Currently, garment owners ensure high productivity by micromanaging each step of the production process through the excessive use of worker supervision. The RMG sector has invested more on monitoring and managing than on the labourers' wellbeing as well as productivity enhancing initiatives for these staff. The real wages of labourers are thus below the minimum standard.

Despite an upward movement in the manufacturing sector, it has been reported that a large number of medium and small industrial mills and factories have been shut down. The tendency towards being dependent on a particular sector and a lack of other progressive and alternative sectors expose the economy to collapse during any economic crisis. The RMG sector has also been confronted with other difficulties recently. Bangladesh has been facing fierce competition from Vietnam and Cambodia. The Trade War between United States and China has benefitted these countries as industries from China shifted to these locations. Aggressive technology acquisition and a skilled work force has also resulted in higher productivity among the South East Asian nations. On top of it, the garments industry is concentrated in only a few products (Titumir 2020). Ten garments products accounts for 68% of the total export of readymade garments. As a result, the sector is extremely fragile to shocks. Exports in RMG sector has declined by 7.74% between July and November compared to the same period of the previous year (EPB 2019). RMG export earnings totalled 13.08 billion US dollars in the first five months of this fiscal year. It is 13.63% lower than the target.

61 garment factories were shut down before November of 2019, leading to 31,600 job losses (BGMEA 2019).

Sustainability Conditions

Human beings and nature co-exist in a mutual and interdependent relationship. Nature contributes to human life through resources, ecosystem goods and services as well as enormous gifts. On the other hand, human beings make and transmit laws, policies, regulations, norms, and values. When institutions function virtuously along with the supply of the factors of production from humans to the economy, the economic system works in a circular flow, by providing economic goods and services to human beings in return. Both institutions and the economy play their role as anthropogenic drivers and affect nature such that when these drivers perform positively, both humans and nature become beneficial to each other and human beings thrive in harmony with nature. The sustainability framework of growth provided in this book underscores the positive attributes of anthropogenic drivers, which benefit both humans and nature (Fig. 1.6).

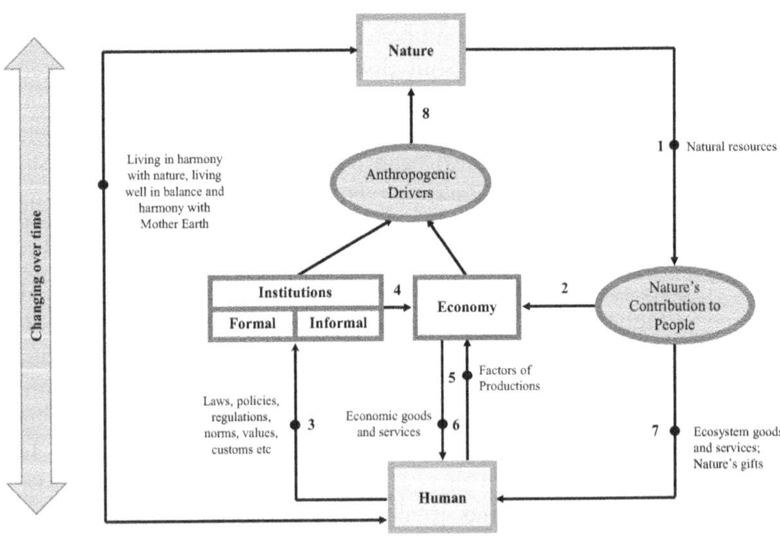

Fig. 1.6 Sustainability framework (*Source* Author)

Institutions for Conservation of Natural Resources

Nature has been a source of both blessings and sufferings for Bangladesh. While the riverine land has experienced great fertility, the country has seen the rage of nature as well in the form of disasters. Rivers play a crucial role in the agriculture of the country. The issue of living in harmony with nature, however, has always been neglected in the development process of the country. Human beings consider nature as the supplier of mere commodities that provide monetary value, which therefore lead to over extraction of natural resources as well as little concern for nature's wellbeing. The relationship between nature and humans have become lopsided as more natural resources are extracted without pondering on the consequences. For example, the lack of institutional oversight regarding environmental protection has enabled sectors like shipbreaking to have detrimental impacts on the environment. The shipbreaking industry might be contributing to the economy, but at the cost of devastating the ecosystem. Forest area in the country has reduced to 1883 thousand hectares in 2020 from 1920 thousand hectares in 1990. Naturally regenerating forest has also declined in the same period from 1845 thousand hectares to 1725 thousand hectares (FAO 2020).

The world's largest mangrove forest, the Sundarbans, is at risk from the Rampal coal-based power plant as well as other newly sanctioned power plants which are in the ecologically critical area. Moheshkhali, the only hilly island of Bangladesh, has also become threatened due to the plans of establishing 15 electric power plants by the government. As a result, the harmony of nature will breakdown and many other rare animals, zooplankton, phytoplankton and coral reefs will be endangered due to environmental degradation.

Restoring natural resources can be done through strengthening both formal and informal institutions. Informal institutions denote the relationship between locals and the nature. Customs and values have made it possible for the locals to live in harmony with nature.

With renewed interest on the environment, it has become extremely difficult to ignore the environment impacts in pursuit of growth. It is in the best interest of Bangladesh to adopt environment-oriented policies. Renewable energy has already become accessible and affordable. Investing heavily in fossil-fuel based power plants when other countries are abandoning the technologies does not look future proof and sustainable.

Growth and the Environment

The air quality of Dhaka has been ranked the worst in the world, raising serious concerns for public health. Bangladesh has emerged as the most polluted country in the world where average PM2.5 concentration was 97.1 $\mu g/m^3$. Dhaka ranks as the second highest polluted capital whereas Delhi stands first (IQA AirVisual 2018).

Bangladesh has been identified as being at risk from climate change due to its exposure from sea level rise, and extreme events prevalence leading to concentrated multi-dimensional poverty. Bangladesh's population at risk of sea level rise is predicted to grow to 27 million by 2050 (IPCC 2014).

In the Environmental Performance Index (EPI), Bangladesh ranks 179 among 180 countries with a score of 29.56 out of 100. Bangladesh plans to introduce 29 coal-fired power plants with a capacity of 33,200 MW to meet its energy demand. The only existing coal-fired power plant in Bangladesh, the Barapukuria Subcritical Plant, has had detrimental effects on the environment. The coal ash pond contaminated land and water in the region with toxic heavy metals (Market Forces 2019). The Barapukuria Power Plant was closed down briefly last year due to a mismanagement of coal, which caused a shortfall. Poor management in this case caused a power shortage in the national grid. 22 out of the 29 proposed power plants have a capacity which is two times or higher than that of Barapukuria and any mismanagement in operating the power plants will significantly affect the national power grid. It is worth mentioning that SDG 16 is about institutions and governance.

Extractive institutions and poor governance of the country have emerged as potential bottlenecks in achieving SDGs, which therefore pose threats to sustain growth as well as harmonious coexistence of human beings and nature. Political institutions are crucial to achieve the SDGs and face the climate related challenges. Bangladesh seems to lag behind in terms of evolving its institutions, politics and development activities towards natural sustainability.

Concluding Remarks

Analysing the drivers of growth, this chapter argues that, labour is a major source of growth in Bangladesh. The inflows of remittances are what fuels this growth. A boom in the RMG sector in the early 1990s also this fuelled growth. Both the RMG and remittance are labour intensive and the economy is still propelled by the two, due to restricted productive expansion in the economy. The discrepancies in national income accounting indicate fragility in macroeconomic indicators as well as poor institutional capacity of the agencies. The RMG sector, which contributes most to the exports of the economy, is on the decline. The lack of investment is a hindrance towards productive expansion of the economy. Governance systems of the country are also on the negative margin resulting in weak regulation and enforcement of laws. The results of weaker institutions present in the country can also be observed from the fact that poverty is on the ascent.

This chapter identifies several fragilities, which need to be addressed in order to move to next phase of development. The productive expansion of the economy as well as the enforcement of regulations by the government can be identified as the crucial factors to the transformability and sustainability of growth. Transformation conditions of economic growth, as explained, depend on strong and functioning institutions.

There is a need to maintain the rigidity and reliability of the national statistics. Discrepancies in the statistics will pose problems in policy design. Bangladesh Bureau of Statistics is primarily responsible for collection and dissemination of statistics. It is imperative for the organisation to work independently to maintain the credibility of the statistics. Overestimating statistics may lead to inappropriate policy formulation.

It is clearly evident that the country has chosen fossil fuels as the main resource for energy generation. This defies the global march towards renewable energy. Such policies clearly work against the SDGs and will have serious environmental impacts on a country which is already earmarked as one of the most vulnerable to climate change. Fossil fuels may energise the economy in the short run. However, in the long run, it will clearly hamper biodiversity and the relationship between humans and nature.

This chapter further underscores that the growth in Bangladesh is not a surprise, conundrum or paradox. If the necessary conditions are met, quantitative achievement occurs. Rather, there is a deficiency in attaining the sufficient conditions for growth, understood as institutions and political settlement, which can transform the economy into the desired form. In order to achieve transformational and sustainable growth, inclusive institutions and a competitive political system is a must.

References

Acemoglu, Daron, Simon Johnson, and James A. Robin. 2001. The Colonial Origins of Comparative Development: An Empirical Investigation. *American Economic Review* 91 (5): 1369–1401.

ADB. 2016. *Bangladesh: Looking Beyond Garments-Employment Diagnostic Study.* Asian Development Bank.

ADB. 2020. *Asian Development Outlook 2020.* Asian Development Bank.

Asadullah, M.N., A. Savoia, and W. Mahmud. 2014. Paths to Development: Is There a Bangladesh Surprise? *World Development* 62: 138–154.

Barai, M.K. 2020. Bangladesh's Economic and Social Progress From a Basket Case to a Development Model.

BBS. 2011. Report of the Household Income & Expenditure Survey 2010. Bangladesh Bureau of Statistics. Ministry of Planning.

BBS. 2017. Statistical Yearbook 2017. Statistical Report, Bangladesh Bureau of Statistics.

BBS. 2019. Final Report on Household Income and Expenditure Survey 2016. Statistical Report, Bangladesh Bureau of Statistics.

BGMEA. 2018. BGMEA Trade Information. www.bgmea.com.bd/home/pages/Tradeinformation.

BGMEA. 2019. BGMEA Trade Information. www.bgmea.com.bd/home/pages/Tradeinformation. Accessed December 2019.

BMET. 2018. Remittance Inflows: Country wise in 2018–19. Statistical Reports, Bureau of Manpower, Employment and Training.

BMET. 2019. Overseas Employment in 2019. Statistical Report, Bureau of Manpower, Employment and Training, Statistical Report.

EPB. 2019. Export Data. Export Promotion Bureau. www.epb.gov.bd/site/view/epb_export_data/. Accessed December 16, 2019.

EPB. 2020. Export Data. Export Promotion Bureau. www.epb.gov.bd/site/view/epb_export_data/. Accessed October 20, 2020.

FAO. 2020. Global Forest Resource Assessment 2020. Food and Agriculture Organisation.

GFI. 2019. Illicit Financial Flows to and from 148 Developing Countries: 2006–2015. Global Financial Integrity.

ILO. 2020a. ILOSTAT. https://ilostat.ilo.org/data/. Accessed October 25, 2020.

ILO. 2020b. Global Wage Report 2020–21. Wages and Minimum Wages in the Time of COVID-19. ILO.

IPCC. 2014. Climate Change 2014: Impacts, Adaptation and Vulnerability. Fifth Assessment Report, United Nations Intergovernmental Panel on Climate Change.

IQA AirVisual. 2018. World Air Quality Report-Region & City PM 2.5 Ranking. Switzerland: IQAir AirVisual: Goldach.

Islam, N. 2003. Urbanization, Migration and Development in Bangladesh: Recent Trends and Emerging Issues. Demographic Dynamics in Bangladesh Looking at the Larger Picture. Centre for Policy Dialogue and UNFPA. Dhaka, pp. 125–146.

Kaufmann, D., A. Kraay, and M. Mastruzzi. 2020. The Worldwide Governance Indicators 2020.

Khan, Mushtaq. 2013. Bangladesh: Economic Growth in a Vulnerable Limited Access Order. 24–69.

Market Forces. 2019. Choked by Coal: The Carbon Catastrophe in Bangladesh. Market Forces.

Marshall, M.G., T.R. Gurr, and K. Jaggers. 2020. Center for Systemic Peace. Polity IV Project.

Ministry of Finance. 2019. Bangladesh Economic Review 2019.

National Board of Revenue. 2019. Revenue Collection Report.

Quddus, M., and S. Rashid. 2000. Entrepreneurs and Economic Development: The Remarkable Story of Garment Exports from Bangladesh. University Press.

Rodrik, Dani. 2013. The Perils of Premature Deindustrialisation. Project Syndicate 11.

Salma, U., M.M. Hasan, and M.I. Sultana. 2020, February. A Regression Model-Based Approach to Identifying Determining Factors for GDP Growth in Bangladesh. In *2020 International Conference on Emerging Trends in Information Technology and Engineering* (ic-ETITE), 1–6. IEEE.

Sonobe, Tetsushi, Khondoker Abdul Mottaleb, and MD. Nurul Amin. 2018. The Miraculous Development of the Garment and Pharmaceutical Industries in Bangladesh. In *Economic and Social Development of Bangladesh*, 27–51. Cham: Palgrave Macmillan.

Subramanian, Arvind. 2009. India's Turn: Understanding the Economic Transformation. OUP Catalogue.

Subramanian, Arvind. 2019. Validating India's GDP Growth Estimates. Center for International Development at Harvard University.

Titumir, Rashed Al Mahmud. 2020. Diversification—The Pathway for Economic Recovery, 2020. https://www.cipe.org/wp-content/uploads/2020/07/Titumir_Diversification.pdf.

Titumir, Rashed Al Mahmud, and Zahidur Rahman. 2017. Changes in Population Age Structure and Economic Development: The Case of Bangladesh. *Florya Chronicles of Political Economy* 3 (1): 1–54.

UNCTAD. 2020. World Investment Report, 2020. UNCTAD.

United Nations. 2017. *Sustainable Development Goals Report 2017*. New York: Department of Economic and Social Affairs.

Unnayan Onneshan. 2020. Whither Bending the Curves for Life and Livelihoods: A Rapid Assesment of National Budget 2020–21.

World Bank. 2011. *Gender Equality and Development' World Development Report 2012*. Washington, DC: World Bank.
World Bank. 2017. *End Poverty: End Extreme Poverty, Boost Shared Prosperity. Annual Report*. Washington, DC: World Bank.
World Bank. 2019. *World Development Indicator*. Washington D.C.: World Bank.

CHAPTER 2

Agriculture in Bangladesh

Introduction

The chapter ushers that the economy of Bangladesh has made inroads in agricultural production. However, productivity in agriculture has declined. Land is now more fragmented because of inheritance by descendants. Additionally, agriculture is still the sector with the highest employment and remains a ways from achieving structural transformation. The prices of inputs have increased, impacting profitability of the farmers. The green revolution has undoubtedly increased the yield but only in cereal production, and has thus created a concentrated output basket. The cereal production may have allowed Bangladesh to achieve self-adequacy, but high retail prices, mostly due to high margin gobbled up by the intermediaries, serve as a major hindrance in attaining food security for the huge majority of people, including the poor. Fertilisers and pesticides in the production process result in higher outputs but only at the cost of degradation of land and loss of biodiversity. In addition, the increased use of deep tubewells and pumps in irrigation has led to a significant decrease in the subterranian water levels. In such a scenario, the agricultural sector has fallen into the crisis of meeting sustainability conditions which are progressively looming ominously. This chapter, thus, attempts to examine the sustainability of agricultural growth in Bangladesh.

R. A. M. Titumir, *Numbers and Narratives in Bangladesh's Economic Development*,
https://doi.org/10.1007/978-981-16-0658-8_2

Since its independence, Bangladesh has depended on agriculture for both the growth of its GDP and the employment of its population. Agriculture contributed almost 60% of the GDP in the 1970s (Ministry of Finance 2019). However, the contribution of agriculture to the GDP started to fall at the start of the 1980s, as the doors for the manufacturing sector opened. During this period, the agricultural sector employed almost 70% of the population whilst agricultural total factor productivity index (TFP) was only around 98 (Fuglie 2015). Bangladesh started moving out of the subsistence level in the 1990s. The share of employment in agriculture fell at the start of the twenty-first century and currently stands at around 40% (BBS 2018). The slow decline in agricultural employment shows that the country is still in the transition stage in attaining structural transformation.

In terms of output, the government of the newly born country directly participated in pricing and distribution by erecting import tariffs on food products, demonstrating its commitment to promote the agricultural sector. The Government set policies like the minimum price programme in the distribution of agricultural produce only to forfeit the programme later. The output of agriculture was still very concentrated within cereal production. The production of jute declined greatly, thus making cereals the only major crops of the country.

During this period, the government established institutions like BRRI and BARI to carry out research and innovation in agriculture. The outcome of these research institutions was the high-yielding varieties of many crops. The growth in farm mechanisation in Bangladesh was mainly generated by enabling policy reforms. Rural mechanisation gained momentum in the 1990s and spread all over the country. Rural labour shrank as workers migrated to the formal sector and other non-farm jobs, raising rural real wages and thereby enhancing total labour earnings. As a result, rural farmers got the opportunity to get escalated real wages, which later improved food security and livelihoods, and helped the poor escape poverty.

The fertilisers used in agriculture were imported for the most part, distributed and subsidised by the Bangladesh Government until the 1990s and thus farmers received fertilisers at much lower prices. The fertiliser sector, however, was greatly affected by the market liberalisation and privatisation efforts of the Government in the 1990s. As a result, private businesses started selling fertilisers in the market extensively after importing them from abroad. This allowed mass use of fertilisers in agricultural production and resulted in higher outputs. However, such initiatives had negative outcomes as well. The privatised market for the inputs often created price fluctuations due to uncertainty (Islam 2003). In addition, they were impacted by the asymmetric information characteristics of the market, which affected the use of fertilisers in the 1990s (Islam 2003). The price of fertilisers soared and government again took back control of the market to stabilise prices. After several years, urea, the most widely used fertiliser, was produced in the country, resulting in lower prices due to the subsidies provided by the Government.

Higher growth in agricultural outputs propels the growth of the manufacturing sector of a country through shifting surplus labour and capital from agriculture to manufacturing (Lewis 1954). In Bangladesh, the structural transformation has been occurring at a dawdling pace. Employment in the agricultural sector is still 40.1% of the population. Technology and mechanisation are only at the primary level of production. Coupled with low productivity, this implies that there exists some form of underemployment in this sector.

Poverty rate among agricultural workers was 50% in 2005, which decreased to 32.6% in 2016. The rate of reduction in poverty, however, declined during this period. From 2005 to 2010, rural poverty reduction was 69% and in the next five years, it dropped to only 27% (World Bank 2019a). Lower farm wages exacerbate the situation, creating income inequality and have minimised access to public goods and services. Farmers have been deprived of fair prices due to the engineering of middlemen and powerful syndicates.

Food supply per capita has increased in Bangladesh over the years and has surpassed the average dietary energy requirement. The availability of food though does not ensure food security as prices of food has gone up, hampering its affordability. Because of higher prices, there is a severe food insecure population in Bangladesh. The unavailability of nutritious food and the variability of intake puts them in a vulnerable condition.

Agriculture is dominated by small farms. The number of small farm holdings increased in the 1990s and there was a sharp slump in large farm holdings. Nevertheless, land fragmentation started gaining pace since average farm sizes decreased significantly. However, only one fifth of the agricultural land was arable under some form of irrigation system.

The availability of agricultural land is on the decline because of rapid urbanisation. Arable land in the country has shrunk to 7.7 million hectares from 9.133 million hectares in 1972 (FAO 2019). As land becomes more fragmented over time, the number of smaller land holdings increase. Households with smaller land holdings fail to specialise and create enough surplus to buy more land and inputs. Eventually, they fall victims to a vicious cycle.

During the covid-19 pandemic, the farmers of Bangladesh have faced a loss of more than BDT 565 billion in the last one and half months (BRAC 2020). As Bangladesh is heavily dependent on food imports, it may face a severe crisis in food availability as the pandemic severely impacts agriculture production across the world. Global prices of farm produce will be increasing as a result. The scenario indicates that food security may be in serious threat if the limited drive for diversification in agriculture is persistent (Unnayan Onneshan 2020).

The objective of this chapter is to discuss the conditions that have caused low agricultural productivity and frustrated sustainability conditions. The factors related to agricultural production include the inputs, outputs and technology. Each of these determines the productivity of agriculture. A decline in agricultural productivity can be imputed to these factors. The inputs in the agricultural sector primarily comprises agricultural land, labour, capital stocks, fertilisers, seeds and energy. On the other hand, the goods produced are the outputs gained from the inputs. Technology has been treated as a separate factor due of its sheer importance in production. Machineries, irrigation methods and harvesting methods are a few elements of technology.

Both the absolute values and the price of inputs have consequential effects on productivity. The use of more inputs than necessary will lower productivity. The chapter proceeds to find the conditions required to increase the productivity to a level which will meet the current demands and propel agriculture towards sustained growth. These conditions include output diversification, efficient use of land, optimum use of fertilisers, formal credit to smaller farms, land irrigation etc., which can maximise agricultural output. Finally, the conditions which help to sustain the productivity levels to fulfil future demand as well as income sources from agriculture are also delineated. Higher spending in research, reduction in the use of ground water, use of bio fertilisers and sustainable agriculture methods are required to keep up with the higher production requirements in the face of upcoming challenges.

The framework denotes three conditions—stability, transformability and sustainability. Stability conditions can be derived from three factors which are inputs, outputs and farm mechanisation. Inputs comprise price condition of inputs, land, fertiliser and agricultural credit. The variation in the output basket is included in output and farm mechanisation consists of the use of technology and machines (Fig. 2.1).

The appropriate functioning of stability indicators contributes to the efficient use of land, optimum use of fertiliser and credit to small farms, which ultimately leads to transformation. When variation in the output basket satisfies stability conditions, it results in output diversification and the production of cash crops, creating output transformation. In terms of technology and machines, transformation occurs when the prevalence of increased land irrigation and mechanisation in all levels of farming takes place. The outcomes that result from the transformation process march towards sustainability, signifying the presence of sustainable methods of production, reduction in the use of ground water, use of bio fertilisers,

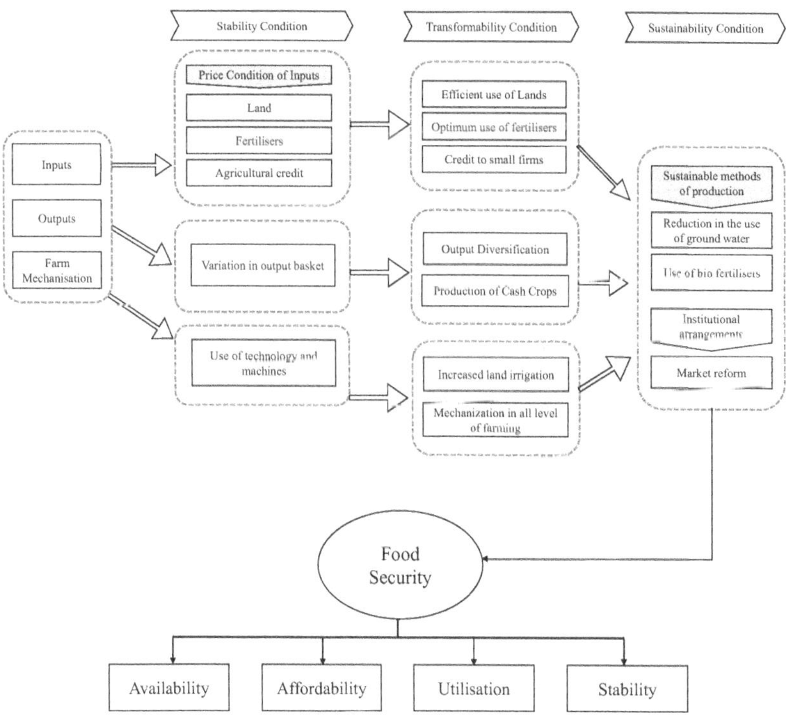

Fig. 2.1 Stability, transformation and sustainability framework (*Source* Author)

institutional arrangements and market reforms. It is to be noted that institutions play a crucial role during all the stages, as without institutional support, rules, regulations and policies as well as the achievement of transformability and sustainability become precarious and gruelling. Sustainability ensures food security which is comprised of four elements—availability, affordability, utilisation and stability. Food security can be ensured once all of these elements are aligned and achieved.

Stability Conditions

Stability condition determines the current state of different indicators and associated risks of the agricultural sector. The analysis of the stability conditions includes inputs and outputs of agricultural production. Inputs include traditional factors like land and labour as well as modern technology used in agriculture.

Fragility in Food Security

In terms of food security, comprised of four pillars—availability, affordability, utilisation and stability, Bangladesh has only achieved the first pillar—availability of food. The threshold for undernourishment in Bangladesh is 1,960 kcal/per capita per day and the average dietary energy requirement for Bangladesh is 2,290 kcal/per capita per day. The food supply per capita per day has increased in the country in the last decade. Food supply per capita now stands at 2,450 kcal/per capita per day (FAO 2019). The supply of food is now well beyond the minimum and average requirement for the country. Even though the net production of food in the country may have surpassed the demand, the prices of food may hamper its affordability—the second pillar of food security, to all households. The prevalence of severely food insecure populations is 10.2% in Bangladesh, even though the country has a net production of food well above the minimum required (FAO 2019). This means that one in ten people cannot afford the minimum food requirement. For European countries, the percentage is less than one.

The utilisation of food in Bangladesh is also in a pitiable condition. The diminishing rate of undernourishment has slowed down due to the lack of a comprehensive increase in crop production. As a result, intake of essential nutrients has worsened simultaneously, signified by an increase in wasting in children under 5, from 11.8% in 2005 to 14.3% in 2016 (FAO

2019). The share of dietary energy derived from cereals and roots and tubers is 80% in Bangladesh. In high income countries, it is 31% (FAO 2019). From 2010 to 2018, milk production increased 237 times, yet the consumption of milk has reduced to 27.31 grams in 2016 from 33.72 grams in 2010. During the same time, production of meat has increased 277 times, but the consumption increased slightly by 0.7 grams.

The stability of food security is vulnerable, as a high percentage of the population remains undernourished and suffers from fatal food insecurity. Bangladesh ranks 88th among 117 countries in the Global Hunger Index and thus has serious hunger problems (GHI 2019). In the Global Food Security Index, Bangladesh stands 83rd among 113 countries, the lowest in South Asia (*The Economist* 2019). Thus, these indices indicate that food adequacy has not ensured food security in Bangladesh.

Slow Rate of Structural Transformation

The growth that the agriculture sector has seen in Bangladesh over the last 25 years needs to converge to a level where the outputs from agriculture will not only ensure food security but also provide income for the population involved in it. The goal of agriculture is not only to ensure food security but also to speed up structural transformation. The share of agriculture in GDP stood at 13.32% in 2017–2018, declining from 17.71% in 2010–2011 (Ministry of Finance 2019). The rate of growth in the agricultural sector is in decline. The rate of growth has gone down to 3.51 in 2018–2019 from 4.19 in 2017–2018 (Ministry of Finance 2019). Employment in agriculture has also been shrinking but at a slower rate than the contribution to GDP.

The beginning of structural transformation is evident from the percentage of labour employed in agriculture. The share of total employment in agriculture was 45.1% in 2013 and it has gone down to 40.6% in 2016 within 3 years (ILO 2019). The rate of employment in the agricultural sector has declined in the last decade (Fig. 2.2). In 1999–2000, employment in the sector was 50.76% which came down to 45.1% in 2013. The growth in persons employed in the agricultural sector has been in reversal since 1999–2000. In 1999–2000, the rate of growth of employment was 1.53% per year which became 4.29% in the 2005–2006 to 2010 period, and again decreased to 0.60% in 2010–2013 (ADB and ILO 2016).

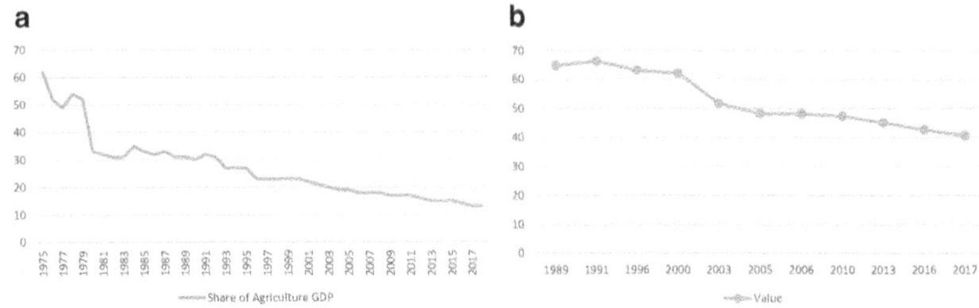

Fig. 2.2 **a** Share of agriculture in GDP (World Bank 2019b); **b** Share of employment in agriculture (*Source* BBS, Labour Force Survey 2016)

The output growth in the agricultural sector has lessened to 3.28% in 2010–2013 from 5.32% during the period of 1995–1996 to 1999–2000. Although the manufacturing sector has become more labour intensive than before, the agricultural sector has not been on the same path. The employment elasticity plunged to 0.1951 in 2010–2013 from 0.7293 during the period of 1995–1996 to 1999–2000 (ADB and ILO 2016). Non-agricultural sources now contribute more than agricultural sources in rural households. The contribution from agricultural income is now 38.21% (BBS 2019).

Increasing Land Fragmentation

Land has been on the decline as a result of aggressive industrialisation and urbanisation. Agricultural land can be categorised in two ways. Croplands are those in which different types of crops are grown regardless of the quality of the land as Bangladesh is situated in the Ganges delta and thus has one of the most fertile lands in the world. In Bangladesh, there has been a decline in all types of land over the years. Size of lands are getting smaller due to fragmentation as a parcel of land being divided amongst the descendants due to inheritance. This process has also caused waste of land used to create boundaries for demarcation amongst the successors of the family land. Smaller lands make farm mechanisation difficult and inefficient, as tractors and tillers cannot function efficiently in lands with smaller and irregular dimensions. Most importantly, this restricts achievement of economies of scale, causing a massive impediment to enhancing growth in productivity.

Table 2.1 Farm holdings

Farm holdings	*1983/84 (million)*	*1996 (million)*	*2008 (million)*
Small farms (0.5–2.5 acres)	7.07	9.42	12.53
Medium farms (2.5–7.5 acres)	2.48	2.08	2.11
Large farms (7.5+ acres)	0.50	0.30	0.23
Average farm size	0.81	0.60	0.50

Source BBS (2009)

The number of small farms has almost doubled in 25 years and at the same time, the number of large farms has reduced to half (Table 2.1). The number of medium farms has also declined, but at a slower rate. The average farm size has waned in this period, currently standing at 0.50 acres. The percentage of rural households without any land is 7.84% and the percentage of rural households in tenancy is 22.06%. Average farm sizes have decreased over the years for most of the developing countries but increased for the OECD countries and a few East Asian countries (FAO 2014). The average farm size of Bangladesh is lower than that of Japan, Thailand, and Vietnam where it was 1.2, 3.2 and 0.7 hectares respectively in 2000, compared to only 0.3 hectares in Bangladesh. At the same time, the average farm size in the United States and the United Kingdom is 178 and 70 hectares respectively.

The risk in the agriculture sector is associated with the size of farms in the country. The nature of risk often determines the outcome in this sector. Small farmers tend to be risk averse and hence opt for products which have the least risk and variability. Small farmers emphasise more on rice and wheat because of the least price volatility of these two goods in Bangladesh. As a result, small and medium households have the highest percentage in growing rice only (Hoque and Ahmed 2020). This works as a significant impediment towards diversification in the agricultural sector.

The landless population has increased over the years and thus contractual renting of land has increased. As the contracts usually span from one to three years, farmers have little incentive in investing in the lands. This also adds to the risk averse nature of the farmers as they have to pay rents regardless of any natural calamities or shocks that hamper production.

The smaller farmers have higher productivity but only within a very narrow range of productivity. The compulsion to maintain subsistence forces peasants to resort to intensive production and smallholding agriculture continues to increase in Bangladesh. These problems are not addressed by market reforms, although agriculture in the country is already largely liberalised, deregulated and privatised. If markets are to drive productivity growth, the expectation is that land transfers should be to smaller farmers. The peasants do not have the capacity to buy land due to high land prices as a result of purchases made by people who are either remitting income from cities or abroad, or people who are buying for industry or other purposes. Thus, the land has become an instrument of savings rather than investment, and the latter could have increased productivity (Titumir 2021).

Overuse of Fertilisers

The agricultural production process now depends more on fertilisers because of two reasons: firstly, the amount of land for agriculture has been decreasing, and land crops are now grown round the year with major and minor seasonal crops. Such high intensity of crop production has significantly deteriorated the quality of agricultural land. Secondly, there are high yielding varieties of crops grown in the country requiring large amounts of fertilisers, causing deterioration in the long run.

Bangladesh uses a greater quantity of fertilisers per hectare of arable land than India, while the rate of consumption has also increased significantly in recent years. Fertiliser consumption as a percentage of production is the highest in Bangladesh (Table 2.2). The overuse or inefficient use of inputs leads to increased cost of production and thus

Table 2.2 Fertiliser consumption

	Fertiliser consumption (% of fertiliser production)		*Fertiliser consumption (kg per hectare of arable land)*	
	2005	*2015*	*2005*	*2015*
Bangladesh	165	477	198	299
South Asia	136	155	124	164
East Asia and Pacific	136	109	270	328
OECD	86	90	121	132

Source World Bank (2019b)

raises the output prices. Subsidies in agriculture mostly go to the procurement of fertiliser and thus keeps the price within the capacity of the small farmers. This too has been a key factor in the overuse of fertilisers in the country. The Government provided subsidies worth USD 700 million in 2018–2019 season which accounts for almost 25% of the Ministry of Agriculture's budget. Government policy regarding subsidies in fertilisers has also contributed to the apparent concentration of output as 80% of the fertilisers is being used in rice production (World Bank 2020).

Differential Access to Credit

Higher credit allocation in the agricultural sector allows farmers to use better and higher quality inputs such as seeds, fertilisers etc. While the availability of credit has increased over the years, they fail to adequately reach the small farms. Agricultural land and productivity have an inverse relationship (Fan and Chan-Kang 2005). The smaller farms tend to have a higher productivity. The productivity is likely to increase with access to credit since credit allows access to better inputs needed for production. The majority of farm holdings in Bangladesh are small, with land areas less than 2.5 hectares. Farmers with small land holdings do not produce enough surplus output to be invested for the following year (Fig. 2.3).

Agricultural credit has seen a rise in recent years both in terms of its target and the disbursement amount. The disbursement exceeded the target for credit allocation. Recovery rate of credits is also higher in the recent years. Access to financial services is still skewed towards large farmers. 13.35% of the large and medium farmers have access to agricultural credit whereas only 7.15% of the small and marginal farmers have access to credit according to a nationwide household survey by IFPRI (*The Daily Star* 2017).

Declining Agricultural Productivity with Concentrated Output Basket

Agricultural production has, no doubt, increased in quantity during the last decade but the growth rate of output has declined. Agricultural output growth dwindled to 2.1% during 2010–2014 from 3.7 during the 2001–2010 period. Total Factor Productivity, an indictor measuring the efficiency of inputs, has therefore also decreased to 0.7 from 0.9 in the same period (IFPRI 2018). The production of rice, the main agricultural product of the country, has soared to 50 million tonnes in 2017 from

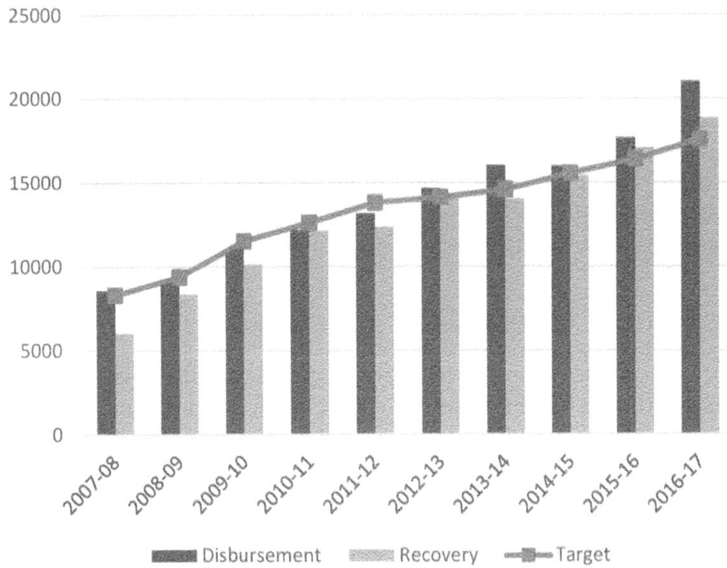

Fig. 2.3 Credit in agriculture (*Source* BBS 2019)

18 million tonnes in 1975, while the value of agricultural production has tripled in the same period.

In terms of agricultural production, rice paddy is the most grown crop in the country. Other crops consist of maize, roots and tubers, pulses and vegetables. In 2017, the quantity of rice paddy produced in the country was around 50 million tons. Maize amounted to 10 million tons and was the second highest agricultural good produced (FAO 2019). Bangladesh ranks high in the Crop Production Index compared to other regions. Once renowned for jute production, the country has shifted towards crop production because of the ability to grow all through the year. In recent years, Bangladesh has achieved food adequacy through the production of rice, which has increased significantly because of the introduction of the High Yielding Varieties (HYV) of rice.

Crop production of Bangladesh has greatly improved in the last decade and has surpassed South Asian and East Asian countries (Fig. 2.4). This is due to the high crop production intensity. Yield per hectare of land significantly increased after 2005, as farms started using technologies and

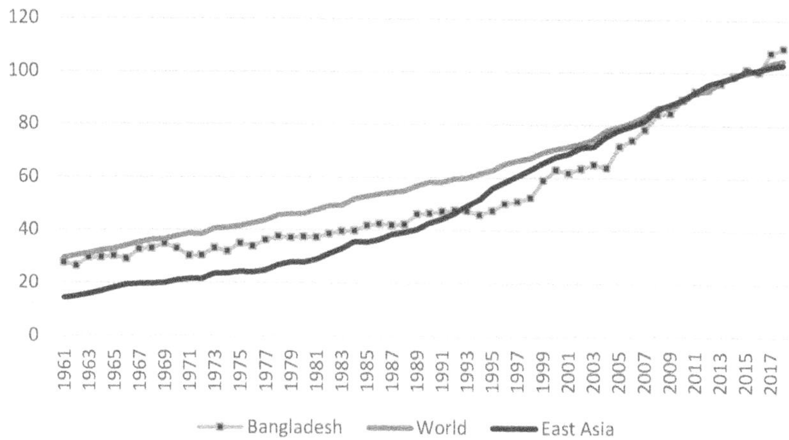

Fig. 2.4 Crop production index (*Source* FAO 2019)

HYV seeds in their production processes. High intensity production has enabled the country to attain self-adequacy in foods. An increase in the production of rice does not necessarily signify an increase in the production of all other crops. However, export earnings from agriculture are currently facing a steep decline. The cereal produced in the country is used primarily for consumption. Although jute has contributed most to the export value in agriculture, in recent years, the export value from jute has been on a downward trajectory.

The lack of farmers' capacity to bargain for fair prices of produce results in lower profits. As the small and medium farm holdings do not have access to better management, they are dominated by intermediaries. Stringent requirements for agricultural procurements by the government also force them to sell their produce at lower prices to intermediaries as small farmers often fail to fulfil those requirements (Mondal 2010).

Low Utilisation of Technology

High population density, fertile soil and deltas, the monsoon economy and the distribution of land and other assets have also shaped the crop farming system technologies (Mandal et al. 2017). The mechanisation process started from the irrigation of lands and has slowly spread to other farm activities. Agricultural mechanisation to a large part depends on R&D in the agriculture sector. Mechanisation in the country was the result of scientific research in institutes such as BARD, BADC, BRRI, BARI. In Bangladesh farm machinery includes machines driven by diesel engines or electrical motors and manually-operated modern farm implements. Engine- or motor-driven equipment includes shallow tube wells, deep tube wells, and low-lift pumps for irrigation; two-wheel power tillers and four-wheel tractors for land preparations; and combines harvesters and reapers for harvesting. Manually operated modern farm machineries include pedal threshers, pesticide and weedicide sprayers, briquette (guti) urea fertiliser applicators, seed drillers, weeders, and so on. Although mechanisation has increased rapidly, most machines concentrate on irrigation and land preparation. Even within the irrigation process, most of the machines are run by diesel and fuel which increases cost and is susceptible to shocks. Low cost sources of irrigation tools are still underused. Size of farms and incapabilities of small farmers handicap the use of modern technologies in crop harvesting. Hence, manual labour is required during harvesting period which increases the cost of production.

Loss from Covid-19

The covid-19 pandemic has hit the economy on all fronts. The agricultural sector suffered the worst blow as disruption in the supply chain due to the shutdown has caused massive losses for the producers. A study by BRAC suggests, around 88% of the farmers incurred losses during the lockdown in the country and amounts to BDT 565 billion (BRAC 2020). Nationwide shutdowns disrupted supply to the consumers resulting in a price hike. Increased food prices coupled with income erosion has worsened food insecurity in the country. The same study mentions that food expenditure in both rural areas and urban slums reduced by 28%.

Lockdown has also affected the production side because of disruption in the supply of inputs. Restrictions on movement has affected labour migration and caused a labour crisis in rural areas. This has caused an income erosion for the migrant agricultural labourers. At the same time, production cost rose as a shortage of migrant labour has increased the cost of labour. The cost of labour rose by 17% and the overall production cost increased by 13% according to a survey by BRAC (*The Financial Express* 2020). Mechanisation is still limited to land preparation and irrigation. Harvesting tools and machines are not widely used, which is also a reason behind the high cost of production. Further, producers of vegetables and non-rice crops, which are perishable items, also faced a declining price due to market shutdowns from the pandemic.

The Government has intervened to tackle the crisis in the agricultural sector. Most of the problems are now a result of institutional fragilities, which existed before the pandemic hit. The agricultural market has been a cause for concern as farmers faced low prices of outputs while consumers were paying higher prices in the market. The government's initiative to stabilise the market is limited within setting a price, direct purchasing and trade restrictions. During the pandemic, only 1% of the farmers sold rice at the price set by the government (*The Financial Express* 2020). The governments' rice procurement plan does not benefit the small farmers as it mostly procures 'boiled' rice from rice mills owned by large farmers. The state's policy to set output price accrues little benefit in the absence of any market monitoring.

The Government has come forward with a set of fiscal policies to mitigate the shock vide its stimulus package announcement for the agricultural sector with a focus on providing agricultural credit to the farmers. It plans to continue providing subsidies to this sector, especially in farm mechanisation. Such policies though fail to reach small and medium farmers. Access to financial services is critical for the small farmers. The ongoing crisis will no doubt lead to income losses for the farmers if this is not tackled. Without the proper financial ammunition, the ability to invest in the next farming season will remain an uncertainty.

Transformability Conditions

Transformability conditions entail the factors which are required for overcoming the major challenges identified in the previous section. In a bid to achieve food security and structural transformation, the issues discussed in the section merits meticulous startegies and actions.

Diversification of Output

To enhance farmers' income through the production of high-value crops and maintain a better soil structure for long-term sustainability, the country needs a departure from "rice-led" growth to a more diversified production base that includes several non-rice crops. Most of the production, other than rice, are minor crops and are only grown in a particular season (Table 2.3).

Table 2.3 Crop production

	Year ('000 tonnes)			
	1985	*1995*	*2005*	*2015*
Rice, paddy	22556	26399	39796	51805
Maize	3	3	356	2272
Pulses	546	532	316	384
Roots and tubers	1842	1903	5167	9509
Vegetables	1074	1390	2471	5058

Source FAO (2019)

In addition, the present yield potential of non-rice crops is very low. It can be increased to the level of HYV wheat if hybrid varieties are used, adequate demand is created and fair prices to the growers can be ensured. The Bangladesh Agricultural Research Institute (BARI) has already developed five high yielding medium duration maize varieties with grain yield potential of 5–7 Mt/hectare. These are suitable for flood prone areas.

Integrated Irrigation

Irrigated land is twice as productive as rain fed land after controlling for other factors (Fuglie 2008). One of the key factors in agricultural productivity growth in the Green Revolution of India was public investments in irrigation (Evanson et al. 1998). In sub-Saharan Africa, average yields on irrigated fields are 90% higher than on nearby rain fed fields (Fuglie and Rada 2013).

In Bangladesh, the percentage of irrigated land has increased in the 1990s. Availability of irrigation equipment allowed barren lands in the country to be converted into arable land. However, a large portion of land still remains out of the irrigation process (Fig. 2.5).

Irrigation in the country mostly depends on tube wells and power pumps, which is not sustainable as it causes groundwater table depletion. Therefore, an integrated water management system which combines rain harvesting and water from canals and rivers is required.

Bangladesh also suffers from lack of water management systems as 80% of the country gets flooded during the monsoon season. On the other hand, the north-eastern part of the country suffers from a deficiency in irrigation water during the non-monsoon seasons. Diversification towards

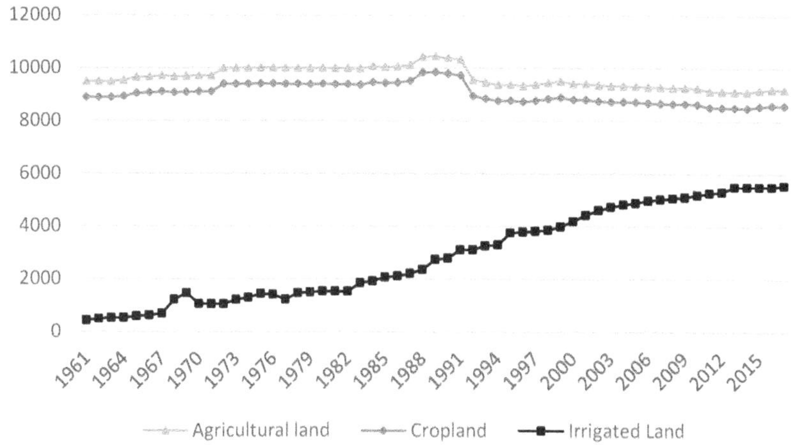

Fig. 2.5 Land pattern (*Source* FAO 2019)

non-cereal crops like vegetables and fruits also require better water management systems.

Optimum Use of Fertilisers

As the amount of agricultural and arable land is decreasing and the same land is used throughout the year for production, the soil is losing its quality. This has led to an increased need for fertilisers to retain productivity.

Bangladesh consumes more fertilisers compared to other South Asian nations but less than the East Asian nations who have higher productivity than Bangladesh (Fig. 2.6). The overuse of chemical fertilisers has a negative impact on the land, reducing its fertility and most importantly, making produced crops detrimental to human health in the long run. Soil salinity from excessive use of fertilisers may cause a decline in output by 15.6% (Dasgupta et al. 2014).

The marginal efficiency of fertilisers also decreases with increased use in production. When a similar parcel of land is used several times a year by means of intensive chemical fertilisers use, it will become infertile and fragile leading to a lower production of crops. If this phenomenon continues, the land can no longer be used.

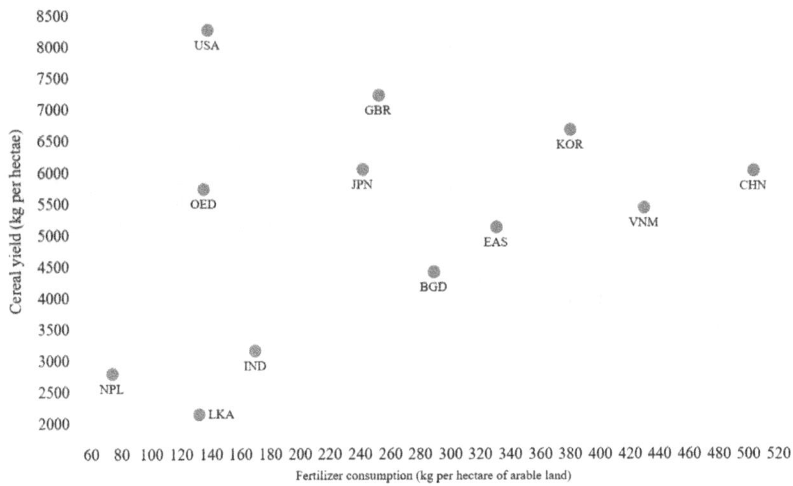

Fig. 2.6 Cereal crop yield vs fertiliser application (BGD = Bangladesh, IND = India, LKA = Sri Lanka, NPL = Nepal, CHN = China, JPN = Japan, VNM = Vietnam, KOR = Korea Republic, GBR = Great Britain, USA = United States of America, EAS = East Asian Average, OED = OECD Average) (*Source* Author's calculation)

OECD countries have higher crop yields than Bangladesh and use less fertiliser (Fig. 2.6). In comparison, East Asian countries have higher yields with higher use of fertilisers. Bangladesh's performance surpasses other South Asian countries in terms of crop yield per hectare. However, the efficiency of fertilisers is decreasing as the persistent use of these products eventually leads to diminishing returns.

The efficiency of fertilisers has declined in the last few years. Efficiency is the ratio of output per hectare and fertilisers used per hectare (Fig. 2.7). It is evident that the higher use of fertiliser is reducing agricultural output. Fertilisers are overused in the production process which raises the production cost and causes significant degradation of the land. This reduction in land fertility forces farmers to use more fertilisers. This has increased the overall use of fertilisers in Bangladesh, causing the land to lose fertility and increasing the cost of production. This eventually creates a vicious cycle which impacts soil productivity.

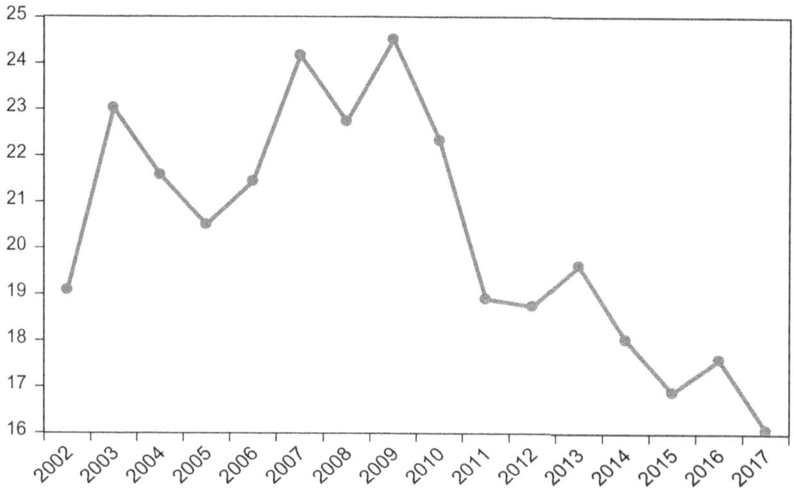

Fig. 2.7 Efficiency of fertilizers (*Source* Author's calculation)

Formalising Credit

Although informal sources of agricultural credit charge higher interest rates than their formal counterparts, they are widespread in rural areas. Borrowing from informal sources is popular among landless and marginal farmers. Medium and large farms borrow more from formal sources like the specialised state-owned Krishi Bank, NGOs and private banks. The proportion of agricultural credit borrowed from NGOs are much higher than the amount that is borrowed from banks (Table 2.4). This provides evidence of the tendency of households to opt for less formalised credit sources. Small farmers believe that the limited number of bank branches and less cooperation from branch officers are the main reasons behind their decision to opt for informal sources of credit (Barkat et al. 2010). Since most farm holdings in Bangladesh are small, informal credit is significantly more popular.

Mechanisation in Harvesting

While irrigation, tillage and threshing operations are almost fully mechanised, there has been modest mechanisation of two important operations

Table 2.4 Disbursement of agricultural credit according to division

Name of division	*Number of households with agricultural loan*	*Agricultural credit from banks (%)*	*Agricultural credit from NGOs (%)*
Barisal	413142	37.74	52.47
Chattogram	953300	31.82	58.80
Dhaka	1043585	29.03	59.79
Khulna	844554	23.36	70.51
Mymensingh	493598	23.30	48.39
Rajshahi	1084697	20.06	72.00
Rangpur	998860	20.36	74.81
Sylhet	481149	32.48	46.57
Total	6312885	26.03	63.28

Source BBS (2019)

i.e., transplanting/seeding and harvesting operations. These operations usually require more labour in the production process and it is often difficult for producers to hire labour during the off season. In addition, research on the size of farm holdings have shown that fragmentation has not significantly affected the expansion of irrigation and tillage mechanisation or productivity gains (Mandal et al. 2017).

The number of tillers and pumps portrays the use of technologies in irrigation (Table 2.5). Other machines like tractors and harvesters are not commonly used in Bangladesh. Bangladesh needs to opt for a full-scale

Table 2.5 Machineries used in agriculture

Machines	*Number*	*Number/'000 ha*
Tractor	35000	2.32
Power tiller	700000	46.42
Pump (DTW)	35322	2.34
Pump (STW)	1523609	101.04
Pump (LLP)	170569	11.31
Rice transplanter	400	0.03
Reaper	500	0.03
Combine harvester	200	0.01
Closed drum thresher	220000	14.59
Open drum thresher	15000	9.95

Source Alam (2016)

modernisation of the agriculture as the factor inputs of land and labour are expected to decline in the future.

Integrated Agricultural Marketing System

A fragile and complicated supply chain of agricultural products exists in the country. Agricultural products reach consumers after travelling through various intermediate markets; from village markets to the rural wholesale markets to the wholesale markets in the cities and finally from the wholesale markets to the corner shops in the cities. Intermediaries in various points of the supply chain in the agricultural markets results in rent seeking activities. Because of intermediaries, information asymmetry exists between producers and sellers. As a result of the above factors, producers do not get the right price for their products. Producers in the recent years have been regularly facing losses, especially in the *boro* seasons. Farmers on an average lost BDT 1.2 per kg in *boro* rice during the 2018–2019 season (World Bank 2020).

The price for consumers on the other hand has only increased in the same period. Hence, intermediaries are taking away profits from the producers because of the existing market structure and distribution system in the country.

Sustainability Conditions

The existing process of accumulation has resulted in a non-sustainable agriculture because of market failures caused by asymmetries of power, diseconomies of scale, and unstable property rights, resulting in arrested productivity growth. This has been further aggravated by climate change. Certain indications of climate change are already visible in the forms of salinity intrusion, river erosion, excessive rains, changes in the seasonal patterns, etc. It is imperative for the country to move towards sustainable agriculture.

Sustainable Irrigation Methods

There can be no denying the imperative to move towards sustainable irrigation methods. Increased land irrigation has a negative impact on the environment as irrigation generally involves use of groundwater and therefore causes decline in groundwater levels. At present, around 75% of the irrigation water comes from under ground whereas only 25% comes from surface sources like rivers and canals (FAO 2019). Increased use of surface water in irrigation is therefore needed for sustainable agricultural production. The daily use of water will increase by 0.8 mm/day at the end of this century because of climate change in the northwest region of the country. Irrigation rate will be 8.8 mm/day in the year 2025 (Shahid 2011). This will significantly lower the groundwater level, leading to desertification. Decline in the level of groundwater also affects the cost of production as pumping water from deeper levels will require more energy.

Ground water levels decline every year at the rate of 0.01 to 0.5 metres, particularly in the regions where *boro* rice is cultivated. Excessive use of groundwater has caused a 32% decline in the 10 years between 2003 and 2013 (Khaki et al. 2018). Ground water is primarily used for irrigation for *boro* rice cultivation, where around 25–75 deep tube-wells are planted per square kilometer—a process that originated in the 1960s. During the 1980s and 1990s, the installation of shallow tube-wells spiked, leading to a further increase in the groundwater extraction rate (Timsina et al. 2018).

Shifting Towards Bio-Fertilisers

For Bangladesh, developing sustainable conditions for agriculture remains a challenge due to a reduction in land and high input costs. By 2050, agricultural land is expected to be reduced by 17%, which will lower food production by 30% (Field 2014). Productivity and income from agriculture will only increase if the prices of inputs are lowered. Much of the demand is met by importing these fertilisers, raising input costs. Bangladesh has a much higher fertiliser consumption as a percentage of fertiliser production, which greatly increases the cost of production.

While analysing the quantity of fertilisers produced in Bangladesh and imports of fertilisers, it is clear that only the production of urea locally is more than the quantity imported (Fig. 2.8). Important fertilisers like muriate of potash (MoP) and superphosphates are mainly imported. To maintain sustainable productivity in agriculture, increased fertiliser production in Bangladesh is essential in reducing prices. By 2050, the demand for paddy rice will be 68.09 million tons. 1.71 million tons of chemical fertilisers will be required in order to meet this demand. The

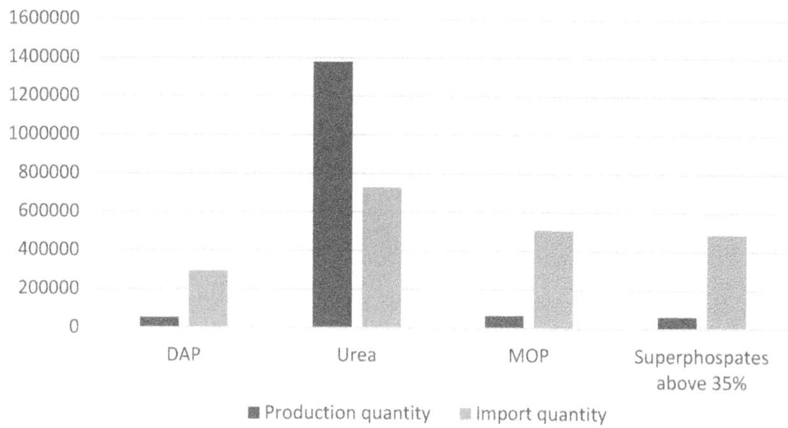

Fig. 2.8 Fertilisers by product (*Source* IFA 2018)

Table 2.6 Differences between recommended and actual fertiliser usage

Type of crop	*Recommended usage of fertiliser*			*Actual usage of fertiliser*			*Percentage of over-use/under-use*		
	Urea	*TSP*	*MoP*	*Urea*	*TSP*	*MoP*	*Urea*	*TSP*	*MoP*
T.Aus	141	101	69	135	28	17	4.26	72.28	75.36
T.Aman	166	101	69	135	30	24	18.67	70.30	65.22
Boro	269	131	121	192	47	37	28.62	64.12	69.42

Source Basak et al. (2015)

increased use of chemical fertilisers reduces the fertility of lands in the long run.

The use of bio slurries or organic fertilisers has the ability to contribute more than 30% of nutrient supply and more than 15% of the total demand of urea, TSP and MoP (Basak et al. 2015) (Table 2.6).

Diversification Towards Cash Crops

Sustainability also requires greater emphasis on the production of cash crops like jute and tea. This raises the value of products as these goods are both exported abroad and consumed in Bangladesh. The production

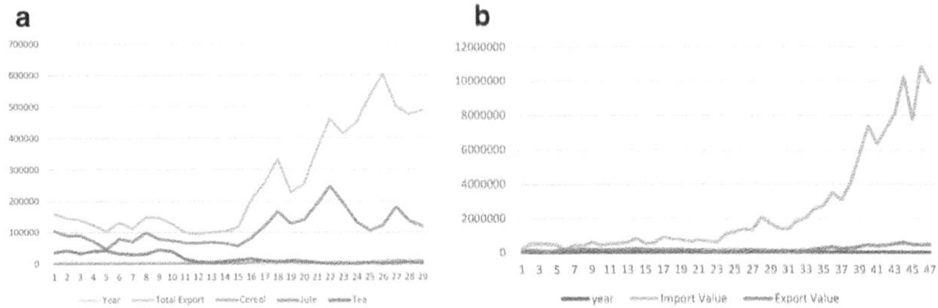

Fig. 2.9 Agricultural trade value (*Source* FAO Statistics 2019)

of jute and minor crops declined in previous decades, but growth has recently increased. Jute has the highest Revealed Comparative Advantage (RCA) score for Bangladesh with a score of 446.3 (UNCTAD 2019). RCA measures the relative comparative advantage of a country in producing and exporting a good to other countries. Hence, production and export of jute accrues the highest benefit for Bangladesh (Fig. 2.9).

To sustain agricultural mechanisation and the process of rural development, more research is needed in mechanisation to reduce drudgery in smaller scale rural enterprises, machinery safety, changing food systems and cropping patterns and the diversification of rural enterprises. It is imperative to maintain the mechanisation process and investments in R&D must increase.

Concluding Remarks

The pace of structural transformation is slower than expected. Traditional methods are still used in agriculture, which requires more labour. The migration from agriculture to manufacturing and service sectors has slowd down in recent years, but in the future, it is likely to create additional pressure in maintaining a sustainable productivity level.

The productivity level is declining in Bangladesh. The reduced farm sizes, coupled with high intensity of crop production, cause land degradation. In the case of agricultural inputs, price is the main concern in Bangladesh because the price of fertilisers and seeds raise the cost of production. Lower fertility of land and higher input prices result in lower agricultural productivity. Agricultural output can also increase total factor productivity since a diverse crop basket may generate more income for

Table 2.7 Summary of the major indicators in agricultural sector

Indicators	*Remarks*
Stability	
Land fragmentation	Land is getting fragmented. In 1983–1984 period, average farm size was 0.81 million acres which came down to 0.50 million acres
Efficient use of fertilisers	Fertiliser consumption has increased in 2015 (477% of fertiliser production) from that of 2005 (165%)
Access to credits	Small farms do not get sufficient access to credit
Variation in output basket	Concentration of crop production, particularly on rice. Declining export earnings. Incapability of bargaining is lessening profit for farmers
Use of technology	Increased mechanisation and less innovation in machineries
Transformation	
Import and production of fertilisers	Increased demand of fertilisers met through import thus raising the production cost
Land irrigation	Quantity of irrigated land has increased but by mostly using ground water
Credit formalisation	Most of the small farms borrow money from informal sectors at higher interest rate due to lack of access to formal banking
Mechanisation in farming at different levels	Tillage and threshing are almost fully mechanised but transplanting/seeding and harvesting operations are still very moderate. There is a lack of efficient labour force to use modern mechanisation methods
Sustainability	
Use of ground water	Ground water level is declining every year at the rate of 0.01 to 0.5 meter in the regions where boro rice is cultivated. Increase in installation of deep and shallow tube wells has exacerbated the problem further
Use of bio fertilisers	Random import and use of chemical fertiliser is occurring in lieu of using bio fertilisers. Detrimental impact of chemical fertilisers on soil, water, flora and fauna

(continued)

Table 2.7 (continued)

Indicators	*Remarks*
Food security	Bangladesh has ranked 83rd, lowest among South Asian countries in the Global Food Security Index-2019. Specially, quality and safety of food indicator is very moderate

the producer. Lastly, technological progress can greatly reverse the trend in productivity through mechanisation in all forms of agriculture.

Productivity plays an immense role in creating a surplus for the producers since the majority of the agricultural producers reside in the rural areas and live below or close to the poverty line. Increased agricultural productivity can serve as a major vehicle to eradicate rural poverty.

An important objective of agriculture is to ensure food security for the population. Food security cannot be ensured just through higher production; the price of foods must be kept at a level that people from all economic classes have access to these products. Food prices in Bangladesh have been increasing steeply but the primary producers of the food barely get the price due to a lengthy supply chain where non-producer-intermediaries get the majority of the profit.

Current production methods are not suitable for sustainable agriculture in Bangladesh. The high use of chemical fertilisers negatively impact biodiversity and land fertility. Chemical fertilisers increased production in the short run. However, its high use in the long run will lower production due to reduced land fertility. Groundwater levels in the country are also receding due to intensive land irrigation methods. The impact of climate change on Bangladesh will cause a loss of land, due to rising sea levels. The use of bio fertilisers and underground water to keep nature safe must be managed to ensure that sustainable production is maintained and food security is assured.

There is also a need to maintain statistical coherence for better policy formulation. Agricultural statistics relies on a single survey and census, last published in 2008. In terms of statistics for consumption and food security, the Government relies on the Household Income and Expenditure Survey. The discrepency between the various organisations questions the reliability of these statistics. As such, they pose a bottleneck in the adoption of the appropriate policies in the sector.

References

Alam, M. 2016. *Status of Agricultural Mechanisation in Bangladesh. A presentation in a workshop on Appropriate-Scale Mechanisation Innovation Hub-Bangladesh*. Held at Bangladesh Agricultural University, 20–21 March 2016.

ADB and ILO. 2016. *Employment and the Labour Market in Bangladesh: Overview of Trends and Challenges*. Asian Development Bank, International Labour Organisation.

Barkat, Abul, Rushad Faridi, Syed Naimul Wadood, Shubhash Kumar Sengupta, and SNM Ehsanul Hoque. 2010. A Quantitative Analysis of Fertiliser Demand and Subsidy Policy in Bangladesh. *NFPCSP, FAO*.

Basak, Jayanta Kumar, Rashed Al Mahmud Titumir, and Khosrul Alam. 2015. Future Fertiliser Demand and Role of Organic Fertiliser for Sustainable Rice Production in Bangladesh. *Agric. For. Fish* 4: 200–208.

BBS. 2009. *Census of Agriculture 2008*. Bangladesh Bureau of Statistics.

BBS. 2018. *Labour Force Survey 2016*. Bangladesh Bureau of Statistics.

BBS. 2019. *Final Report on Household Income and Expenditure Survey 2016*. Bangladesh Bureau of Statistics.

BRAC. 2020. *Impacts of Covid-19 Pandemic on Agriculture and Implications for Food Security*. BRAC.

Dasgupta, S., M.M. Hossain, M. Huq, and D. Wheeler. 2014. *Climate Change, Soil Salinity, and the Economics of High-Yield Rice Production in Coastal Bangladesh*. Washington, DC: The World Bank.

Evanson, R. E., C. Pray, and Mark W. Rosegrant. 1998. *Agricultural Research and Productivity Growth in India*. Research Report, International Food Policy Research Institute.

Fan, S., and C. Chan-Kang. 2005. Is Small Beautiful? Farm Size, Productivity, and Poverty in Asian Agriculture. *Agricultural Economics* 32: 135–146.

FAO. 2019. *FAOStat*. www.fao.org/faostat/en/#data/. Accessed December 2019.

FAO. 2014. *The State of Food and Agriculture: Innovation in Family Farming*. Rome: Food and Agriculture Organisation.

Field, C.B. 2014. *Climate Change 2014–Impacts, Adaptation and Vulnerability: Regional Aspects*. Edited by C.B. Field. Cambridge University Press.

Fuglie, Keith. 2015. Accounting for Growth in Global Agriculture. *Bio-Based and Applied Economics* 4 (3): 201–234.

Fuglie, Keith. 2008. Is a Slowdown in Agricultural Productivity Growth Contributing to the Rise in Commodity Prices? *Agricultural Economics* 39: 431–441.

Fuglie, Keith, and N. Rada. 2013. Resources, Policies, and Agricultural Productivity in Sub-Saharan Africa. *USDA-ERS Economic Research Report*, 145.

GHI. 2019. *Global Hunger Index Report 2019*. Concern Worldwide.

Hoque, M., and M. Ahmed. 2020. *Agricultural Diversification in Bangladesh: Trends, Spatial Patterns, and Drivers". Background paper for "Agriculture Strategies Development in Bangladesh*. World Bank, Washington, DC: Agriculture and Food Practice.

IFA. 2018. *International Fertiliser Association*. http://ifadata.fertiliser.org/ucSearch.aspx. Accessed December 2019.

IFPRI. 2018. *Global Food Policy Report 2018*. International Food Policy Research Institute.

ILO. 2019. *ILOSTAT*. https://ilostat.ilo.org/data/. Accessed December 2019.

Islam, Nurul. 2003. *Making of a Nation, Bangladesh: An Economist's Tale*. The University Press Ltd.

Khaki, M., E. Forootah, M. Kuhn, J. Awange, F. Papa, and C.K. Shum. 2018. A Study of Bangladesh's Subsurface Water Storages Using Satellite Products and Data Assimilation Scheme. *Science of the Total Environment* 625: 963–977.

Lewis, W.A. 1954. Economic Development with Unlimited Supplies of Labour. *The Manchester School* 22 (2): 139–191.

Mandal, M.A. Sattar, D. Stephen Biggs, and Scott E. Justice. 2017. *Rural Mechanisation: A Driver in Agricultural Change and Rural Development*. Edited by M.A. Sattar Mandal, D. Stephen Biggs, and Scott E. Justice. Institute of Inclusive Finance and Development (InM).

Ministry of Finance. 2019. *Bangladesh Economic Review 2018*. Ministry of Finance.

Mondal, M.H. 2010. Crop Agriculture of Bangladesh: Challenges and Opportunities. *Bangladesh Journal of Agricultural Research* 35 (2): 235–245.

Shahid, S. 2011. Impact of Climate Change on Irrigation Water Demand of Dry Season Boro Rice in Northwest Bangladesh. *Climatic Change* 105 (3–4): 433–453.

The Daily Star. 2017. Agricultural Credit, Extension Services: Marginal Farmers Have Least Access.

The Economist. 2019. Global Food Security Index. https://foodsecurityindex.eiu.com/Index.

The Financial Express. 2020. Boro Farmers Report 40pc Deficit Between Actual and Expected Profit. https://www.thefinancialexpress.com.bd/economy/bangladesh/boro-farmers-report-40pc-deficit-between-actual-and-expected-profit-1594053305.

Timsina, J., J. Wolf, N. Guilpart, L.G.J. Van Bussel, P. Grassini, J. Van Wart, A. Hossain, H. Rashid, Saiful Islam, and M.K. Van Ittersum. 2018. Can Bangladesh Produce Enough Cereals to Meet Future Demand? *Agricultural Systems* 163 (2018): 36–44.

Titumir, R.A.M. 2021.

Unnayan Onneshan. 2020. Whither Bending the Curves for Life and Livelihoods: A Rapid Assesment of National Budget 2020–21.

World Bank. 2019a. *Bangladesh Poverty Assessment: Facing Old and New Frontiers in Poverty Reduction*. Washington, DC: World Bank.

World Bank. 2019b. *World Bank Development Indicators*. https://datacatalog.worldbank.org/dataset/world-development-indicators. Accessed December 2019.

World Bank. 2020. *Promoting Agri-Food Sector Transformation in Bangladesh*. World Bank Report. Washington, DC: World Bank.

CHAPTER 3

Manufacturing Industry of Bangladesh

Introduction

The chapter scrutinises the current state of the manufacturing industry in Bangladesh and seeks to identify the transformability conditions, given that the sector is concentrated within a narrow product basket and low market diversification. A sustainable industrial sector is necessary for the long-term economic development of a country. Both historical and cross-country evidence suggest that rapid GDP growth with extensive job creation requires a high-performing and diversified manufacturing sector in the early stages of the take-off period.

Bangladesh's economy is following the conventional path. Historically, textiles and apparel are the first industries to "take off." The ready-made garment (RMG) sector contributes the highest among all the manufacturing industries of Bangladesh. Moreover, the RMG sector contributes more than any other sector in terms of growth and foreign exchange earnings. Despite its stellar success story, the sector faces a number of challenges.

The chapter is built on a conceptual framework containing the stability, transformability and sustainability conditions for the manufacturing sector of Bangladesh (Fig. 3.1).

R. A. M. Titumir, *Numbers and Narratives in Bangladesh's Economic Development*,
https://doi.org/10.1007/978-981-16-0658-8_3

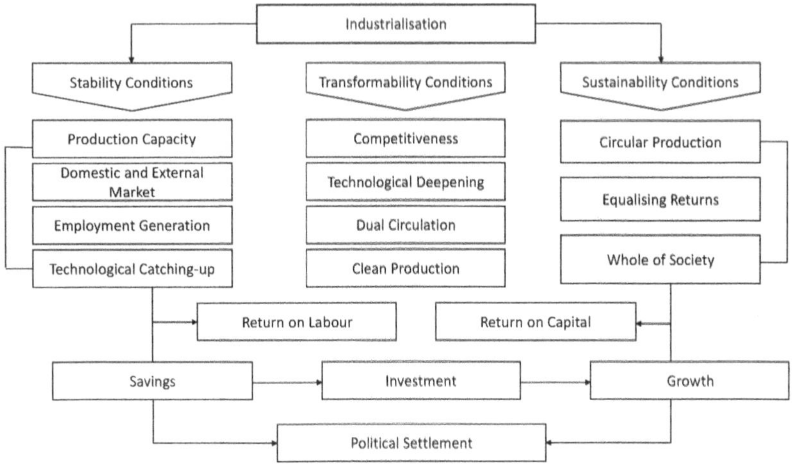

Fig. 3.1 Conceptual framework (*Source* Author)

The stability conditions seek to understand the current scenario in manufacturing. The stability of the sector is measured here by its production capacity for the domestic and external markets, employment generation and technological catching-up. Production capacity indicates the current state of productivity, product diversification and growth of the sector whereas domestic and external market focuses on the exports and market diversification situation of the industry. The shift in the labour force is understood by the capacity of employment generation of the industry and technological catching-up discusses inclusion of technology in the industry.

The transformability conditions entail the necessary settings for transforming the sector into a steadier and more competitive one. In order to do so, four key indicators are presented. The competitiveness entails the capacity in making inroads into the global market. Technological deepening provides the importance of coping with the technological revolution to maintain a competitive edge. A strategy of dual circulation is a development pattern for striking a balance between domestic and international markets to complement each other for absorbing shocks, if any, that arise out of excessive dependence on any one market. Clean production has been included in the necessary conditions for transformation of the industry for minimising waste and emissions as well as for optimising output.

In the era of covid-19, building back better and attaining Sustainable Development Goals (SDGs) is a matter of great import for all. Three indicators are laid out as sustainability conditions. Circular production epitomises a green industrialisation strategy in which raw materials, components and products lose their value as little as possible and renewable energy sources are used, with a sustainable relationship between human beings and nature at the core. Second, a conscious effort for diminishing the inequality between return on labour and return on capital can enhance economic growth by leading to higher savings and investment, alongside moving towards the goal of achieving a more harmonious society. Finally, ensuring sustainability requires nothing short of a whole of society approach with multi-layered engagement and meaningful participation of different stakeholders, driven by appropriate institutions and an inclusive political settlement. An inclusive political settlement is not merely about incentive structures, rather the relations between the state and society, the social contract. Such a contract needs to be robust and legitimate by balancing the distribution of power between contending social groups and social classes, on which any state is based.

Stability Conditions

In order for the country to maintain a steady growth rate, the need for a stable manufacturing industry is crucial. In this section, stability of the manufacturing industries is measured by four indicators—(i) production capacity, (ii) market diversification, (iii) employment generation and (iv) technological catch-up.

Production Capacity

The overarching goal for the country's industrialisation, as Perspective Plan of Bangladesh 2010–2021 has noted, lies in enhancing industrial contribution to the GDP to 40% over the next decade, with a contribution of 30% from the manufacturing sector (Planning Commission 2009).

Bangladesh witnessed decades of sluggish economic growth until 1990. The growth rate started to rise from the early 1990s. During the first decade of the twenty-first century, the average economic growth rate approached 6% per annum. Despite the rise in economic growth, the average growth rate for Bangladesh during the 2000s was much lower than those of China, India and Vietnam (Ministry of Finance 2018).

The contribution of the industrial sector to the GDP is increasing. Yet, Bangladesh's manufacturing was slow to respond to the decline in the contribution of the agricultural sector in increasing the GDP over time.

The contribution of the broad industry sector to the GDP has been estimated to be 33.66% in fiscal year 2017–2018 which was 32.42% in 2016–2017 (BBS 2019). Among the broad industry sectors, the contribution of the manufacturing sector is the highest at 22.85% in 2017–2018, increasing from 21.74% in 2016–2017 (Ministry of Finance 2018) (Table 3.1).

Growth remains steady at around 8% for both sizes after the 1990s and the contribution of large and small size enterprises to the growth of manufacturing remains at 70 and 30% respectively. Again, labour and capital productivity as well as profitability are higher in small and medium enterprises. Small manufacturing units need special attention, due to their greater flexibility and higher labour absorptive capacity (BBS 2012) (Table 3.2).

Table 3.1 Decadal average of some key indicators of the manufacturing industries

Indicators		*Period*		
		1991–2000	*2001–2010*	*2011–2018*
Industry Value Added (% of GDP)		22.36	23.76	26.68
Employment in industry (% of total employment) (modelled ILO estimate)		11.05	14.31	19.55
Annual growth rate (%)	Small and cottage	***	6.93*	8.75
	Medium-large	***	7.24*	11.67
	Total	***	7.17*	11.26
Manufactures exports (% of merchandise exports)		86.34	91.41	95.06
Manufactures imports (% of merchandise imports)		66.93	61.72	63.61
Growth Rate of number of RMG Factories		15.96	4.71	-0.62
Growth Rate Export Share of RMG (% of total export)		6.57	0.21	1.02

Note *Data started from 1998; ***Data not available
Source Ministry of Finance (2019), World Bank (2019), BGMEA (2019)

Table 3.2 Gross outputs by size of manufacturing industries

Category	*No of establishments*		*Gross output*	
	Number	*Col %*	*(In million Tk.)*	*Col %*
Total	42,972	100.0	534,905	100.0
Micro	17,384	40.6	275,818	5.1
Small	15,666	36.6	1,203,267	22.3
Medium	6,103	14.3	1,408,342	26.1
Large	3,639	8.5	2,507,478	46.5

Source BBS (2012)

A Decelerating Trend

The number of large and medium manufacturing industrial establishments in Bangladesh declined significantly in 2019, even though the curve of their contribution to the GDP headed upwards. The contribution of the manufacturing sector to GDP is estimated to be nearly 20% in 2018–2019, up from nearly 15.5% in the 2012 (BBS 2019). The decline in the number of large and medium manufacturing units indicates that the industrial sector faces numerous challenges and could result in negative consequences for employment generation. The number of large industries employing 250 or more people fell by 608 units from 3,639 in 2012 to 3,031 in 2019. On the other hand, the number of medium-sized plants fell drastically by 51% from 6,103 in 2012 to 3,014 units in 2019. The number of small industries employing less than 100 people each, however, increased sharply from 15,666 in 2012 to 23,577 in 2019 (BBS 2019).

Medium-sized industries are believed to be the backbone of Bangladesh's industrial strength. However, both the number of people employed and the number of industrial units have declined significantly. These industries usually employ between 100 and 250 people per firm. The number of jobs fell to 0.461 million in 2019, less than a half of 1.04 million in 2012. However, employment in large industries increased from 2.96 million in 2012 to 4.02 million in 2019 (BBS 2019).

The number of RMG factories in Bangladesh has declined in the last 10 years. As a result, the average growth rate of the RMG sector's contribution to the total exports has also declined during the same period. The average manufacturing export volume has increased over the years but the growth rate of exports has declined (Table 3.1).

Table 3.3 Manufacturing value added (MVA) as a percentage of GDP and annual growth of Bangladesh in recent years

Year	*Manufacturing, value added (% of GDP)*	*Manufacturing, value added (annual % growth)*
2005	14.744	7.856795
2006	15.30756	10.81066
2007	15.93407	10.53512
2008	16.12437	7.331292
2009	16.48019	6.693401
2010	16.12123	6.646766
2011	15.99673	10.01339
2012	15.91422	9.955216
2013	16.44202	10.30689
2014	16.61271	8.766757
2015	16.78867	10.31058
2016	17.03025	11.69082
2017	17.30064	10.96521
2018	17.95814	13.40215

Source World Bank (2019)

Manufacturing value added (MVA) indicates the net manufacturing output in a year. MVA as a share of GDP shows an increasing trend (Table 3.3). Despite having a large labour force as well as a comparative advantage in manufacturing as a labour-intensive sector, the growth rate is low. Over the years, manufacturing output has contributed to economic growth, but the rate was inconsistent. Low productivity, a narrow product basket and export concentration are the important factors behind this inconsistency (Fig. 3.2).

A Below Mark Productivity

Bangladesh, being the second-largest garment exporter, is also the second lowest in terms of productivity, calculated as the value of GDP produced per hour at constant price. The hourly productivity of Bangladesh is valued at USD 3.4 while that of China, the largest exporter, was recorded at USD 11.1, according to the data of the Asian Productivity Organisation (APO) for the year 2019 (Table 3.4). The highest labour productivity was calculated in Sri Lanka at USD 15.9, followed by Indonesia at USD 12.3. Labour productivity in other apparel producing countries such as

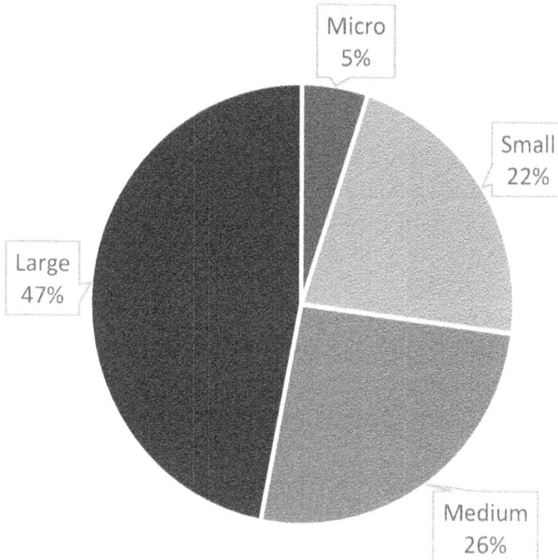

Fig. 3.2 Distribution of gross output by size (*Source* BBS 2012)

Table 3.4 RMG worker productivity in Asian countries

Country	*Per hour productivity in value (in USD)*
Sri Lanka	15.9
Indonesia	12.3
China	11.1
Philippines	8.7
India	7.5
Vietnam	4.7
Myanmar	4.1
Bangladesh	3.4

Source APO (2020)

the Philippines, India, Vietnam and Myanmar was also higher than that of Bangladesh (Uddin and Halder 2020).

Different studies have identified that a low literacy rate, lack of formal institutionalised and non-institutionalised training are the main reasons behind the low productivity. In addition, lower wage rates act as a key impediment toward achieving higher productivity. The other challenges currently faced by RMG industries of Bangladesh is to ensure better working conditions for the millions of garment workers which might have salient impacts in accelerating productivity to compete in the global export market.

Finally, insufficient skilled labour works as a major hindrance, necessitating a robust, educated labour force, despite having an abundance of labour, with most of them unskilled or semi-skilled.

A Narrow Product Basket

Currently, at the 6-digit Harmonized System (HS) code level, only 10 RMG products account for 68% of total RMG exports. HS is an international nomenclature for the classification of products, allowing participating countries to classify traded goods on a common basis for customs purposes.

The corresponding figures for China, India and Vietnam are 36, 46 and 42%, respectively (UNIDO 2019a). Production has concentrated in lower value products.

The concentration of products around textiles and garments is also reflected in the IMF's export diversification measures, which include an extensive and intensive margin. Extensive export diversification, which has been negligible, shows an increase in the number of export products or trading partners; intensive export diversification considers the shares of export volumes across active products or trading partners. The degree of concentration has revealed that it had a more intensive margin than extensive margin diversification (Raihan et al. 2017) (Table 3.5).

Table 3.5 IMF Bangladesh Export Diversification Index (2005–2014)

	Year									
Indicator	*2005*	*2006*	*2007*	*2008*	*2009*	*2010*	*2011*	*2012*	*2013*	*2014*
Export Diversification Index	4.64	4.68	4.65	4.72	4.82	4.81	4.8	4.89	4.94	4.95
Extensive margin	0.07	0.08	0.08	0.08	0.07	0.07	0.06	0.07	0.06	0.06
Intensive margin	4.56	4.6	4.58	4.65	4.75	4.69	4.74	4.83	4.88	4.89

Source IMF (2017)

Bangladesh is the second-largest producer of jute in the world after India. Diversifying jute-made products can expand the industrial base of the country. The pharmaceutical industry has become a potential sector for earnings in the recent year with astonishing growth.

Regulatory Uncertainty and Lack of Transparency

The political environment of the country has been the cause of concern. Any sort of uncertainty in the political climate of the country results in a decline in investor's confidence. Deeply rooted corruption and inefficiency cost the country around half a billion USD annually and poor management cost the country roughly one billion USD annually. To increase investors' confidence, government must formulate and enact policies to ensure transparency and accountability.

Transitional Challenges from LDC to a DC

The process of transition from the United Nations list of Least Developed Countries (LDCs) to developing countries, may bring new challenges in the export of goods for Bangladesh. As soon as that happens, exporters will have to face intense competition, losing market advantage due to loss of generalised system of preferences, including duty and quota free access to European Union economies as a LDC. Under the pressure of additional tariffs, export earnings could fall by USD 536 million which is about 14.28% of the country's total exports (Table 3.6) (Shah and Karmaker 2020).

Table 3.6 Amount of export and export loss in terms major products due to LDC graduation

Manufacturing products	*Export (average of 2016–2018)*	*Export loss due to Transition*
RMG	3581.50 (85%)	484.45 (15%)
Textiles	258.20 (6%)	18.39 (8%)
Leather and leather products	133 (3%)	16.31 (14%)
Fish and frozen food	61.20 (1%)	11.45 (20%)
Chemicals	27.5 (1%)	–

Source Shah and Karmaker (2020)

Market Diversification

On the basis of market orientation, the manufacturing sector of Bangladesh can be broadly defined by two sub-sectors; external market oriented and domestic market oriented. The export-oriented market is dominated by the RMG sector (Fig. 3.3). The RMG sector exports 95% of the production to foreign markets. Other export-oriented industries include transport equipment (82%), leather and leather goods (74%) and textiles products (57%). Domestic market-oriented industries comprise refined petroleum, machinery and equipment, motor vehicles etc. (CPD 2018).

Much of the export growth has been driven by the knitwear and woven garments sector, which gained further momentum in the post multi-fibre arrangement (MFA) era. Exports from Bangladesh suffered during the global economic crisis but fared better than many competitors. Exports strongly rebounded in 2011 after the crisis due to stronger demand from both traditional markets (EU and USA) and non-traditional markets. The newest economic crisis brought forth by the covid-19 pandemic however is likely to put a dampener on export earnings as export destinations restrict their trade boundaries, and competing countries who fared better

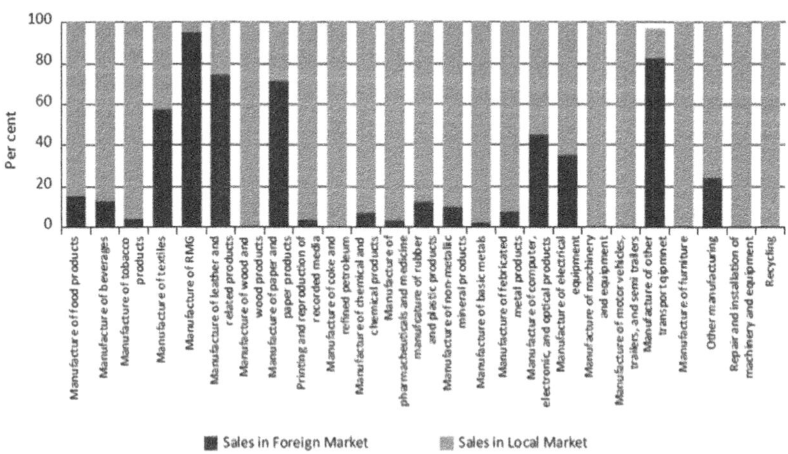

Fig. 3.3 Ratio of market exposure of different manufacturing industries (*Source* CPD 2018)

in managing the pandemic will gain a competitive advantage in regards of safety standards.

Garments sector of Bangladesh is a source of vulnerability because of high export concentration. The concentration intensifies within the garments sector as only five garments products constitute 87% of total exports. A sudden decline in the demand would send shock waves throughout the economy. Diversification within the garments sector is required to avoid any catastrophe (Ministry of Finance 2018).

Concentration in Export Market

Ready-made garments destinations are limited to the European and North American countries. The export in the European countries is stacked up in a few countries like France, Germany, United Kingdom and Italy. A shock in the importing country can adversely affect the export. The Balkan region and Eastern European countries can be the next potential market for export. It is also time to explore developing countries for export markets. Trade with South American countries is still very miniscule. Trade with neighbouring countries remains low as well.

Bangladesh has to maximise benefit from the existing policies for LDCs, as it is expected to graduate from this tier by 2024, implying that strategies need to be devised in order to utilise the existing benefits.

It is also evident that Bangladesh's export products and markets may take a hit once it graduates from LDC status. For example, the EU is the destination for 82% of RMG. Bangladeshi exports enter the market without any duties as these enjoy duty free access under the GSP facility. The tariff free entry has permitted the ready-made garments products to have an advantage over competitors. Everything but Arms agreement of EU allowed tariff free entry to the largest export destination. Once the country moves out of the LDC status, additional 7–8% of tariffs will be charged thus significantly dampening the competitiveness of the firms. GSP + comes with tougher conditions like workers' rights and standards which are precarious. Bangladesh needs to ramp up its diplomacy to ensure tariff free entry to the markets through Free Trade Agreements (FTAs).

Employment Generation

The structural transformation has gained a steady pace in Bangladesh with employment shifting from agriculture to the service sector. Manufacturing sector is slowly absorbing surplus labour. Employment in the service sector has increased by 26.5 percentage points and in manufacturing industries by 7.3 percentage points (Fig. 3.4). Most of the employment in the manufacturing sector has gone to industries like textile, agro and food processing and light engineering (BBS 2012).

Small and micro manufacturing enterprises account for 93.3% of manufacturing enterprises and provide 47% of manufacturing employment as observed in the 2002 Economic Census by the BBS. Large manufacturing enterprises, on the other hand, constitute 6.7% and provide 53% of manufacturing employment (Small and micro manufacturing enterprises employ 1–49 persons and large enterprises employ 50 & above on an average as per definition of Economic Census). Another important observation is that the share of manufacturing in non-farm establishment and employment increases with the size of the enterprise, from 12.6 and 26.4% respectively in micro and small enterprises to 32.7 and 52.4% respectively in large sized manufacturing. It is, therefore, evident that Bangladesh's manufacturing sector is characterised by a dualistic pattern. Hence, a dualistic approach is instrumental in financing the enterprises, marketing the products as well as making decisions for choice of technology and technology upgradation (BBS 2012).

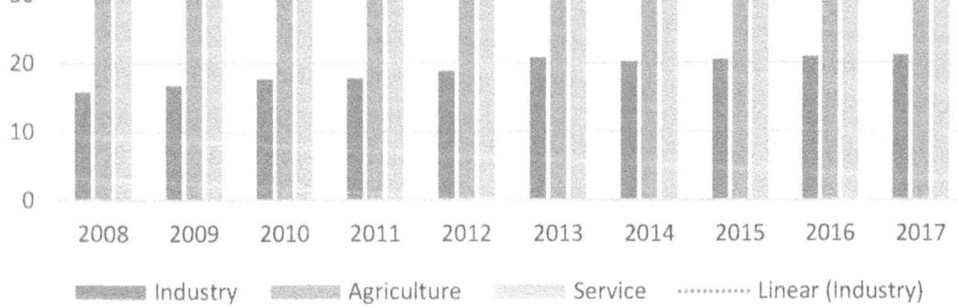

Fig. 3.4 Sectoral share of employment in Bangladesh (*Source* World Bank 2019)

Table 3.7 Number of manufacturing establishments by size and TPE

Size class	*No. of establishments*	*Total Persons Engaged—TPE*		
	Number	*Both sex*	*Male*	*Female*
Total	42,72	5,015,936	3,062,009	1,953,928
Micro	17,384	271,644	229,407	42,237
Small	15,666	738,801	615,426	123,374
Medium	6,103	1,041,220	673,821	367,399
Large	3,639	2,964,272	1,543,355	1,420,918

Source BBS (2012)

The number of manufacturing establishments in the country stood at around 43,000 in 2012. Micro industries had the highest share with over 17,384 establishments followed by 15,666 in small, 6103 in medium and 3639 in large types. Micro industries employed well over 272 thousand and large industries employed around 3 million persons (Table 3.7) (BBS 2012).

Micro and small industries were the most prevalent type accounting for more than 77% of the total manufacturing industries of the country whereas those industries absorbed only 20% of total persons engaged (Fig. 3.5). The large industries constituted only 8.5% of the total and constituted 59.1% of the total persons engaged.

The large industries constituted only 8.5% of the total industry and provided 61.3% of the wages and other benefits paid to employees. On the other hand, micro industries included 40.6% of the total industry and constituted only 4.9% of wages and benefits (Fig. 3.6).

A Dominant Informal Sector

The informal sector dominates in terms of employment. About 88.4% of the employed population is in the informal sector and this has increased over the years (Table 3.8). Limited job opportunities in the formal sector push people to engage themselves in the informal sector. The working conditions of informal sector workers are unsafe and unhealthy. They work long working hours and have low wage rates (BBS 2012).

Formality accrues costs to the firms such as taxes, cost of compliance with regulation etc. However, being informal is not free either. There is also a significant amount of costs associated with informal sector such as bribes, risk of eviction, lack of credit etc. Beside the cost–benefit

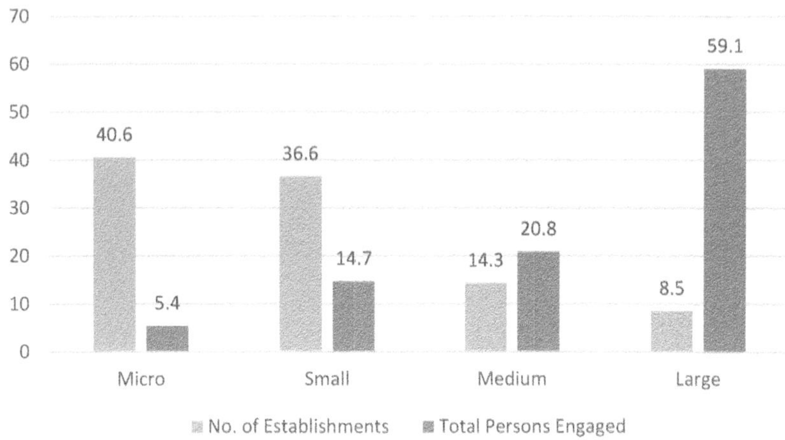

Fig. 3.5 Distribution of manufacturing establishments and persons engaged by size (*Source* BBS 2019)

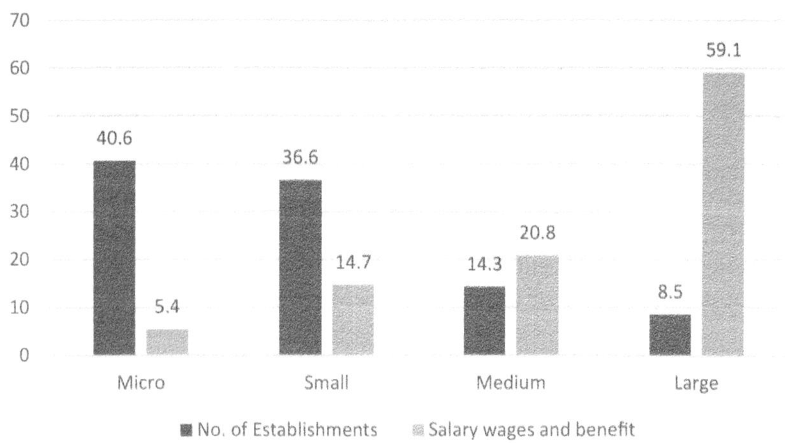

Fig. 3.6 Percentage distribution of establishments and salary and wages paid by size (*Source* BBS 2012)

Table 3.8 Trends in informal employment in the manufacturing sector (%)

Year	*2016*	*2013*	2010
Formal employment	11.6	8.9	9.7
Informal employment	88.4	91.1	90.3
Total	100.00	100.00	100.00

Source BBS, LFS, various years

trade-off between formal and informal sector, there are some other non-cost considerations to remain informal such as lack of information, lack of access to registration facilities etc. Employees of informal sector face various levels of discrimination. Employees of informal sector receive little to no benefit, both financial and non-financial, compared to formal sector. Besides, small entrepreneurs in the informal sector have very low profit margins. Large and medium enterprises generally keep a part of their operations informal in order to avoid high tax rate, complex procedures of paying tax liability, and weak rule of law. Therefore, by reducing taxes and strengthening regulatory framework the evasion may be tackled (Hassan 2019). More importantly, the impact of policies is not limited to the informal economy, but also have ramifications for the formal economy.

Technological Catch-Up

Successful technological catch-up largely depends on a committed state, which can orchestrate industry development with a relatively uniform set of policies, including R&D support, subsidies, trade restrictions, and local content requirements. In contrast, recent contributions from the technology lifecycle literature have argued that policies should be tailored to differing technological characteristics in industries. These suggest that policy makers in newly industrialising countries (NICs) should avoid drafting generic sector plans, but should tailor plans to individual industries, and respond to changing policy support needs as technological capacities and global competitiveness develop (Binz et. al. 2017).

Southeast Asian countries have emerged as the new manufacturing base in the continent and have become the alternate source for Chinese products. These countries faced insufficient technology that paralysed the manufacturing sector. Initially Southeast Asian countries had to rely on foreign investment and technologies for manufacturing growth. Relocation of Chinese industries to the Southeast Asian countries have also brought the technologies along with it. With proper policy formulation, these countries have now acquired much of the market for technology. Malaysia for instance relied on its small and medium enterprises for innovation as competition among companies forced them to keep innovating (Na and Kang 2019).

Developing countries in particular face an uphill task in upgrading technologies. The problem lies in financing new technologies, training of workers and physical infrastructure. Government policies play an important role in bringing new technologies to the fore but developing countries lag behind due to institutional barriers.

Financing of the new technologies is the most pressing problem in technology upgradation. The risk entailed with financing new technologies act as a deterrent for investors as return from the investment comes late. Setting up new technologies are subject to right processes and alignment. Lack of risk-sharing instruments in the financial sector also discourages investors. Market failure, alongside the lack of risk-sharing instruments, slows down investment in technological upgradation.

Incorporating new technologies depends on the training of workers. Optimal use of new machines and tools requires informed workers. The state of technical and vocational education in Bangladesh remains in a primitive stage. As a result, the productivity of the workers and absorption of new technologies remain low in the country thus affecting the return on capital and labour. Market failures also come from the fact that the social return to training is higher than the private return to the entrepreneur who is asked to pay for it, and the result is a low take-up of the available training. Government policies can overcome the market failure (Khan 2008).

COVID-19: A Havoc in the Manufacturing Industry

The characteristic of being a one-sector based manufacturing sector has made the business climate more susceptible to shocks, especially after the advent of the pandemic. Small and medium level owners are failing to acquire opportunities to avail loan from banks to establish and run their factories (Unnayan Onneshan 2020). There is negligible diversification in products and markets which results in a negative motion of export growth. Against the backdrop of recent predicaments, export of RMG has decreased by USD 4.48 billion during March, April and May of 2020 from that of the previous year.

The covid-19 pandemic has caused a serious damage to the manufacturing industry. The industry forms the economy's backbone, accounting for 84% of all exports. But the global pandemic has disrupted supply of raw materials, delayed shipments, cancelled or suspended orders and led to factory closures (UNDP 2020). International buyers have either cancelled or suspended USD 3.16 billion worth of shipments involving 1,142 factories as of 18 April 2020 (ADB 2020).

Almost 7 million workers stare at joblessness as the collapse in global demand has caused a decline in new orders. Reportedly, 1 million workers have already been fired or furloughed. A survey conducted by BRAC University states high level of uncertainty among the RMG workers. 47% RMG workers reported that they did not receive their wages. In spite of the USD 5.8 billion provided as stimulus by the government, almost half the number of employees have lost their jobs (ADB 2020). The industry has lost USD 4900.55 million of exports in the first three months (March, April and May) of the pandemic in 2020 which estimates a 56.9% loss of export compared to the same three months of 2019 (UNDP 2020).

The covid-19 pandemic is set to cause a major blow to the industrial, consumer and service sectors. Presently, there are 1,461 manufacturing units in the textile-value chain, of which 425 are in yarn manufacturing, 796 in fabric production and 240 in dyeing-printing-finishing operations. There are also a large number of accessories suppliers, mostly small and medium enterprises (SMEs), who are providing buttons, zippers, hangers, threads and other accessories (ADB 2020).

The RMG sector is deeply rooted in other economic sectors as well. The financial sector depends largely on garments industries. Around 98% of garments factories are clients of commercial banks. Financial institutions provide insurance to the factories as well. Around 87% importers and 15% of exporters get insurance from financial institutions. A major share of export income comes from RMG, on an average 40% of the total. The 4.1 million workers in the industry have also created a large demand for low-cost consumer goods, such as cosmetics, dresses, footwear, utensils and other products. Thus, losses in RMG sector will disrupt the chain of economic activities (ADB 2020).

The CMSMEs have been facing a significant crisis due to the global pandemic. During the first three months (March, April and May of 2020) of the shutdown activities, about 52% of SMEs have to shut down their businesses since generating zero revenue and revenues of 28% of SMEs have dropped by at least 50%. In the Service industry, 40% SMEs experienced a heavy hit of considerable revenue loss by 50% or more. About 14% of the SMEs have already laid off all their employees (LightCastle 2020). Deficient financial access was a major obstruction in the development of the SMEs and even in this pandemic, lack of financial access is worsening the situation persistently.

Government has announced a stimulus package of 2.35 billion USD (200 billion BDT), of which 1.17 billion USD (100 billion BDT) is exclusively allocated for SMEs as credit line facility at the subsidised interest rate of 2.0%. Of the total amount under the package, the share of micro and small industries would be 70.0% and the remaining 30.0% would go to medium-sized industries (*The Financial Express* 2020). SMEs would get a working capital loan at 9% interest rate with the government giving 5% subsidy. How these packages are being distributed is the main matter of concern here (Mamun 2020). On another level, of the total package offered by the government, only USD 495 million will be available for the garments sector. To put this figure in context, it is slightly more than one month's wages (USD 423 million) that the garments sector pays to all of its workers (UNDP 2020).

Small women entrepreneurs may be more adversely affected than other groups. Access to finance has been a serious concern for the women entrepreneurs. Women entrepreneurs have been facing difficulties in getting credits; 15% of total credits within the SME sector as promised by government policies. The key barriers are related to collateral requirements and guarantee, trade license and rigidity of loan procedures and mind-set of the bankers toward women entrepreneurs (*The Financial Express* 2020).

Transformability Conditions

Over the last two decades the growth of the manufacturing industry is noteworthy. Thus, transforming the manufacturing sector into a more competitive and vigorous one, the economy can be advanced to a steadier level in the post covid-19 period. The transformability conditions discuss four key indicators- (i) competitiveness, (ii) dual circulation, (iii) technological deepening and (iv) clean production.

Increasing Competitiveness

The term competitiveness has different meanings at the firm and at the country level. At the firm level, "competitiveness" denotes to the ability of firms to compete. This includes their capacity to sell products in local or international markets. However, competition between countries in international markets is not a zero-sum game: all countries can compete and at the same time—as alleged by David Ricardo around 200 years ago (Ricardo 1817)—and at the same time benefit from international trade.

In terms of human capital, Bangladesh is better positioned than India and Pakistan but worse than countries like China, Vietnam and Thailand. However, the level of skills is worse in Bangladesh than the other countries (Table 3.9). Moreover, business dynamism and innovation capability indicators signal that Bangladesh has not achieved sufficient competence in these prospects. These factors adversely impact Bangladesh's manufacturing industry.

The Competitive Industrial Production (CIP) Index is a method developed by UNIDO to measure the industrial competitiveness among the countries of the world. Germany, Japan and China have achieved the top three positions respectively. Bangladesh ranked 72nd amongst all the countries in the CIP index—with a score of 0.03 (Table 3.10). Bangladesh is ranked 1st among the LDCs, which clearly documents how the lack of progress in Bangladesh's manufacturing sector compared to the developed countries (UNIDO 2019b).

Table 3.9 Comparison of some selected countries in terms of global competitiveness

Indicators		*Rank of the country*					
		Bangladesh	*India*	*China*	*Pakistan*	*Vietnam*	*Thailand*
Human Capital	Health	93rd	110th	40th	115th	71st	38th
	Skills	117th	107th	64th	125th	93rd	73rd
Innovation Ecosystem	Business Dynamism	121st	69th	36th	52nd	89th	21st
	Innovation Capability	105th	35th	24th	79th	76th	50th
Overall Score		105th	68th	28th	110th	67th	40th

Source World Economic Forum (2019)

Table 3.10 The CIP rank, score and quintile of selected countries

Competitive industrial performance index	*CIP rank*	*CIP score*	*CIP quintile*
Germany	1	0.51	Top
Japan	2	0.4	Top
China	3	0.37	Top
Korea	4	0.36	Top
USA	5+	0.36	Top
Singapore	12	0.26	Top
UK	17	0.21	Top
Malaysia	21	0.17	Top
Thailand	27	0.15	Top
India	3	0.08	Upper Middle
Vietnam	43	0.07	Upper Middle
Bangladesh	72	0.03	Lower Middle

Source UNIDO (2019b)

A country's shares in world manufacturing value added (MVA) and in the world trade of manufactured goods determines the position of that country in the global market. Countries with higher values receives benefit from agglomeration and scale effects as well as greater negotiating power in trade agreements.

The MVA of manufacturing industry of Bangladesh is so small in comparison to the other Industrialised and Newly Emerging Economies that its index value is nearly zero. This implies that while China is influencing the world trade of manufacturing as the highest scorer of the index, Bangladesh fails to affect the world in these indicators, despite its ranking as first among the LDCs in CIP index (Table 3.11).

In order to make products from Bangladesh more competitive and sustainable, and thereby fostering economic growth, there are some issues that need to be addressed urgently. Improving connectivity can raise the competitiveness of the country. Improvement in the capacity of seaports will boost the international trade by reducing the lag time. Increased railway capacity will enhance intra-boundary trade. Increasing airfreight capacity and airport facilities will ensure the fastest delivery of sample goods and other accessories. Uninterrupted supply and balanced price of utilities such as power and gas can also improve competitiveness. Bangladesh lags behind in terms of skilled labour in the workforce.

Table 3.11 Manufacturing Value Added (MVA) indices of some selected countries

	MVA per capita index	*Share of world MVA index*	*Share of MVA in GDP index*	*Share of medium and high-tech activities in total MVA index*	*Industrialisation intensity index*
Germany	0.42	0.26	0.62	0.79	0.71
Japan	0.42	0.41	0.62	0.73	0.67
China	0.09	1	0.92	0.53	0.72
Korea	0.31	0.12	0.84	0.81	0.82
USA	0.25	0.62	0.33	0.6	0.46
Singapore	0.39	0.02	0.51	1	0.76
UK	0.14	0.07	0.23	0.57	0.4
Malaysia	0.11	0.03	0.68	0.56	0.62
Thailand	0.07	0.04	0.81	0.52	0.66
India	0.01	0.14	0.49	0.55	0.52
Vietnam	0.01	0.01	0.49	0.49	0.49
Bangladesh	0.01	0.01	0.6	0.12	0.36

Source UNIDO (2019b)

Training programs for labour can raise the productivity of the workforce and reduce the gap in competitiveness with the rival countries.

The rival countries for Bangladeshi export has been adopting technology and thus gained higher competitiveness than Bangladesh. A special fund for technological upgradation can boost the competitiveness of Bangladeshi products. Government intervention is required for small and medium industries to adopt technologies in production that would increase efficiency.

Augmentation of Technological Deepening

Technological deepening refers to the accumulation of new and improved methods of producing goods through various innovative measures. Augmentation of technology leads to an increase in productivity of labour and capital. Technological spill-overs and low vulnerability to price shocks imply that the more technology-intensive the goods being produced are, the higher the expected benefits from producing (and further exporting) them. As a measure of competitiveness, technological deepening and upgrading are much essential and can be measured by two composite indices. First, the degree of industrialisation intensity, serves to estimate the complexity of production processes given by the share of medium- and high-tech (MHT) value addition in total MVA (*MHVAsh*). Higher complexity of manufacturing process results in higher likelihood of knowledge spillovers as seen in the case of East Asian countries. Second, the export quality, *MQual*, measures the quality of the integration process in the country's manufacturing sector. The export quality, *MQual*, is estimated based on the share of MHT manufacturing exports in total manufacturing exports, (*MHXsh*), and the share of manufacturing exports in total exports (*MXsh*). Higher manufacturing export share denotes higher competitiveness as the country's export faces competition in the global market (UNIDO 2019b).

In the Asian countries, the share of MHT manufacturing exports was considerably higher in 2016 than in 1990, ranging from 41% in Thailand to nearly 78% in Singapore. In the case of Bangladesh, it is just ten per cent (Table 3.12).

China's surge to being the manufacturing superpower was the result of structural change in the form of an enterprise reform. Technological

Table 3.12 MHT MVA share in total MVA and MHT exports share of selected countries

Country	*Medium- and High-tech Manufacturing Value Added share in total manufacturing value added (%)*	*Medium- and High-tech manufactured exports share in total manufactured exports (%)*
Germany	0.62	0.74
Japan	0.57	0.81
China	0.41	0.6
Korea	0.63	0.75
United States	0.47	0.64
Singapore	0.78	0.71
United Kingdom	0.44	0.7
Malaysia	0.44	0.63
Thailand	0.41	0.64
India	0.43	0.34
Vietnam	0.39	0.51
Bangladesh	0.1	0.02

Source UNIDO (2019b)

upgradation occurred at both the private and public firms which stimulated technological progress (Walheer and He 2019). There is an upward trajectory in China in manufacturing capability development, research and development commitment, and human capital investment (Li 2017). Thus, there is a need for accelerating the process of technological deepening in Bangladesh in order to achieve competitiveness.

Dual Circulation and Market Diversification

The term 'dual circulation' indicates the circulation of manufacturing products into both domestic and external market. The industry can be transformed into a more productive and competitive one through market diversification for its products. The United States and the European Union dominated the export market for garments products. These two destinations generate more than 90% of the total RMG export earnings of Bangladesh. European Union overtook United States as the prime export destination after the tragedy of 'Rana Plaza' when the United States Senate suspended generalised system of preference on Bangladeshi export. The shares of other importers such as Australia, Canada, China, Japan and the Russian Federation as well as countries in the Middle East in the total RMG export earnings of Bangladesh are minimal. The Eastern bloc of Europe and the South American countries remain untapped.

Bangladesh has to utilise its labour to convert into its competitive edge. This requires establishing labour-intensive industries for domestic and external consumption through massive training programmes, backward and forward linkage, improving utility services, installing state-of-the art laboratories for controlling and testing the quality, setting up product-based industrial zones or clusters, confirming easy availability of raw materials and disseminating updated information to the producers on markets and technology on a regular basis.

Clean Production

The concept of clean production relates to the environmental and economic performance of the industries. On the economic front, the concept means maximising resources for optimal and efficient production. On the environmental front, the concept deals with minimising waste disposal and rehabilitation requirements. The idea behind clean production is to gain as much from factors of production without harming the environment. Cleaner production includes less waste, recovery of valuable by-products, improved environmental performance, increased productivity, better efficiency, reduced consumption, and an overall reduction in costs.

Clean production can reduce operating costs, improve profitability and worker safety, and reduce the environmental impact of the business. It is obvious that cleaner production techniques are good business for the industry because it will reduce costs from waste, raw materials, and health safety & environment (HSE) damage. Thus, the performance of firms will improve, leading to competitiveness at the local and international markets. Compliance with environmental protection regulations will improve the public image too.

On a broader scale, cleaner production can help alleviate the serious and deteriorating problems of air and water pollution, ozone depletion, global warming, landscape degradation, solid and liquid waste, resource depletion, acidification of the natural and built environment, visual pollution, and reduced bio-diversity.

Accompanying this strategy of clean production, the manufacturing industry of Bangladesh can complete the transformation to a more sophisticated sustainable level of productivity. The garment industry in Bangladesh has already adopted greener technologies as the country now has the highest number of green apparel factories with 67 Leadership in Energy and Environmental Design (LEED) certified factories (*The Dhaka Tribune* 2020).

Sustainability Conditions

A sustainable manufacturing industry is a pre-requisite for the long-term economic development of a country. Once the industry has become stable and fulfilled the transformability conditions, its journey for attaining sustainability begins, though such can be advanced simultaneously. In order to cope with the global industrial revolution, a country's manufacturing industry has to fulfil, at least, three sustainability conditions—(i) circular production, (ii) equalising returns and (iii) whole of society.

Environmental sustainability in trade remains elusive in Bangladesh. Even though Bangladesh scored higher than neighbouring India and Pakistan in the Sustainable Trade Index 2020, the environmental standard in trade is lowest because of deforestation and water pollution.

Labour standards is the lowest ranking as well for Bangladesh (Economist Intelligence Unit 2020).

Circular Production

Circular production is the centre of creating a circular economy where the productivity of the industry depends only on its actual demand. Producing the amount of manufactured goods which is necessary for the economy in terms of both domestic and external market is the essence. Through circular production, resources such as human resources, environmental resources etc. can be utilised in a more equitable way and the economy can keep its balance between context and firms (Fig. 3.7).

While there is an urgency for the industrialised economies to move fast with the circular flow of industrial production to put the brakes on the

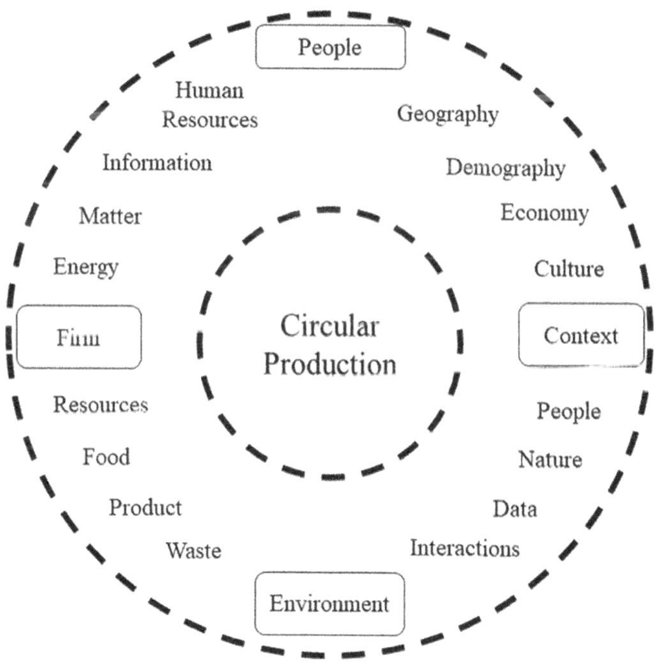

Fig. 3.7 Circular production in economy (*Source* Prepared by Author)

climate crisis, a developing country like Bangladesh must chart its road map as well to achieve the process of circular production.

Equalising Returns

There is a circular relationship between firms and individuals. Firms are generally considered as the capital owners whereas, the individuals are the labour. Firms get the factors of production from the households and the households receives the output by the firms. The households generally maintain the relationship as consumer-producer with the firms. The households consume the products produced by the firms. On the other hand, the firms have to give wages to the labour force as their income source (Fig. 3.8).

The prevailing system shows that capital owners, i.e. the firms get larger shares as a return to capital while they exploit the workforce through providing them lower wages as empirically evident in the case of Bangladesh and many other countries. There is a necessity for reversal of the inequalising trend. This can be achieved through institutional regulations backed by a favourable political settlement.

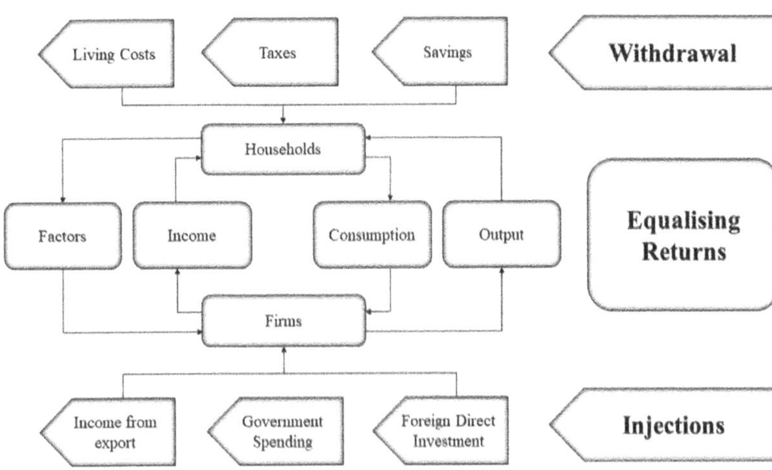

Fig. 3.8 Conceptual framework for equalising returns (*Source* Prepared by Author)

Whole of Society

A sustainable economy is comprised of all the stakeholders. Thus, the demand for a sustainable manufacturing industry needs to accommodate the participation of everyone in the society. Enterprises (producers and their suppliers, retailers, recyclers and waste management companies) choose how resources are extracted, processed, sold and managed. These choices are influenced by the choices of consumers as well as by financial institutions through lending policies and ratings and by governments through taxes, regulations and laws.

Governments, civil society and NGOs, consumers and enterprises all have important roles to play in fostering sustainable consumption and advancing circular production. The government can perform its role by adhering to international agreements, enacting national policies, regulations and laws, providing fiscal structures and incentives, infrastructure and services, guiding enterprises and consumers, and ensuring compliance through monitoring, enforcement, etc.

On the other hand, civil society and NGOs can make independent assessments, arrange public campaigns, work as a critics and mould public opinions.

The enterprises have their roles in economic development, legal compliance, sustainable sourcing, production and distribution, eco-efficiency and waste reduction, consumer choice editing and influencing, recycling, innovation and setting examples.

The consumers make purchasing decisions, lifestyle choices, political support, peer to peer influencing, enhancing human capital and social capital etc. Together, all these forces make the whole of society a means of creating a sustainable economy. If one of these forces do not accomplish their role, the economy faces externalities. As a result, inclusion of everyone in the economy as a whole of society is a must for achieving sustainability (Fig. 3.9).

Concluding Remarks

Export expansion has steadily contributed an increasing portion of manufacturing growth. Yet it is concentrated mostly in readymade garments. Narrow domestic capacity has constrained the manufacturing sector.

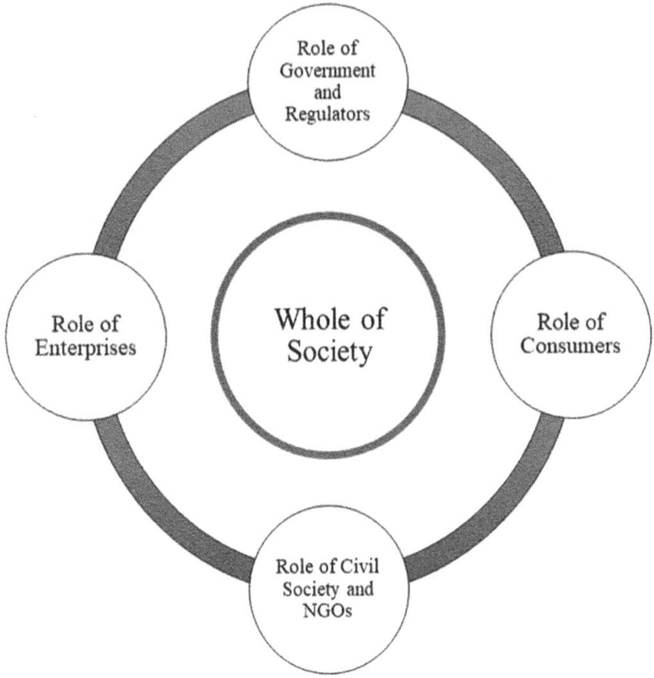

Fig. 3.9 Role of forces in whole of society (*Source* Prepared by Author)

Imports of intermediate goods have been increasing. The manufacturing sector is mostly oriented towards producing final goods. Backward linkages have not established a foothold.

Given the vast domestic demand of more than a 160 million people, enhancement and diversification of domestic capacity is the way forward. Such efforts are, in the long run, preparations for strengthening export competitiveness too. This would result in the creation of decent employment as well as moving away from informal sectors.

The export destinations are heavily concentrated to the European and North American countries. Exports to Europe are concentrated in a few countries like France, Germany, the United Kingdom, and Italy. A shock in the importing country can adversely affect the export. It is now time to search for newer markets. Exports to neighbouring countries, with

Table 3.13 Summary table of major indicators of manufacturing sector

Indicators	*State of Bangladesh*
Stability	
Production capacity	Manufacturing production capacity has maintained a rate of growth over the last decade. The major challenge lies in product diversification and output concentration
Domestic and external Market	The domestic production capacity is concentrated and export market is skewed in few destinations. The country needs to increase diversification and competitiveness to thwart any shock due to concentration
Employment generation	Manufacturing shows a higher trend of employment over the last two decades. Yet there is vulnerability due to excessive concentration in informal sector
Technological catching-up	Bangladesh faces a number of challenges including financing technological catching up and upskilling workforce
Transformability	
Competitiveness	There is a dire need for product and market diversification and technological catching up to transform into competitive manufacturing
Dual circulation	To address the wage inequality as well as informal sector problems, both domestic and external market have to be expanded to transform the industry into a steadier path in the post pandemic era
Technological deepening	Medium and High-tech manufactured exports share is miniscule in total manufactured exports. There is need for augmented investment for technological deepening
Sustainability	
Circular production	Circular production has to be established in order to fulfil the necessity of balancing environment and productivity for the long run success of the industry
Equalising returns	Equalising returns to capital and labour is necessary to augment the economy and maintain social harmony in the long run
Whole of society	A sustainable economy is comprised of all the stakeholders, and thus, needs to ensure participation of everyone in the process

Source Prepared by author

high imports flowing in from China and India, remain low due to non-tariff restrictions. China has recently announced 97% duty free access. The Balkan region and Eastern European countries can be a potential market. Trade with South American countries are still very miniscule. It is also time to explore developing countries with a diversified product base.

Bangladesh must derive maximum benefit from the existing policies for LDCs, as it is expected to graduate from this tier by 2024, implying that strategies need to be devised in order to utilise LDC benefits before these are no longer applicable. Simultaneously, Bangladesh needs to ramp up its diplomacy to ensure tariff-free entry to markets through different mechanisms, including bilateral free trade agreements.

Bangladesh has a huge trade deficit with China and India. At the same time, it has failed to maximise the potential of trade with Nepal and Bhutan. Regional trade agreements would help tap into markets of these countries. Stiff non-tariff barriers and anti-dumping policies in India have been impeding export opportunities for Bangladesh. Export to Nepal and Bhutan can be raised through ensuring third-party connectivity, which is the subject of ongoing negotiations.

Fiscal support in the form of subsidies and tax relief provided to the ready-made garment sector have undoubtedly aided its growth. The cracks in the sector have widened during the general shutdown from covid-19 with garments business owners failing to pay workers. The government again had to intervene in the form of a stimulus package to disburse the dues. The clientelist nature of government policy in providing tax exemptions and subsidies to a certain group aggravates the condition. The government's move to fix the same rate of interest for all sectors irrespective of size will impede SMEs' access to loans as banks may deem such loans riskier. Dedicated supply chain finance in place of traditional bank loans may speed up working capital for manufacturing industries and service sectors.

Bangladesh must continue its efforts to strengthen and modernise the economy through diversification of industry sectors; and it must develop a highly skilled workforce—its human capital—to keep pace with that diversification. Training and education can transform an unskilled and semi-skilled workforce into one that is able to support emerging sectors, such as information technology, pharmaceuticals, and shipbuilding.

As an economic latecomer to the globalising world economy, Bangladesh possesses an advantage towards attaining a sustainable manufacturing industry. The cities, manufacturing industries, energy and transport systems and the institutions can be built in new, more sustainable ways that take the distinctive national characteristics into account fulfilling the sustainability conditions. Newer, improved methods such as circular production can fulfil the necessity of balancing the needs of the environment and productivity for the long run success of the industry.

References

ADB. 2020. *COVID-19 and the Ready-Made Garments Industry in Bangladesh*. COVID-19 Active Response and Expenditure Support (CARES) Program.

APO. 2020. APO Productivity Databook 2020. Asian Productivity Organization.

BBS. 2012. Survey of Manufacturing Industries 2012. Bangladesh Bureau of Statistics. Dhaka, Bangladesh.

BBS. 2019. Survey of Manufacturing Industries 2019. Preliminary Report. Bangladesh Bureau of Statistics. Dhaka, Bangladesh.

Binz, C., J. Gosens, T. Hansen, and U. Hansen. 2017. Toward technology-sensitive catching-up policies: Insights from renewable energy in China. Retrieved September 30, 2020, from https://www.sciencedirect.com/science/article/abs/pii/S0305750X1730102X.

CPD 2018. Growth of Employment in the Manufacturing Sector: Impact of Trade and Trade-related Policies. CPD Working Paper 118. Centre for Policy Dialogue (CPD).

Economist Intelligence Unit. 2020. Sustainable Trade Index 2020. Economic Intelligence Unite and The Hinrich Foundation.

Hassan, H. 2019. Determinants and Effects of the Informal Economy: Bangladesh Perspective. *Janata Bank Journal of Money, Finance and Development* 5: 197–208. Number 1, 2018.

IMF. 2017. The Diversification Toolkit: Export Diversification and Quality Databases. International Monetary Fund. Washington.

Khan, M. H. (2008). Technological Upgrading in Bangladeshi Manufacturing: Governance Constraints and Policy Responses in the ReadyMade Garments Industry.

Li, L. 2017. China's Manufacturing Locus in 2025: With a Comparison of "Made-in-China 2025" and "Industry 4.0". *Technological Forecasting and Social Change* 135: 66–74. October 2018.

LightCastle Partners. 2020. COVID-19: Impact on Bangladesh's SME Landscape. https://www.lightcastlebd.com/insights/2020/04/25/covid-19-impact-on-bangladeshs-sme-landscape. Accessed on June 18, 2020.

Mamun, H.A.R. 2020. Coronavirus Outbreak: Impacts on SMEs. *Daily Asian Age*. https://dailyasianage.com/news/226129/coronavirus-outbreak-impacts-on-smes. Accessed on June 18, 2020.

Ministry of Finance. 2018. Bangladesh Economic Review. 2017. Ministry of Finance. Dhaka, Bangladesh.

Ministry of Finance. 2019. Bangladesh Economic Review. 2018. Ministry of Finance. Dhaka, Bangladesh.

Na, K., and Y. Kang. 2019. Relations Between Innovation and Firm Performance of Manufacturing Firms in Southeast Asian Emerging Markets: Empirical Evidence from Indonesia, Malaysia, and Vietnam. *Journal of Open Innovation: Technology, Market, and Complexity* 5 (4): 98. https://doi.org/10.3390/joitmc5040098.

Planning Commission. 2009. *Perspective Plan of Bangladesh 2010–21.* Dhaka, Bangladesh: Bangladesh Planning Commission.

Raihan, S., A Lemma, B.H. Khondker, and F.B. Ferdous. 2017. Bangladesh Sectoral Growth Diagnostic. Economic Dialogue on Inclusive Growth in Bangladesh.

Ricardo, David. 1817. *On the Principles of Political Economy and Taxation.* London: John Murray.

Shah, J., and S. Karmaker. 2020. ৪৫ হাজার কোটি টাকার রপ্তানি কমবে (Export of 45000 Crore Will Be Reduced) *The Daily Prothom Alo.* https://www.prothomalo.com/business/industry/%E0%A7%AA%E0%A7%AB-%E0%A6%B9%E0%A6%BE%E0%A6%9C%E0%A6%BE%E0%A6%B0-%E0%A6%95%E0%A7%8B%E0%A6%9F%E0%A6%BF-%E0%A6%9F%E0%A6%BE%E0%A6%95%E0%A6%BE%E0%A6%B0-%E0%A6%B0%E0%A6%AA%E0%A7%8D%E0%A6%A4%E0%A6%BE%E0%A6%A8%E0%A6%BF-%E0%A6%95%E0%A6%AE%E0%A6%AC%E0%A7%87?fbclid=IwAR1oXlMW0qXp7SIGkd_xbVf8NEvWYSgS8mdrUqRUhuAJOOSXfZ2SMfY6F_k. Accessed on 8th October, 2020.

The Financial Express. 2020. SMEs in Promoting Sustainable Growth. https://www.thefinancialexpress.com.bd/views/smes-in-promoting-sustainable-growth-1576305701. Accessed on June 18, 2020.

The Dhaka Tribune. 2020. Bangladesh has the Most Green RMG Factories. https://www.dhakatribune.com/business/2018/03/02/bangladesh-green-rmg-factories/#:~:text=Bangladesh%E2%80%99s%20RMG%20sector%2C%20a%20%2428%20billion%20industry%2C%20has,green%20buildings%2C%20the%20highest%20number%20in%20the%20world.

Uddin, J., and S. Halder. 2020. RMG Labour Productivity yet Behind That of Rivals. *The Business Standard*. https://tbsnews.net/economy/rmg/rmg-labour-productivity-yet-behind-rivals-140554?fbclid=IwAR3obIbolWQ7qrJL4tPPhY6MhDFj59-K1NBzIUvAyFD8UHDymcPm-rhAPgY. Accessed on 8th October, 2020.

UNDP. 2020. Covid-19: A High-Stakes Test for the RMG Sector. United Nations Development Programme. https://www.bd.undp.org/content/bangladesh/en/home/stories/covid-19--a-high-stakes-test-for-the-rmg-sector.html. Accessed on 30th September, 2020.

UNIDO. 2017. Data Base of Individual Countries. United Nations Industrial Development Organization.

UNIDO. 2019a. Data Base of Individual Countries. United Nations Industrial Development Organization.

UNIDO. 2019b. The Competitive Industrial Performance (CIP) Report 2018. United Nations Industrial Development Organization.

Unnayan Onneshan 2020. Whither Bending the Curves for Life and Livelihoods: A Rapid Assesment of National Budget 2020–21.

Walheer, B., and M. He. 2019. Technical Efficiency and Technology Gap of the Manufacturing Industry in China: Does Firm Ownership Matter? *World Development* 127: 104769. March 2020.

World Bank. 2019. World Development Indicators. Washington, DC.

World Economic Forum. 2019. Global Competitiveness Report 2019: How to End a Lost Decade of Productivity Growth. World Economic Forum. Davos, Switzerland.

CHAPTER 4

Financial Sector of Bangladesh

Introduction

The banking system and the capital market are the two main subsectors of the financial sector and are closely linked with each other. The ultimate objective of the financial sector is to maintain the virtuous cycle of growth through capital formation.

Bangladesh's economy clearly relies on a bank dominated financial system. Direct financing through issuing equity is insignificant and the other financing mechanisms, including bonds is nearly non-existent. These sectors have been facing a number of serious challenges due to malpractice, scams and heists, even though Bangladesh's banking sector has expanded over the years in terms of number, instruments, and volumes of assets. Malpractice has impacted the overall performance of the sector, reflected through various efficiency and soundness indicators. Repeated concerns have been expressed regarding the constant deterioration of banking performance and its potential implications for the sustainability of the sector.

Bangladesh's capital markets are afflicted by extreme volatility, price manipulation, insider trading. Thus, it tempts high speculation in the absence of a strong regulatory framework. Poor management, unethical practices, and over leveraging also discourage bona fide investors from entering the market. This is further exacerbated by a majority

R. A. M. Titumir, *Numbers and Narratives in Bangladesh's Economic Development*,
https://doi.org/10.1007/978-981-16-0658-8_4

of people lacking awareness of how capital markets function, and as a result, educated investors are in short supply. These ground realities make the stock market an unviable investment option and means of financial intermediation.

The conceptual framework of the financial sector illustrates the relationship among the households, firms, banking sector and the capital market. This relationship leads to capital formation and growth if the indicators function in a stable way (Fig. 4.1).

The function of households in this framework is investing in the firms through the banks and the capital market. The firms pay interest to the bank and share their profits with stakeholders. Thus, capital is formulated and can then be used in, amongst others, by the firms in technological upgradation and gains in their productivity. Households get better goods and services. Both households and firms keep reinvesting in the banks and capital market, thus maintaining the circular flow. These processes are the building blocks of the growth of the economy.

Risk management and regulation is an integral part of this process to maintain continuity. Therefore, regulations and policies must be closely monitored and properly implemented. The Central Bank and the Securities Exchange Commission (SEC) are two principal regulatory bodies that establish the checks and balances in this dynamic process through

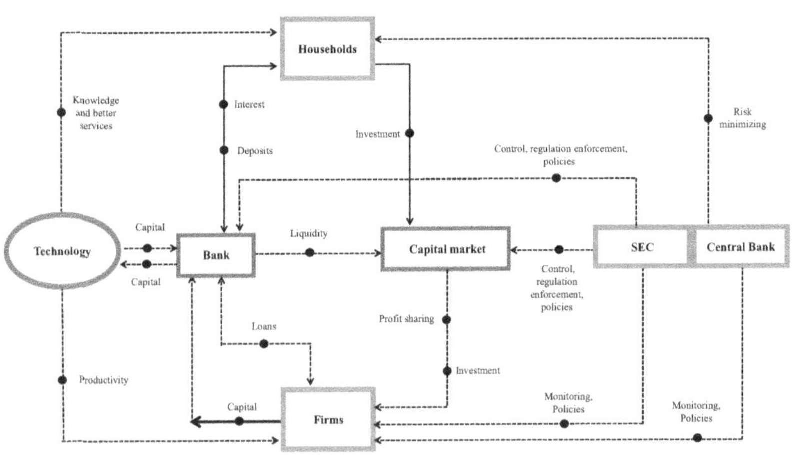

Fig. 4.1 Conceptual framework (*Source* Prepared by Author)

prudential regulations. The whole system becomes unstable and vulnerable without the enforcement of these regulations. As mentioned in the framework, a well-established financial system relies on the effectiveness of the relationships among the stakeholders.

This chapter is divided into two broad sections—Banking Sector and Capital Market—and discusses the performance of the sector in terms of major indicators to comprehend the stability, transformability and sustainability conditions. The subsections also explore and analyse key differences between Bangladesh's financial sector and that of other countries through comparative analysis. Finally, a summary of the state of the financial sector is presented as concluding remarks.

Banking Sector: A Framework

The framework denotes the indicators evaluating the necessary and sufficient conditions for the growth of the banking sector of Bangladesh. Access and functioning is one of the two clusters for comprehending the stability of the banking sector. The other cluster entails the quality and soundness of the sector. Performance and profitability along with regulatory reforms are assumed as the conditions for transformation of the banking sector. A diversified investment portfolio as well as interlinkage between the banking sector and capital markets are crucial in creating a sustainable banking sector (Fig. 4.2).

Stability Conditions

'Access and Functioning' and 'Quality and Soundness' are two major dimensions which have been considered for assessing the stability of banks. 'Access and functioning' in Banking are narrowed down by four indicators—(1) domestic credit, (2) credit to private sector (3) branches of banks and (4) Net Foreign assets. At the same time, the 'Quality and soundness' of the banking sector is analysed by four key indicators- (1) capital adequacy ratio, (2) non-performing loans (NPLs), (3) non-performing assets (NPAs) and (4) rescheduled Loans.

Bangladesh scored 38.3 out of 100 and ranked 130th out of 141 countries in terms of soundness of banks. In defining the banks' soundness, weak monitoring, growing default loans, lack of good governance, balance sheets and availability of funds, and capacity to repay are considered. India scored 60.4 and ranked 89th followed by Pakistan ranking

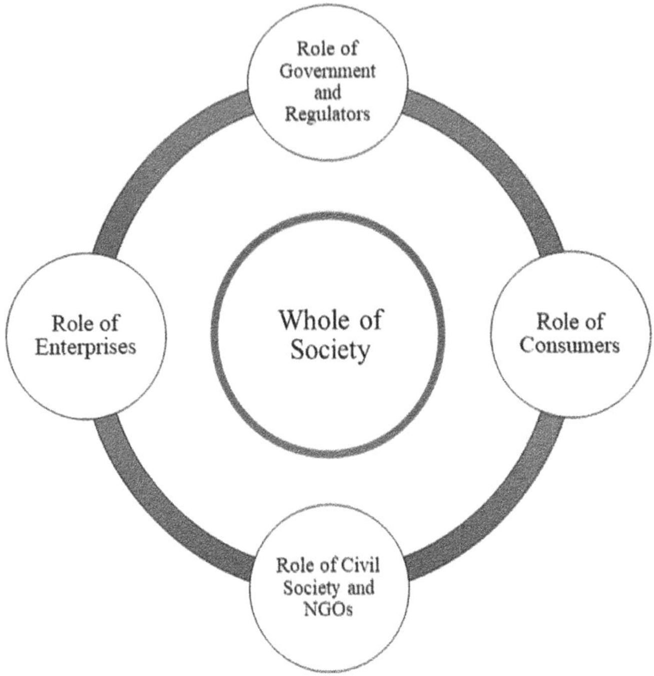

Fig. 4.2 Stability, transformability and sustainability framework in banking sector (*Source* Author)

93rd, Sri Lanka 94th and Nepal 108th. In the global competitive ranking in 2019, Bangladesh scored 105, which was 103rd in 2018. The country's overall score, however, remained unchanged at 52.1 (WEF 2019).

Several indicators like deposit money assets, liquid liabilities and financial system deposits have significantly increased in the decade between 2009 and 2017 compared to the preceding decade. There is a high rate of increment in average domestic credit to the private sector in the decade of 2009–2017, compared to the previous one, when the credit was provided by the banks (Table 4.1). On the other hand, some important indicators like return on assets (RoA), return on equity (RoE) and stock turnover ratio have declined on an average over the decades. The Z score also remained in between 7 and 7.5 over the last two decades and is currently at 7.1 clearly demonstrating the low quality of the banking sector.

Table 4.1 Decadal average of some key indicators of financial sector

Indicators	*Period*	
	1998–2008	*2009–2017*
Private credit by deposit money banks to GDP (%)	23.11	36.69
Deposit money banks' assets to GDP (%)	34.57	52.30
Liquid liabilities to GDP (%)	36.39	53.31
Financial system deposits to GDP (%)	32.35	42.19
Domestic credit to private sector (% of GDP)	26.74	42.82
Domestic credit to private sector by banks (% of GDP)	26.46	82.62
Stock market capitalisation to GDP (%)	5.81	25.48
Stock market total value traded to GDP (%)	0.90	1.45
Bank return on assets (%, after tax)	1.45	1.28
Bank return on equity (%, after tax)	19.63	15.07
Stock market turnover ratio (%)	29.60	25.17
Bank Z-score	7.53	7.54

Source World Bank (2019a)

The strength of a bank means the capacity to withstand against all types of odds, which is measured by the capital of a bank. The banking sector assets reached BDT 14,566.9 billion in 2018, registering a moderate growth of 11.5% from that of 2017 (Bangladesh Bank 2018a). The NPL ratio has increased from 9.3% at end of 2017 to 10.3% at the end-2018. Most of NPLs are in the State-Owned Commercial Banks (SCBs), which stood at 30% at the end of 2018. There has been a growing trend of loan rescheduling and restructuring, including those granted by the central bank, Bangladesh Bank (BB) on an individual basis. Total stressed advances, which include NPLs, restructured and rescheduled loans, now exceed 20% of total loans. This mainly reflects the high stressed assets in SOCBs, even though in recent years the stressed asset ratio has also been increasing in private commercial banks (PCBs). The high level of stressed assets limits the banks' ability to engage in new lending and limits access to credit (IMF 2019).

Deterioration in Quality and Soundness

Capital Adequacy Ratio

Maintaining adequate amount of capital is an integral part of a bank's process of risk management since capital is regarded as the shock absorber.

The banks in the country have already implemented Risk Based Capital Adequacy (RBCA) guideline formulated in line with Basel-II and has begun implementing Basel-III, which was introduced in response to the global financial crisis.

The capital adequacy ratio, also known as capital-to-risk weighted assets ratio (CRAR), a means used to protect depositors and promote the stability and efficiency of financial systems, has declined to 10.5% in 2018 from 10.8% in 2017. 48 banks have maintained a CRAR of 10.0% or higher at the end of 2018 out of 57 scheduled banks. The aggregate asset share in the total assets of banking industry decreased to 73.2% from 76.5% during the period of 2015–2018, even though the number of CRAR compliant banks remained the same as 2017 (Fig. 4.8).

The banks are required to maintain a Capital Conservation Buffer (CCB) above the minimum required CRAR of 10.0% according to the Basel III framework. CCB requirement for banks in Bangladesh was introduced from early 2016 in phased-in manner and to be fully implemented by 2019 when CCB was targeted to be 2.5% above the regulatory minimum compliance requirement of 10.0%. CCB needs to be maintained in the form of Common Equity Tier-1 (CET-1) capital. Banking industry maintained a CCB of 0.5% as of end-December 2018 (Fig. 4.3) against

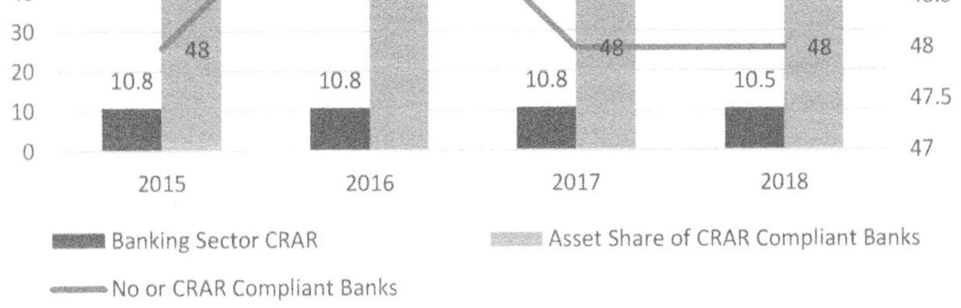

Fig. 4.3 Year-wise CRAR, CRAR compliant banks and their asset share (*Source* Bangladesh Bank 2018a)

Table 4.2 Comparison of capital adequacy indicators of the neighbouring countries

	CRAR (%)				
	2014	*2015*	*2016*	*2017*	*2018*
India	12.8	12.7	13.3	13	13.7
Pakistan	17.1	17.3	16.2	15.8	16.2
Sri Lanka	17.2	15.4	15.6	15.2	15.9
Bangladesh	11.4	10.8	10.8	10.8	10.5

Source Bangladesh Bank (2018b), Reserve Bank of India (2018), State Bank of Pakistan (2018), Central Bank of Sri Lanka (2018)

the CCB requirement of 1.875% for 2018. The previous score was 0.8% at end-December 2017 against the regulatory requirement of 1.25% for 2017. 43 out of 57 banks were able to maintain the minimum required CCB during the review period (Bangladesh Bank 2019).

The cross-country scenario (Table 4.2) shows a lower standard in Bangladesh for this particular indicator. The capital adequacy of the country's banking sector was lower compared to the ratios of neighbouring countries as of end-December 2018.

Non-Performing Loans (NPLs)

A loan is non-performing when the payments of interest and principal are outstanding by 90 days or more, according to the guidelines of the central bank. NPL is a suitable indicator for measuring the asset quality of bank as the lion's share of a bank's earnings is generated from the loans. An increase in the growth of the ratio indicates the deterioration of the asset quality.

The officially recognised figure of the total defaulted loans at the end of June 2019 stood at BDT 1124.25 billion, which is 11.69% of the total outstanding loans, according to Bangladesh Bank (BB). But the actual size is more than double this figure. All troubled assets are not captured in the definition of defaulted loans by Bangladesh Bank. Such loans amounted to BDT 792.42 billion as of January, 2019 if problem assets as well as those in the special mention accounts, which is the precursor to the classified category are counted (*The Daily Star* 2019).

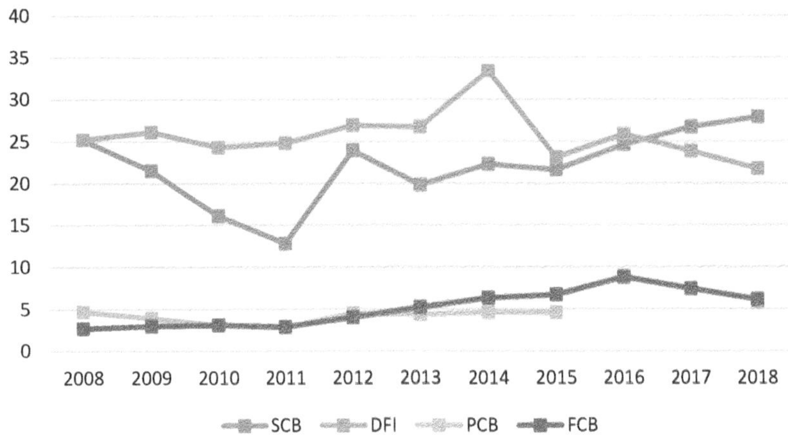

Fig. 4.4 Non-Performing Loan as a share of total loan (*Source* Bangladesh Bank 2018a)

The amount of NPL was exceptionally high in SCBs and in state-owned development financial institutions (DFIs) in 2018. The SCBs had a NPL of 28.2% which is the highest in last ten years as of June 2018 (Fig. 4.4). During the same time, 5 banks had a loan concentration of about 47%. The net NPL is only lower than India and Bhutan as a percentage of total loans outstanding in the banking sector (Fig. 4.5).

Non-Performing Assets (NPAs)

As of June 2019, the total amount of NPAs in the banking sector of Bangladesh stood at BDT 2401.67 billion. This is about more than double the Bangladesh Bank reported amount of defaulted loans according to the IMF (*The Daily Star* 2019). At the end of December 2018, the NPA ratio, which is calculated as the ratio of stressed assets as a percentage of total loans and advances outstanding, stood at 20.5%. The amount was 19% at the end of December 2017. In general, banking sector's stressed assets are defined as the sum of gross nonperforming assets plus restructured and rescheduled standard advances. This increase in the NPAs is mainly attributable to the augmented volume of non-performing assets and rescheduled advances (Bangladesh Bank 2018b).

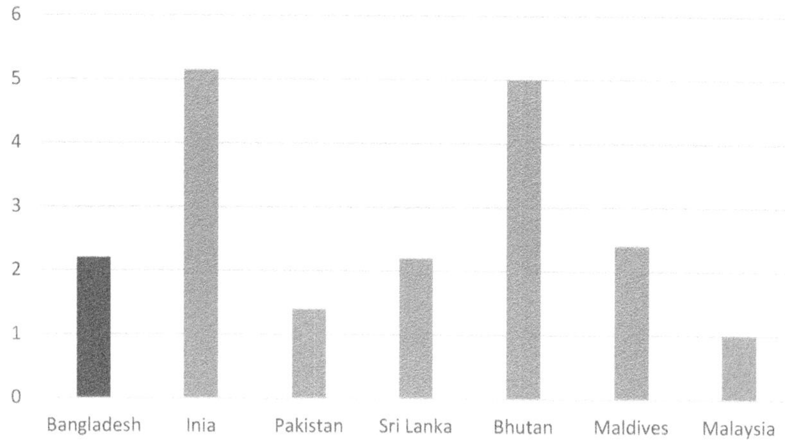

Fig. 4.5 Net NPL ratios in selected countries (*Source* Bangladesh Bank 2018b)

The ratio of NPAs has increased. The distribution of the NPAs ratio (Fig. 4.6) exhibits that 11 banks maintained their stressed assets ratios below 5% at the end of December 2018. In 2017, 15 banks maintained this ratio. At the end of December, 2018, 16 banks maintained NPAs ratio between 5 and 10%. At the same period, 30 banks had this ratio more than 10%. In 2017, the corresponding number of banks at the same performance level was 17 and 25 respectively (Bangladesh Bank 2018a).

Rescheduled Loans

Rescheduling loans by masking the problem loans has become a concern. A large number of the Special Mention loans, which have potential weaknesses that deserve management's close attention and if not corrected may result in deterioration of the repayment prospects, are rescheduled or restructured many times. As a result, the problem loans are disguised to suggest lower amount of NPLs, though the NPLs rise over time. As of June 2019, loans amounting to BDT 271.92 billion are held in Special Mention accounts (Bangladesh Bank 2019). Thus, these defaulted loans are often categorised back as regular loans. Most of these defaults were made by choice rather than facing any unexpected financial problems, as per the IMF (*The Daily Star* 2019).

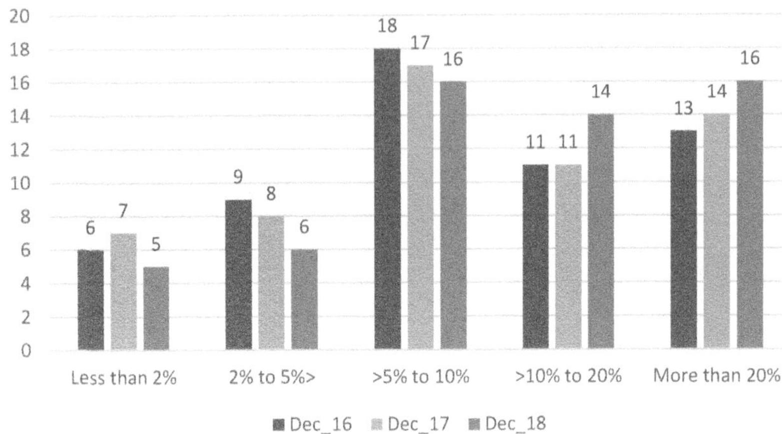

Fig. 4.6 Distribution of stressed assets ratio (*Source* Bangladesh Bank 2018b)

The trend in rescheduled loans for the five years of 2014–2018 indicates a rise in the amount of loans rescheduled (Fig. 4.7). The amount of loans rescheduled in 2018 was BDT 232.1 billion which was 24% higher than that of the amount rescheduled in the year 2017. The

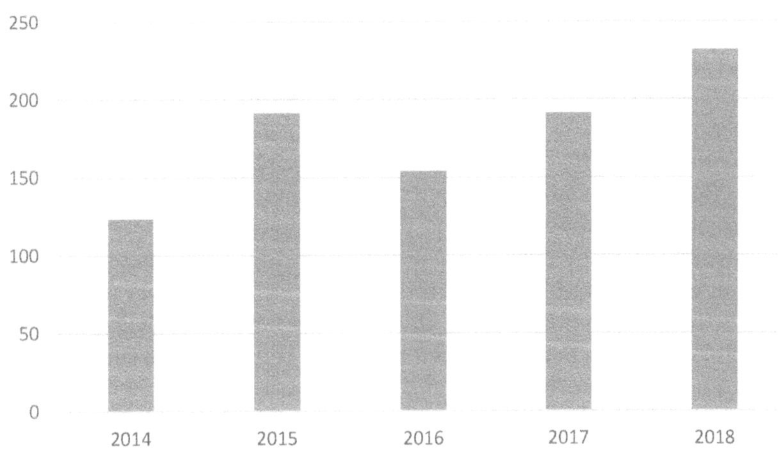

Fig. 4.7 Rescheduled loans (*Source* Bangladesh Bank 2018b)

loans are rescheduled due to over-leverage, slowdown in external demand for export-oriented products, poor due diligence, and negligence in the compliance of risk management practices (Bangladesh Bank 2018b).

Shortfalls in Access and Functioning

Domestic Credit

All credit to various sectors on a gross basis is included in the domestic credit provided by the banking sector. The only exception is the credit provided to the central government. Domestic credit provided by Bangladesh's banking sector increased from 28.3% in 1999 to 64.1% in 2018 growing at an average annual rate of 4.69% (Bangladesh Bank 2018a). For an otherwise bank dominated financial system, private investment is primarily sourced from domestic credit. A sluggish credit growth rate is therefore likely to restrain the growth of investment over the years, pulling the reins on productive capacity expansion (Fig. 4.8).

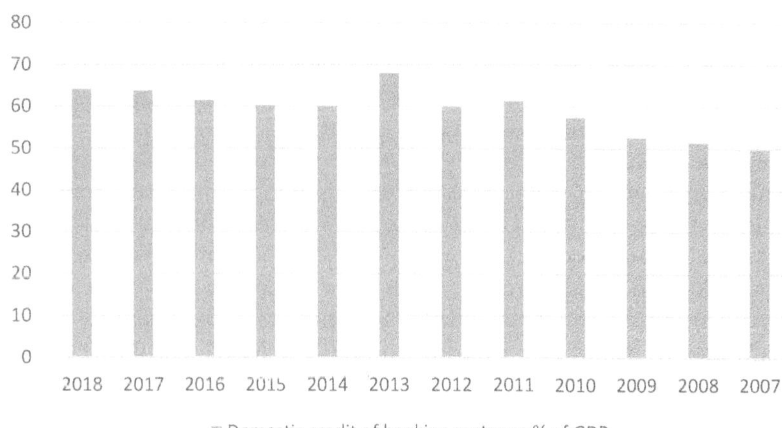

Fig. 4.8 Domestic credit of banking sector as % of GDP (*Source* World Bank 2019b)

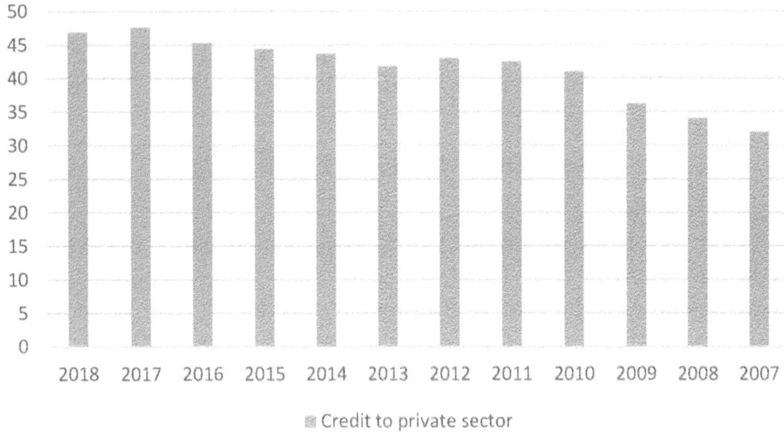

Fig. 4.9 Credit to private sector as a percentage of GDP (*Source* World Bank 2019b)

Credit to Private Sector
Domestic credit to private sector refers to the financial resources provided to the private sector by financial corporations through loans, purchases of non-equity securities, and trade credits and other accounts receivable, that establish a claim for repayment. In 2018, domestic credit to Bangladesh's private sector was 46.9%. This amount increased from 21% in 1999 to 46.9% in 2018, rising at an average annual rate of 4.40% (Fig. 4.9). Private sector credit growth was therefore lower than the annual domestic credit growth, implying a dampener on private investment. During the pandemic-induced economic slowdown, private sector credit growth had in fact dwindled to 8.86% in March 2020, the lowest since December, 2008, portraying a slump in investment due to reduced economic activities.

Branches of Banks
The number of branches of banks denotes the access of the banking sector to the population. Over the last 10 years, 3,228 branches of both private and state-owned banks have been established in Bangladesh. As a result, the total number of bank branches in the country has become 10,114 by June, 2018 which was 6,886 in June, 2008 (Dhaka Tribune 2018).

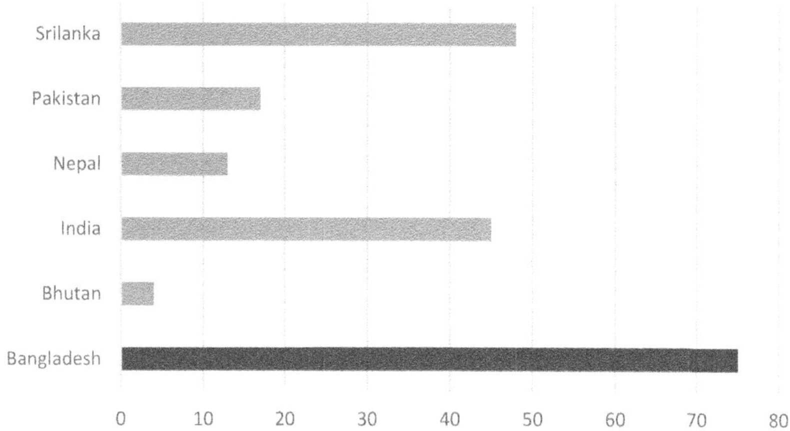

Fig. 4.10 Branches of commercial banks per 1,000 square kilometres in South Asia (2016) (*Source* IMF 2018)

Bangladesh recorded the highest concentration of branches of commercial banks in the South Asian region. There were 75 branches of commercial banks per 1000 square kilometres of land in 2016 (IMF 2018). In the global comparison, Bangladesh ranks 8th in geographic concentration of commercial bank branches, aside from the microstates (Fig. 4.10). A higher number of branches may however increase administrative costs for commercial banks, but may be useful for distributing the risks of non-performing loans which is high and prevalent in the country.

Net Foreign Assets
Net foreign assets are the sum of foreign assets held by the monetary authorities and deposit money banks, less their foreign liabilities. In 2018, net foreign assets for Bangladesh was USD 26.56 billion, which is a 3.14 decrease than that of the previous year. According to the Central Bank, net foreign assets reached USD 28.45 billion in 2017 in Bangladesh. This is 2.47% more than in the previous year. Historically, net foreign assets in Bangladesh reached an all -time high of 28.45 billion USD in 2017 (Fig. 4.11). When compared to Bangladesh's main peers, net foreign assets in Bhutan amounted to 0.87 billion USD, 3,790 billion in China. Bangladesh has been ranked 26th within the group of 145 countries we followed in terms of net foreign assets, 24 places above the

Fig. 4.11 Net foreign assets of banking sector (*Source* World Bank 2019b)

position seen 10 years ago (World Bank 2018). Although the net foreign assets in Bangladesh have been positive over the years, the amount of it is significantly lower than its South Asian counterparts, implying a possible shortfall and untapped resources.

Overall, the banking sector's performance in terms of the stability conditions has been a cause of concern. A string of scandals and high rates of NPLs has put the sector in a liquidity crunch. The level of stressed advances, including NPLs and restructured or rescheduled loans, is at 20% of total funds loaned. The state-owned banks have been doing particularly poorly, with an NPL rate of 30% at the end of 2018. While lending rates have been high, the government has been attempting to reduce it to single digits through appeals and persuasion. However, there are three reasons this has not been working effectively: high and rising NPLs, a need to reduce the advance-deposit ratio from 85 to 83.5%, and the negative impact of the issuance of savings certificates on bank deposits (IMF 2020).

Transformability Conditions

Transformability in the banking sector requires a profitable and efficient banking system with prudential regulations. Bank profitability is critical to form capital, establish adequate loss reserves, manage expenses and provide dividends to shareholders. Both profitability and efficiency measurements are essential for the evaluation of performances of any financial institution. The banking sector's operating profit, without tax and provision, increased from BDT 246.5 billion in 2017 to BDT 266.4 billion in 2018, recording an increase of 8.1%. However, net profit decreased by 57.5% from BDT 95.1 billion in 2017 to BDT 40.4 billion in 2018. This is due to the higher provision requirement, the amount set aside to allow for uncollected loans and loan payments as per the loan classification requirement of the Central Bank. The provisioning requirement increased owing to the swollen NPL.

Performance and Profitability

The banking sector's profitability are generally measured in terms of (1) return on assets (RoA) (2) return on equity (RoE) and (3) net interest margin (NIM).

Return on Assets (RoA)

RoA denotes the efficiency of management in using its financial and real resources to generate earnings. Higher values of the return on assets thus show that the business is more profitable. RoA declined for 29 banks, remained unchanged for 11 banks while it increased for 17 banks in 2018. Notably, 89.5% of the banks had RoA of less than two percent (Fig. 4.12a).

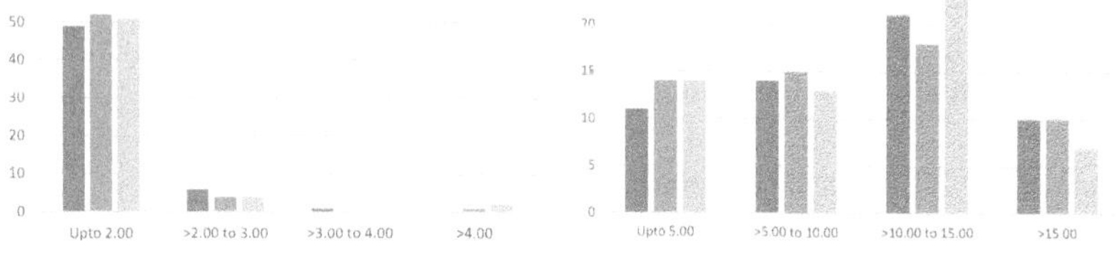

Fig. 4.12 **a** Banking sector RoA. **b** Banking Sector RoE (*Source* Bangladesh Bank 2018b)

Return on Equity (RoE)
RoE shows the net income as a percentage of shareholder equity. A company's efficiency in generating income on new investments is measured by the higher values. RoE reached 4.4% in 2018 from 10.4% in 2017 by decreasing about 6%. This indicates the decline of RoE in 28 banks although it increased for 24 banks and remained unchanged for 5 banks. 52.6% of the banks had ROE higher than 10% (Fig. 4.12b). Total interest income increased by 22.1% whereas total interest expense increased by 22.1% in 2018 compared to 2017. On the other hand, the amount of non-interest income decreased by 4.8%. The main reason for this fall is the decline in investment income from government securities (Bangladesh Bank 2018b).

Net Interest Margin (NIM)
Net interest margin is defined as a measure of the difference between the interest income generated by banks or other financial institutions and the amount of interest paid out to their lenders, relative to the amount of their assets. The NIM increased by 20 basis points from 2.0% in 2017 to 2.2% in 2018 (Bangladesh Bank 2018b). NIM has increased in 2017 to 2.0% by 10 basis points in terms of different components of profitability. In 2016, NIM had increased by 1.9%. The total interest expense also increased by 4.3% in 2017 from that of 2016. The SCBs, however, registered positive NIM in 2018 after experiencing negative NIM for the past two years. There has been a moderate decrease in the NIM of SDBs from 1.3% in 2017 to 0.3% in 2018. On the other hand, the PCBs registered a slight increase in NIM from 2.7% in 2017 to 2.8% in 2018. In 2018, the NIM of FCBs remained higher compared to all other categories of banks (Fig. 4.13). FCBs had a much higher interest income than their interest expense, whereas the interest incomes barely exceeded interest expenses for the SCBs and SDBs (Bangladesh Bank 2018b).

Regulatory Reforms for Reversing the Trends
The monetary policy reforms taken by the Bangladesh Bank are being affected by clientelism. Political patronisation is also modifying the regulatory system in favour of the governing body of the banks, set by political interference. The amendment of the Bank company law in 2018 increased the tenure of members of the governing body as well as increasing the

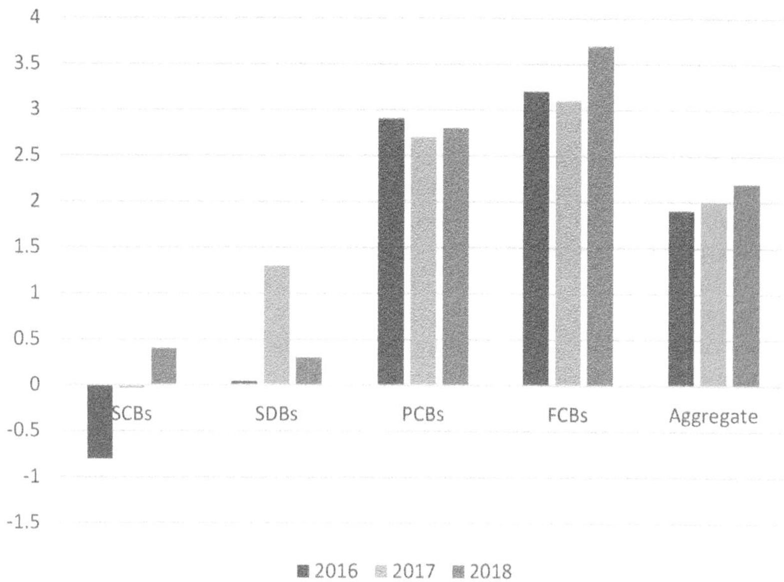

Fig. 4.13 Bank type wise NIM (*Source* Bangladesh Bank 2018b)

provision of having board members from the same family from two to four. As a result, private banks are getting more familial supremacy and with an increase in ownership of multiple banks by the same family, carry along nepotism. Those families are the largest borrowers and as a result, the general depositors are not generating profits from their investments (Titumir 2019).

Bangladesh has ranked 54th out of 133 nations in the Financial Secrecy Index (FSI) 2020, with a score of 72.73, based on the country's high secrecy over jurisdiction and offshore financial services. The index measures different jurisdiction's contribution to global financial secrecy in a way that highlights harmful secrecy regulations. A hundred score means high secrecy and zero means high transparency. The FSI consists of 20 Key Financial Secrecy Indicators in four Key Indicator Categories—Ownership registration, Legal entity transparency, Integrity of tax and financial regulation, and international standards and cooperation. The score indicates how intensely Bangladesh's legal and financial systems allow wealthy individuals and criminals to hide and launder money, according to a study by Tax Justice Network (TJN). Bangladesh maintains very high secrecy in legal entity transparency, achieving a mean score of 95 out of 100. Bangladesh's domestic legal entities maintain a very poor transparency, which has resulted in Bangladesh achieving 9 points higher than the average secrecy score. Bangladesh has zero transparency in public company ownership, accounts, country-by-country reporting and legal entity identifier (*The Business Standard* 2020).

When the existing structure of the banking system fails to fulfil the desired level of economies of scale in operations, reforms play a reshaping role as an inevitable process. Sheng (1996) defines banking sector reform or the restructuring of banks as "the package of macro-economic, micro-economic, institutional and regulatory measures taken to restore fragile banking systems to financial solvency and discipline." There is an existing relationship between reform and bank efficiency through improvements in RoE, RoA, NIM etc. (Fu and Heffernan 2008). Effective and ongoing regulatory reforms can develop the financial system by means of improving competitiveness, mobilisation of savings, and allocation of efficiency and achieving economic growth (Besanko and Thakor 1992; Claessens and Laeven 2004).

The need of the hour is to remove the identified weaknesses of the banking sector if it were to transform and sustain its growth trajectory. The government needs to respond to the urgency by embarking on a comprehensive review of financial assets to analyse the actual performance of the market to develop strict criteria and internal control systems for the NPLs.

A reform of the banking sector will strengthen it as lending will not be haphazard, and stricter regulation will also limit the extent of unethical practices such a bribery and corruption, which have also plagued the sector significantly. Regulatory forbearance needs to be avoided with strict and prompt remedial actions imposed upon banks. Central Bank's independence and autonomy are key for effective regulation and supervision. Efforts to adopt risk-based supervision should continue. A clear entry and exit strategy for banks should be introduced and enforced while establishing an emergency financing facility for solvent but temporarily illiquid banks (IMF 2020).

Sustainability Conditions

Sustainability in the banking sector represents the cycle of fulfilment of the stability and the transformation conditions that generate growth. Any shock in the banking sector inflicts a catastrophic damage to the economy if the sector is not sustainable. The investors do not have a diversified choice of investment source. Thus, the diversification of the investment portfolio is a way of ensuring sustainability in the banking sector.

Diversification of Investment Portfolio

Any single security contains both systematic and unsystematic risk. As more assets which are not perfectly positively correlated are added to the portfolio, the unsystematic portion of the risk goes down. For a properly well-diversified portfolio, it is theoretically possible to remove all the non-systematic risk. Risk can be reduced by constructing portfolios with less correlated assets. But at the same time, return is also a matter of concern to investors. So, the ability to achieve return goals must be considered. Investment Portfolio diversification is only considered to be working in terms of reducing unsystematic risk. Creating a portfolio of assets is the best way to reduce exposure to unsystematic risk. However, investors have to pick assets that are less positively co-related. The banks in Bangladesh do not have the investment space that can focus on their operational efficiency and capital structure to improvise their performance in the stock market.

Bangladesh has the highest percentage of NPLs among South Asian countries (Fig. 4.14). Bangladesh also has one of the lowest percentages in providing domestic credit to the private sector as a percentage of GDP. Compared to the OECD and East Asian countries, Bangladesh fares poorly in terms of the stability of the financial sector. Lower percentage of domestic credit by banks has also resulted in lower manufacturing value added to the GDP (Fig. 4.15). As a result, the Small and Medium Enterprises numbers have started to fall.

Bangladesh ranked 45th from highest to lowest level of risk on the BASEL AML Index in 2019, out of 125 countries (a risk score of 5.0 or above and can be loosely classified as having a significant risk of ML/TF). Bangladesh has scored 5.80 on a scale of 0 to 10 in the index.

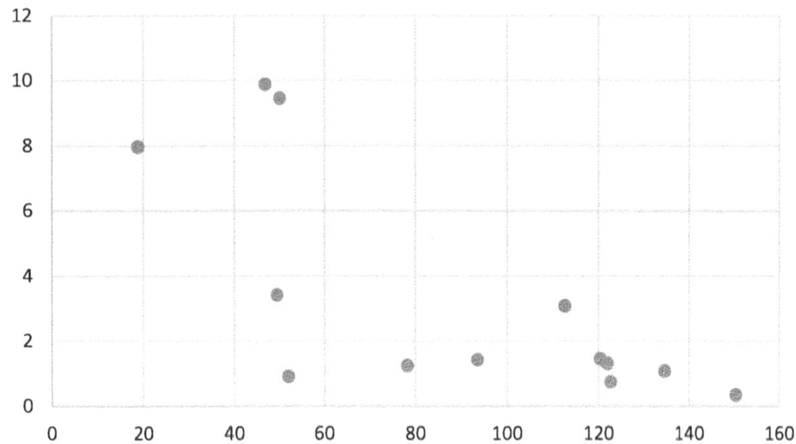

Fig. 4.14 Domestic credit vs. Non-performing loans of some selected countries (*Source* World Bank 2019b)

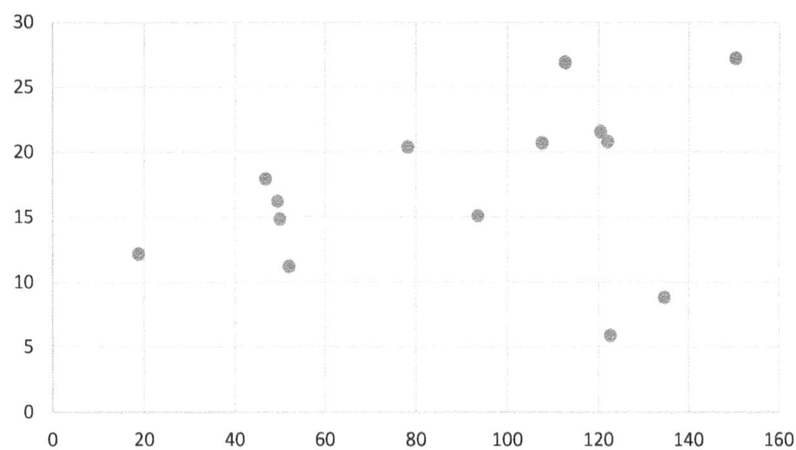

Fig. 4.15 Manufacturing Value Added vs. Domestic credit to private sector of some selected countries (*Source* World Bank 2019a)

Strengthened Policies for Risk Management

In order to achieve stability in the banking sector and thus, transform it into sustainability, Bangladesh Bank should tighten the criteria for rescheduling/restructuring of loans and avoid their repeated use. Clear and well-defined criteria should also help prevent Bangladesh Bank's involvement when banks grant rescheduling/restructuring at their discretion. Banks' corporate governance needs to be strengthened; serious graft cases point to insufficient internal control and risk management. Loan concentration limits should be ensured to be observed. Legal systems should be strengthened to support banks to recover NPLs, particularly those by wilful defaulters. Further strengthening capacity and efficiency of the judicial system could expedite the legal processes and settlements. The role of SCBs needs to be reassessed; a limited number of SCBs with clear public mandates could receive transparent budget support (IMF 2019).

Capital Market: A Framework

Capital market is an integral part of an economy. A sound and efficient capital market can enhance the rapid economic development by providing long-term funds to the entrepreneurs.

The stability of the capital market depends on the size of, and access to, the market (Fig. 4.16). The size of the market incorporates the stock traded and the turnover of shares. Share turnover is a measure of stock liquidity. It is calculated by dividing the total number of shares traded over a period by the average number of shares outstanding for the period. The higher the share turnover, the more liquid company shares are. The trading volume of top firms and the concentration in the market are the key inputs for the access to the market. Both provisions of the market (access and size) consist of market capitalisation.

Efficiency of the market and risk control mechanisms are assumed here as transformability conditions. Efficiency comes through synchronicity and liquidity. Synchronicity refers to the amount that market and company-specific information are reflected in share prices. Market liquidity refers to the extent to which a market (e.g. stock market) allows assets to be bought and sold at stable and transparent prices.

The achievement of efficiency strengthens the market's capacity to formulate risk control mechanisms. Risk control mechanisms are related to volatility in the market and the vulnerability to earnings manipulations.

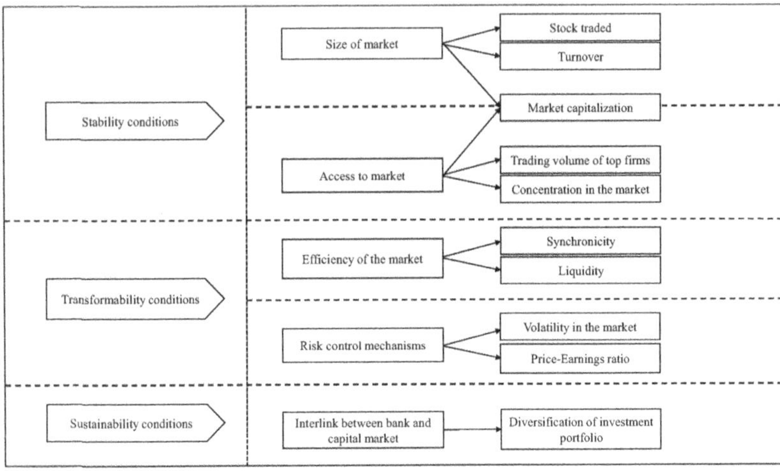

Fig. 4.16 Stability, transformation and sustainability indicators of Money and Capital Market (*Source* Author)

An efficient market can manage the volatility of market and create a strong mechanism so that volatility does not increase. Apart from that, institutional arrangements are very significant to attain sustainability of the capital market as regulatory reforms come from these arrangements.

The sustainability conditions in the capital market emphasises the integration of the banking sector and the capital market. Despite a strong dominance of the banking sector in the capital market, investment portfolio has to be diversified in order to create a sustainable capital market for the achievement of long-term economic growth. Sustainability of the financial sector in Bangladesh will therefore require a harmonisation between the banking sector and the capital market that contribute to the investment portfolio with equal significance.

Stability Conditions

The stability of the stock market can be explained with two sets of dimensions. The first one is the size of the market which can be described by three indicators- (1) Market Capitalisation (2) Turnover ratio and (3) Trade by Foreign Investors. The second dimension, access to market, can be explained by two indicators- (1) Trading Volume of Top firms and (2) Concentration in the market.

Size of the Market

Market Capitalisation Ratio

There is a gradual downward movement of the DSE broad index (DSEX). The DSEX stood at 5385.6 in December 2018 from 6244.5 in December 2017. Similarly, the market capitalisation of DSE decreased to BDT 3,872.9 billion at the end of 2018 compared to BDT 4,228.9 billion at the end of 2017. The fall of both indices and market capitalisation has demonstrated a downtrend in the capital market (Bangladesh Bank 2018b).

Stock market deepening is measured by total market capitalisation as a percentage of GDP. The market capitalisation GDP ratio plummeted to 17.2% in 2018 (Fig. 4.17). The fall in market capitalisation and high GDP growth contributed to the sharp fall in the market capitalisation ratio. Over the years while the market capitalisation ratio recorded a downward trend with moderate fluctuation.

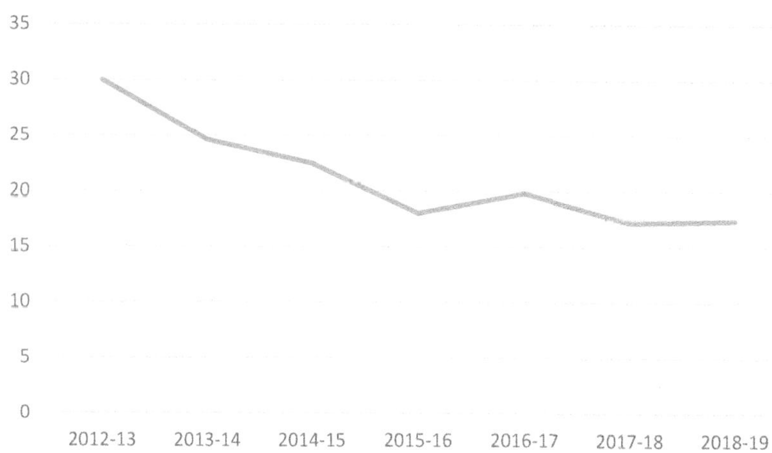

Fig. 4.17 Market capitalisation ratio (*Source* Bangladesh Bank 2018b)

Turnover Ratio
The liquidity in stock market can be measured by the turnover velocity ratio, i.e. traded turnover divided by market capitalisation. The turnover velocity ratio decreased to 34.4% in 2018 compared to 51.3% in 2017. This implies that liquidity was tighter in 2018. This has been the case over the years, excepting a spike in 2017 (Fig. 4.18).

Trade by Foreign Investors
The total trade by foreign investors fell to BDT 92.7 billion in 2018 from BDT 114.5 billion in 2017, recording a fall by 19% in DSE (Fig. 4.19). Total shares bought by foreign investors declined to BDT 43.7 billion in 2018 from BDT 65 billion in 2017 recording a 33.5% decline. On the other hand, the total shares sold by foreign investors increased to BDT 49 billion in 2018 from BDT 48.7 billion in 2017. As a result, net investment became negative in 2018 for the first time in the past five years. Moreover, the value of total foreign trade recorded at 6.9% of the total turnover of DSE during 2018 compared to 8.6% in 2017 (Bangladesh Bank 2018b).

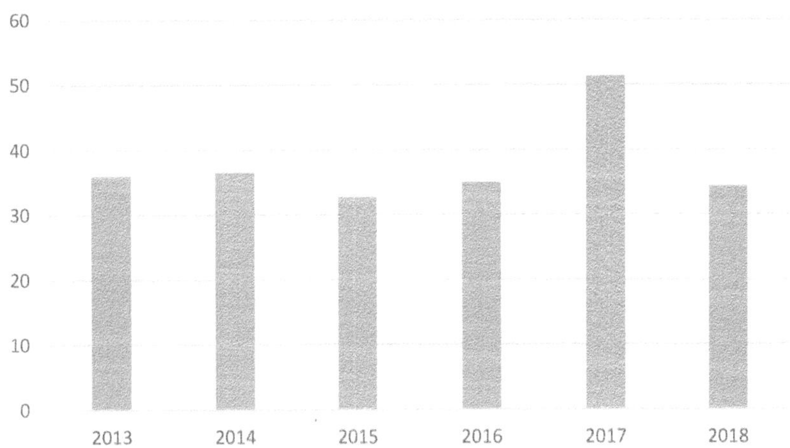

Fig. 4.18 Turnover velocity ratio (2013–2018) (*Source* Bangladesh Bank 2018b)

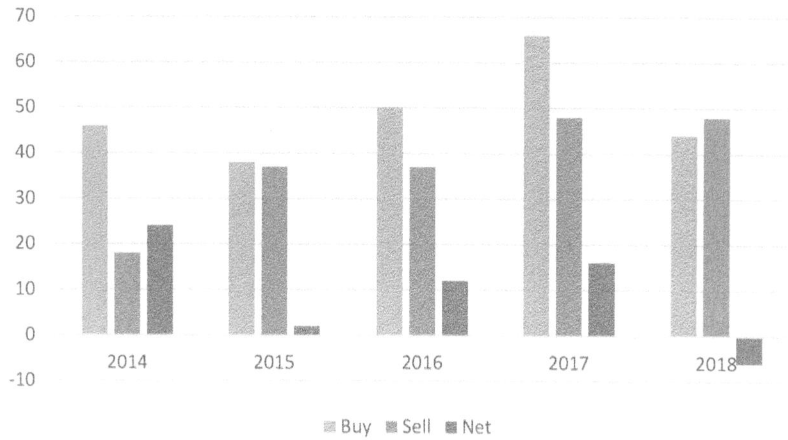

Fig. 4.19 Foreign trade turnover (2014–2018) (*Source* Bangladesh Bank 2018b)

Access to the Market

Concentration in the Market

Concentration in the market can be described by the market capitalisation decomposition. The manufacturing sector dominates the market capitalisation in 2018 capturing 39.1%. Food and allied industries, pharmaceuticals and chemicals, textile and engineering industries are major contributions in the manufacturing sector (Fig. 4.20).

The service and miscellaneous sector captured second largest share, 34.4% of the market capitalisation, in 2018 from 33.5% in 2017. The fuel and power subsectors were the key contributors in this sector. The market share of the financial sector decreased from 29.7% in 2017 to 26.4% in 2018, largely attributable to the negative growth in banks and financial institutions. The growth in banks and financial institutions decreased by 23 and 22% respectively in 2018 compared to those of 2017. The share of the corporate bond sector decreased from 0.16% in 2017 to 0.09% in 2018 (Bangladesh Bank 2018b).

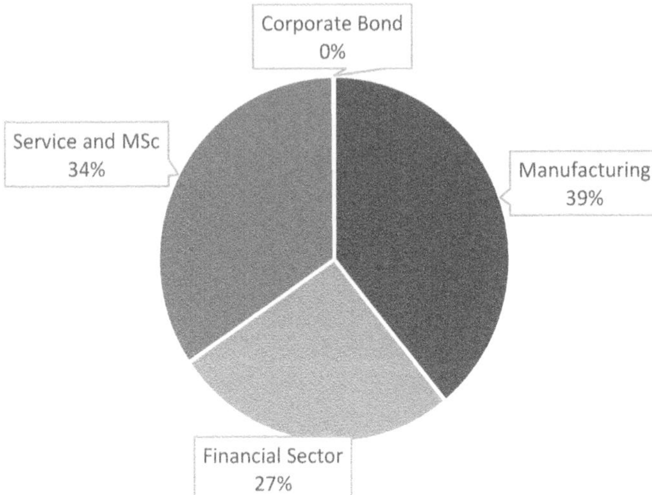

Fig. 4.20 Decomposition of MCap (December 2018) (*Source* Bangladesh Bank 2018b)

Transformability Conditions

Transformability conditions in the capital market denote the mode of transforming the current market into an efficient one. The transformation of the capital market needs significant risk control mechanisms through controlling volatility in the market as well as having a progressive price-earnings ratio. Thus, transformability conditions in the capital market have been discussed in terms of two key indicators—(i) efficiency of the market and (ii) risk control mechanism.

Efficiency of the Market

No market can become vibrant and experience reasonable growth without long-term investors. Other deficiencies, including the shortage of quality issues, have kept this particular section of investors away from the market. However, they are most discouraged by the highhandedness of the manipulators. Large manipulators, with strong political connections, played important roles in 1996 and 2010, leading to the collapse of the market on these two occasions (*Financial Express* 2020).

Regulators have taken some steps in recent years to bring some semblance of market stability. The major step was the demutualisation of the Dhaka and Chittagong Stock Exchanges. There has been a de jure separation of ownership, management, and trading rights, the two stock exchanges, though these are yet to demonstrate that the exchanges are professionally run, and free of vested interests of brokers and dealers. Another major step was the recent entrance of a Chinese consortium, comprising the Shanghai Stock Exchange and the Shenzhen Stock Exchange, as strategic partners of the DSE. The step too has not been able to turn around the market.

Risk Control Mechanisms

Capital market risk control mechanisms can be explained through two indicators- (1) volatility of the market and (2) price-earnings ratio.

Volatility of the Market

For several countries, capital market development has been marred by increasing volatility, despite being denoted as a key challenge for sustainable development of stock markets. Reasons underlying the volatility in capital market are often associated with a lack of efficient regulation of securities market, deficiencies in governance, market bubbles showing 'irrational exuberance' that distort market signals. Besides, the view of speculative actions moves against creating an environment of trust and a sense of fairness in financial markets (Krishnamurti et. al. 2003).

When combined with allegations of market manipulations, insider trading, and outright scams, the speculative nature of the market can be a serious impediment to capital formation, and efficient functioning of the financial markets (Rahman and Moazzem 2011). The level of volatility existing in a market is crucial for business confidence of the average investors. A higher degree of fluctuation will confound the perceptions and anticipations leading to uncertainties and uninformed speculation by investors, further worsening volatility. The stock exchange authority must be cautious in monitoring and forecasting the trends of volatility of DSE (Fig. 4.21).

The key indicators of the major stock exchanges in the country have been encountering worsening volatility over time and the regulations

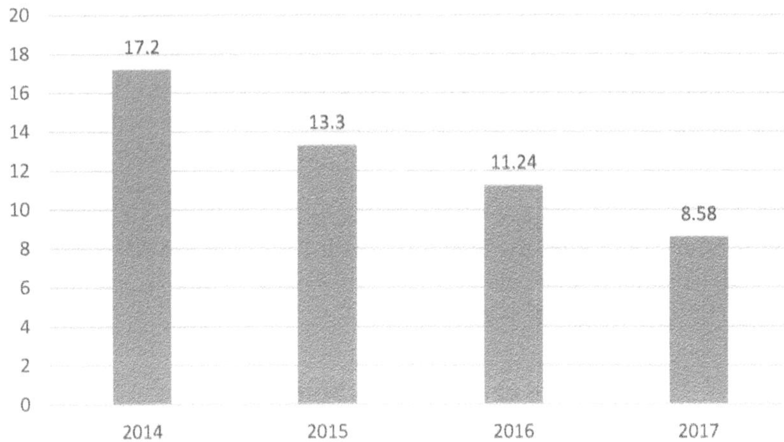

Fig. 4.21 Volatility of stock price (*Source* World Bank 2018)

intended to curb the volatility are largely ineffective. Different jurisdictions have adopted different systems of securities regulation, exemplifying inconsistency (Rahman and Moazzem 2011).

In order to make the market less volatile, SEC itself should be strengthened. A less volatile capital market will enhance predictability and business confidence of investors, improving the market adaptability to rapid unanticipated changes, and thus strengthening the transformability in the overall financial sector.

Price-Earnings (P/E) Ratio

The current market price of the stock divided by its earnings per share (EPS) is known as price earnings (P/E) ratio, which shows how much investors are paying for each unit of earnings. Figure 4.22 shows that the overall weighted average price-earnings (P/E) ratio of the DSE declined from 17.3 in December 2017 to 15.2 in December 2018. The lower PE ratio suggests stocks were less expensive during 2018 than in 2017. This also implies that investors were not optimistic about the future growth of the listed companies.

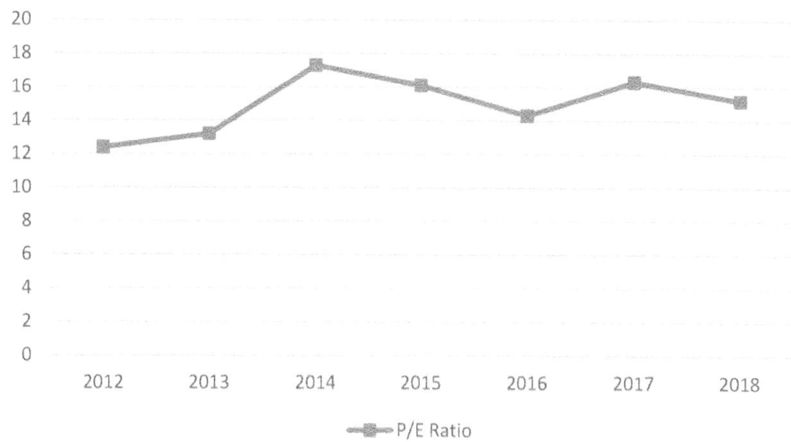

Fig. 4.22 Market Price-earnings ratio (June 2012–December 2018) (*Source* Bangladesh Bank 2018b)

The fluctuating trend of P/E ratio over time represent an unsettling nature of valuation of stocks in the market, moving between being over-valued in 2014 to undervalued in 2016, then rising again the next year and falling the next. A high P/E ratio suggests that shares are high risk and with lower scope of growth in earnings. The observed volatility in the market puts investors in uncertainty and greater speculative tendencies. This requires substantial reckoning on the part of the regulators.

Sustainability Conditions

A sustainable capital market is a prerequisite for maintaining the financial flow in the economy. Both the banking sector and the capital market has to play their role together in order to provide the foundation of a sustainable financial sector. Therefore, sustainability conditions in the capital market analyse the pathway of creating a sustainable financial sector through linking the banking sector with the capital market where the key target is to diversify the investment portfolio.

Linking the Banking Sector and Stock Market

The linkage between the banking sector and the stock market is crucial from the perspective of financial stability. The DSE is largely influenced by the banking sector which holds more than 15% share of the total market capitalisation. A strain on the banking sector is therefore very likely to have detrimental impacts and/or contagion effects on the stock market. Both market capitalisation and index may plunge severely due to a decrease in the bank share price. Both bank turnover and the DSEX had been moving towards the same direction during the past two years, implying that bank turnover had an impact on the index (Fig. 4.23).

Similarly, the performance of stock market has an impact on the banks as well since banks have investment exposure in the stock market. However, the banks' aggregate investment in the capital market remained much below the permissible limit set by the Bangladesh Bank. The banks' capital market exposure was 16.5 and 27.4% of prescribed capital on solo and consolidated basis respectively at end-September 2018 (Fig. 4.24). Considering the lower capital market exposure of the banks, it seems that the equity price shock would not pose any stability threat to the banking sector in the near term.

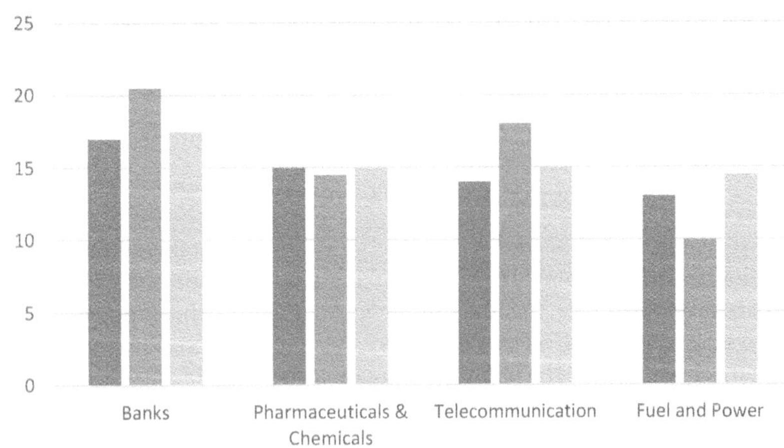

Fig. 4.23 Top four sectors' Market capitalisation in DSE (2016–2018) (*Source* Bangladesh Bank 2018b)

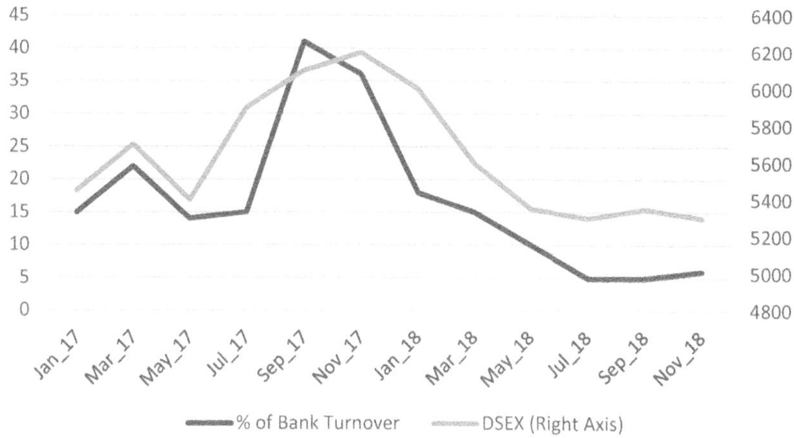

Fig. 4.24 Percent of bank turnover & DSEX movement (2017–2018) (*Source* Bangladesh Bank 2018b)

The capital markets are important for financial intermediation and resource mobilisation, specifically for raising long-term financing and risk capital for infrastructure and entrepreneurial activities. Well-functioning capital markets can reduce the private sector's dependency on bank financing. Bangladesh's capital market needs to be larger, deeper, and more dynamic to encourage enough private sector investment to spur economic growth and enable the country to achieve middle-income status (ADB 2020).

Growing Importance of Financial Sector in Pandemic Era

The financial sector was hit hard by the covid-19 pandemic among many other sectors. Banks in Bangladesh were already struggling with a challenging environment pre-covid. Restoring the economy to pre- covid scenario will require a concerted effort and mix of both monetary and fiscal policy measures.

The banking sector is acting as the main source of finance for the stimulus packages provided by the government for loss-inflicted strategic industries. The banking sector is playing a major role through formulation of different refinance schemes and lending policies in accordance with the government's stimulus. However, effective supervision is needed so that

Table 4.3 Summary of the key drivers of financial sector of Bangladesh

Indicators	*State of Bangladesh*
Banking sector	
Domestic credit	Rate of growth in domestic credit declined
Credit to private sector	Domestic credit to private sector is either stagnant or declined in the last decade
Net foreign assets	Net foreign assets declined
Capital adequacy	Decreasing trend in capital flow
Rescheduled loans	Rescheduled loans have doubled
Bank Z-score	Bank Z-score is very minimum and is lower than countries like India, Nepal, Bhutan, Pakistan, Afghanistan and Vietnam
Non-performing loans	Gross non-performing loans have increased and the highest among neighbouring, East Asian and OECD countries
Capital market	
Foreign trade	Total trade by foreign investors has decreased
Stock market turnover ratio	Stock market turnover ratio decreased
Access to market	Only a few large companies have most of the share in the capital market

Source Prepared by Author

loans under the stimulus package go to eligible entrepreneurs and such loans do not default, making the situation worse by adding to the existing high NPLs.

Concluding Remarks

Financial sectors are an integral part of the growth process. The financial sector of Bangladesh lags behind in this context as it is completely a bank-based financial system. This system has been facing a number of challenges alongside operational expansion. The performance of the banking sector in terms of quality and soundness parameters is degrading due to increasing ratio of NPLs and NPAs in the absence of regulatory reforms. At the same time, the capital market of Bangladesh shows an increasing trend in terms of size of the market but is mired by market downturns, instability and malpractice.

The financial sector of Bangladesh exhibits considerable vulnerability and needs major regulatory reforms in order to gain stability. The linkage between the banking sector and the stock market is crucial from the perspective of financial stability since the banking sector dominates it in terms of market capitalisation. Any stress on the banking sector has, therefore, adverse effects on the stock market, as is the case at present. Both market capitalisation and major indices have exhibited a decline over the years due to a fall in the banks' share prices, implying that bank turnover had an impact on the index. Similarly, the performance of the stock market has impacted banks as well since banks have investment exposure in the stock market.

The problems of stressed assets, rising NPLs, decline in the stock market were pre-existing even before the covid-19 pandemic. The role of financial sector in fighting the pandemic is a necessity for keeping the economy running. Such a move towards the pathway of revival of the economy direly requires reforms in the financial sector.

References

ADB. 2020. Asian Development Outlook 2020. Asian Development Bank.

Bangladesh Bank. 2018a. Annual Report 2017–18. Bangladesh Bank.

Bangladesh Bank. 2018b. Financial Stability Report. Bangladesh Bank.

Bangladesh Bank. 2019. Annual Report 2018–19. Bangladesh Bank.

Besanko, D., and A. Thakor. 1992. Banking Deregulation: Allocational Consequences of Relaxing Entry Barriers. *Journal of Banking and Finance* 16: 909–932.

Claessens, S., and L. Laeven. 2004. What Drives Bank Competition? Some International Evidence. *Journal of Money, Credit and Banking* 36: 563–584.

Central Bank of Sri Lanka. 2018. Soundness Indicators – Quarterly Financial Information, Central Bank of Sri Lanka.

Dhaka Tribune. 2018. Over 3,000 Bank Branches Established in the Last 10 Years. Accessed from https://www.dhakatribune.com/business/2018/11/18/over-3-000-bank-branches-established-in-the-last-10-years.

Heffernan, Shelagh, and Maggie Fu. 2008. The Determinants of Bank Performance in China. SSRN 1247713.

IMF. 2018. Financial Access Survey. 2017. International Monetary Fund. Washington D.C.

IMF. 2019. World Economic Outlook October 2019. International Monetary Fund. Washignton, DC.

IMF. 2020. World Economic Outlook October 2020. International Monetary Fund. Washignton, DC.

Krishnamurti, C., J.M. Sequeira, and F. Fangjian. 2003. Stock Exchange Governance and Market Quality. *Journal of Banking & Finance* 27 (9): 1859–1878.

Rahman, T., and K. G. Moazzem. 2011. Capital Market of Bangladesh: Volatility in the Dhaka Stock Exchange (DSE) and Role of Regulators. *International Journal of Business and Management* 6 (7).

Reserve Bank of India. 2018. Financial Stability Report. December 2018. Reserve Bank of India.

Sheng, A. 1996. *Bank Restructuring: Lesson from the 1980s*. Washington: The World Bank.

State Bank of Pakistan. 2018. Quarterly Compendium: Statistics of the Banking System. December 2018. State Bank of Pakistan.

The Business Standard. 2020. Budget Leaves Fiscal Space in Quandary. https://tbsnews.net/feature/panorama/budget-leaves-fiscal-space-quandary-99790?fbclid=IwAR3tDeUoWlLvlY3xNiIigW0Ye1QqBlkOQmrVayuG9Y1JIyrKQVB62oM-70. Accessed on June 30, 2020.

The Daily Star. 2019. IMF Report on Loan Defaults Alarming. https://www.thedailystar.net/editorial/news/imf-report-loan-defaults-alarming-1806238. Accessed on June 21, 2020.

The Financial Express. 2020. Bangladesh Bank Waives Penalty on Credit Card Dues Until June. https://thefinancialexpress.com.bd/economy/bangladesh/bangladesh-bank-waives-penalty-on-credit-card-dues-until-june-1585992519. Accessed on 4th October 2020.

Titumir, R.A.M. 2019. *Political Settlement and Economic Outcome* (in Bangla). Dhaka: Samhati Publications.

WEF. 2019. Global Competitive Report. World Economic Forum.

World Bank. 2018. Global Financial Development Database 2017–18. World Bank. Washington D.C.

World Bank. 2019a. Global Financial Development Database 2019. World Bank. Washington D.C.

World Bank. 2019b. World Development Indicator. World Bank. Washington D.C.

CHAPTER 5

Education in Bangladesh

Introduction

This chapter examines the state of education in Bangladesh in terms of generating knowledge, creating a skilled workforce and the formation of citizenship in Bangladesh. While the rate of enrolment and literacy has increased, the quality of education provided in Bangladesh remains a matter of concern. Bangladesh has ranked 112th out of 138 countries in the Global Knowledge Index 2020. It has scored 35.9—the lowest among South Asian countries. The GKI, produced annually since 2017, is a summary measure for tracking the knowledge performance of countries based on 133 variables under seven sectors, namely pre-university education, technical and vocational education and training, higher education, research, development and innovation, information and communications technology, economy and the general enabling environment (UNDP 2020).

In Bangladesh, education has been provided largely by the public sector. Even though the private market for education exists in the country, it is still largely regulated by the state. In both primary and secondary education, the curriculum and the policies are formulated by the government. In recent years, there has been a higher enrolment rate. The quantitative development in education has been marred by the deterioration in the quality of education in the country.

R. A. M. Titumir, *Numbers and Narratives in Bangladesh's Economic Development*,
https://doi.org/10.1007/978-981-16-0658-8_5

While in-school disruption is universal during the pandemic, out-of-school learning deprivation is having a variation depending on socio-economic status of the household, access to technology, and parental capabilities. There is likely to be a gendered response in terms of children's learning needs at home as well. If unaddressed, the sudden nationwide shutdown also risks reversing some of the earlier achievements with improved access to education such as close to universal primary school enrolment and attainment of gender parity in secondary education (BIGD 2020). Despite the ongoing crisis due to the pandemic, the Government has allocated only 15.1% of the total budget for FY 2020–2021 which was 15.2% in the previous fiscal year. Development budget in the education sector has slightly increased to 19.4% from 18.1% in 2019–2020. Education and technology sectors take 2.7% of the GDP which is insufficient. The allotted money gets disbursed among several sectors equivocating the presence of the required budget for skill development and life-long training. UNESCO recommends a 6% budget allocation as share of total GDP in education which is not visible in the current trend (Unnayan Onneshan 2020).

The notion of education in state and citizen building comes from the writings of Adam Smith. Smith argues that education can bring a positive change in the living standards of those who suffered economically from division of labour (Smith 1822; Thomas 2018).

There are two distinct ways to achieve human development; 'income-mediated' and 'support-led'. The former works through rapid and broad-based economic growth, which facilitates better standards of living and better provision for social services, while the later works primarily through effective welfare programs that support health, education, and social security (Sen 1999). One way to measure the quality of life is through the capability approach, where a person's life is thought to be a combination of various "doings and beings", better known as functioning and capabilities. Central to Sen's understanding of capabilities is the idea of agency freedom, i.e. that individuals can act to bring about changes that they value. Capabilities thus imply more than simply skills in a narrow sense. They also imply the freedom and opportunity for an individual to convert whatever resources she may have at their disposal into achievements or outcomes of different kinds (Tikly and Barrett 2011).

UNESCO introduced a model by Jacques Delors (2013) for twenty-first century global education. The model proposes four pillars for education which it calls lifelong learning. This chapter conceptualises a framework based on the ideas of capability and the four pillars of education (Fig. 5.1).

The first element of the framework is access to basic education, which is required for functioning and capabilities as well as 'learning to know' as per the UNESCO framework. The second element, education for skill formation and innovation, also results in functioning and capabilities as well as the second pillar which is 'learning to do'. The third element is citizenship education. Agency and the last two pillars from the UNESCO framework imply the role of education in creating a global citizen with personal fulfilment.

The stability conditions of education can be termed as a functioning stage which consists of three main factors—access, skill formation and innovation and citizenship formation. Access incorporates enrolment, completion, repetition and the adult literacy rate. Skill and innovation are formed and developed through greater enrolment in tertiary and vocational education and sufficient years of schooling. Citizenship education can be burgeoned through a high tax-GDP ratio and social cohesion. Social cohesion implies an individual's responsibility towards the nation, ethics, norms, values, honesty, refraining from evil and harmful acts, such as corruption, tax evasion, bribery, threatening law and order, sedition etc.

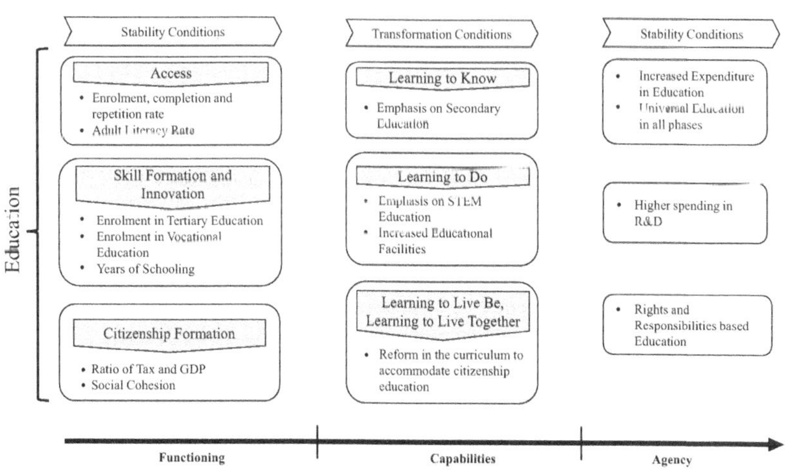

Fig. 5.1 Conceptual framework (*Source* Prepared by Author)

Afterwards, the proper occurrence and functioning of the stability stage conduces transformation where learning to know, learning to do and learning to live as well as learning to live together become prime factors. This stage can be entitled with the capabilities, inspired from Amartya Sen's capability approach. In Sen's framework, learning to know indicates an emphasis on secondary education. Learning to do emphasises on STEM education. STEM education is a curriculum based on the idea of educating students in four specific disciplines—science, technology, engineering and mathematics—in an interdisciplinary and applied approach and increased educational facilities. Reform in the curriculum to accommodate citizenship ascertains learning to "be" and learning to "live together". After the successful establishment and continued practice of capabilities, sustainability comes with the provision of agency. In addition, higher spending in R&D is mandatory to ensure more innovation and skill formation. Citizenship education is moulded to rights and responsibility-based education, which ensures sustainability.

The chapter is outlined with four sections. The stability conditions examine the core state of the education of Bangladesh. The transformability conditions discuss the pathway to transform the gaps with specific emphasis on secondary and STEM education. The penultimate section discusses the measures to be executed in order to establish a sustainable education system for long-term development. The chapter ends with concluding remarks.

Stability Conditions

This section looks at the current state of education in Bangladesh and compares with other countries, including East Asian and OECD countries. In doing so, it looks at three sets of indicators. Firstly, education should be available and accessible to the population of the country. The rationale for universal education is not only confined to the 'human capital' perspective. Education has redistribution characteristics and has the capability to reduce inequality. Higher quality of primary education has resulted in reduced inequality in East Asian countries, which, in turn, has a positive effect on economic growth (Birdsall et al. 1995). The enrolment rate in education at different levels depicts the scenario of availability and accessibility of education. Secondly, skill formation is considered as the precondition for growth in any economy. A skilled workforce increases productivity of the economy through optimising the capital and labour inputs. It is also necessary for the economy to invest in innovation to move forward. Labour and capital have diminishing marginal returns and that is why technology can propel the production process in the economy. Developed countries and the newly developed East Asian economies reached the apotheosis of their economic growth through higher investment in innovation. Thirdly, the importance of education in fostering citizenship values in the economy is one of the prime factors for the public provision of education. If the education sector is left to the private markets, there will be an inevitable tendency of profit maximisation by the providers and as citizenship and intrinsic values are mostly spread through externalities, there will be a reduced focus on such values by the private providers of education.

Increasing Access to Education

The enrolment rate in the primary education in Bangladesh has seen a surge in the last decade, largely because of higher government spending in primary education. Net Enrolment in primary education in the country is in a stable condition. Net enrolment increased by ten percentages points in the last 13 years and stands at 97.85% in the country (BANBEIS 2019). Average net enrolment in high income countries is 96.15 (UNESCO 2020) (Fig. 5.2).

However, Bangladesh does not fare well in terms of its average time spent, calculated by the mean and expected years of schooling. In Bangladesh, this rate is very low, even compared to countries like India, Nepal, and Sri Lanka. The difference between Bangladesh and the OECD countries is vast (Fig. 5.3).

The mean years of schooling in Bangladesh is 5.8 years whereas for OECD countries it is beyond 11 years. East Asian countries also have high mean years of schooling. Even after achieving universal primary education, low mean years of schooling means that students do not continue education for longer (Table 5.1).

Enrolment in primary education is the most basic indicator and does not reflect the quality of education in a country. High enrolment rate and literacy rate will only be useful when there is a higher enrolment in secondary education. While net enrolment in primary education has been close to 100%, in secondary education the enrolment is around only 60%. In 2018, the enrolment reached 72% (UNESCO 2020) (Fig. 5.4).

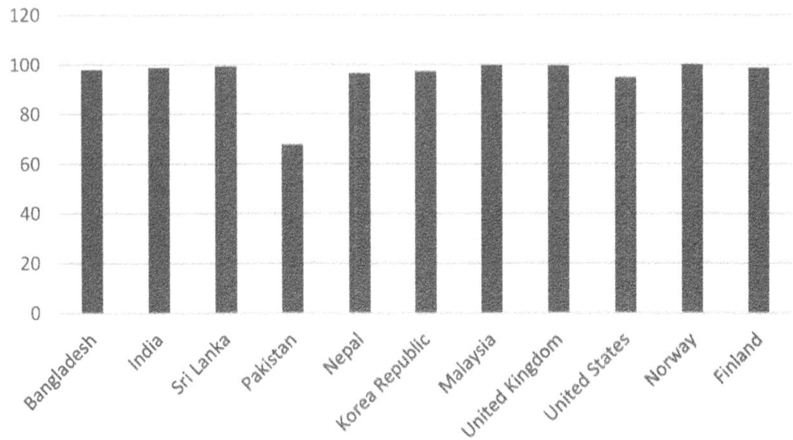

Fig. 5.2 Net enrolment rate in primary education (*Source* UNESCO 2020 and BANBEIS 2019)

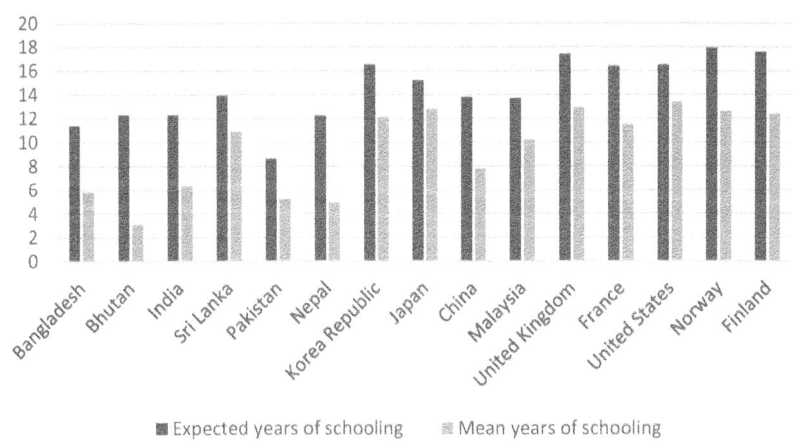

Fig. 5.3 Years of schooling (*Source* UNESCO 2020)

A UNICEF analysis on the allocation of public education resources in 2015 asserted that in low-income countries, 46% of the resources went to the top 10% of the students with the highest level of education. In lower-middle income countries, the percentage was 26%. These figures

Table 5.1 Percentage of repeaters

Country	*Primary education*	*Lower secondary education*
Bangladesh	4.74	2.16
India	0.57	0.38
Pakistan	2.25	1.73
Sri Lanka	0.99	0.80
Singapore	0.16	0.63
Thailand	1.73	3.91
Finland	0.25	0.35
United States	1.61	1.91

Source UNESCO (2020)

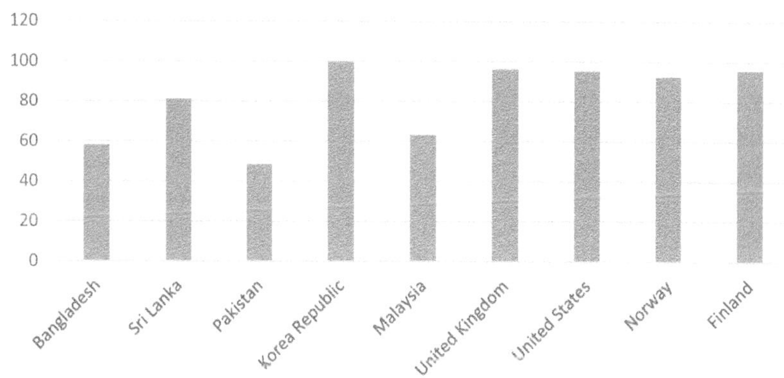

Fig. 5.4 Net enrolment in secondary education in 2016 (*Source* UNESCO 2020)

demonstrate that children from the wealthiest households were disproportionately favoured since they were numerously represented among those with highest levels of education (UNICEF 2020). 65% of the total students of public universities are represented by the richest 20% class. The poorest 20% constitute only 5% in public universities. In private universities, 57% of the students are from the richest 20% class while only 5% are from the poorest 20% class and 3% are from the lower middle-income group. The scenario is worse in case of government colleges, where only 2% students come from the poorest 20% class and 60% come from the richest 20% category. 42% of the students at the university level come from urban/semi urban level whereas 34% come from rural families (World Bank 2019).

Low Skill Formation and Innovation

The current labour force of Bangladesh can be described as mostly low-skilled. International Standard Classification of Occupations (ISCO) of the International Labour Organisation (ILO) defines skill as a function of the complexity and the range of tasks performed in an occupation. It has three classifications of skills based on the education achieved by the workers. According to the ILO estimates, only 8% of the labour force is highly skilled while 74% of the labour force is in the medium skill level (Table 5.2).

Eventually, the level of skills depends on the education of the labour force. Those in the higher echelon of the skills have generally completed tertiary education. If the labour force participation rate of Bangladesh is analysed by the level of education, tertiary education has higher rate of labour force participation meaning that 80% of the tertiary graduates join the workforce. Secondary education has the lowest rate in the labour force participation and even lower than the primary education. Nevertheless, the high participation rate is in primary education. This suggests that a good number of students have dropped out from formal education and entered into jobs that require low level of skills. The participation rates of

Table 5.2 Skills level of the labour force

	Skill level 3 (high skilled)	*Skill level 2 (medium skilled)*	*Skill level 1 (low skilled)*
Bangladesh	8	74	17
India	16	59	25
Pakistan	11	72	16
Japan	25	66	7
Korea Republic	22	65	13
Finland	47	46	6
United Kingdom	49	42	9
United States	47	43	10

Source ILO (2020)

Table 5.3 Labour force participation rate in different levels of education

Level of education	*Male*	*Female*	*Total*
No schooling	84.2	38.1	59.0
Primary	91.5	39.7	66.2
Secondary	71.3	32	51.5
Tertiary	89.4	56.9	79.4
Total	80.5	36.3	58.2

Source BBS (2018)

the tertiary graduates show that higher levels of education result in higher chances of employment (Table 5.3).

The correlation between education and skill level is depicted in the scatterplot (Fig. 5.5). The scatterplot has been computed using schooling data taken from UNESCO and the skill level data has been gathered from the ILO.

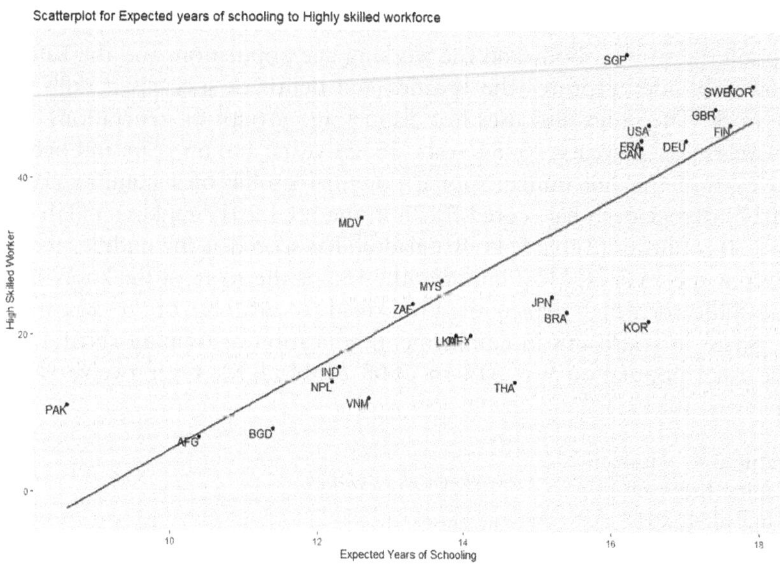

Fig. 5.5 Scatterplot for expected years of schooling and high skilled workforce (*Source* Author)

The OECD countries are in the top of the plot, having higher amount of skilled labour force with higher years of schooling. The trend line in the plot shows a high positive correlation between expected years of schooling and skilled workforce. Bangladesh in this plot stands quite a long way below countries like India, Vietnam and Nepal.

Universities too in Bangladesh have failed to achieve their desired outcome. According to the latest labour force survey, 46% of unemployed youths are tertiary education graduates (BBS 2018). Unemployment amongst university graduates is 11.2% which is more than those of secondary or post-secondary levels (6.4%) (World Bank 2019). 39% of the university graduates remain unemployed for 1–2 year after graduation, which is more than the students of polytechnics (32%) (World Bank 2019).

Human Capital Index (HCI) by World Economic Forum (WEF) is a complex measure of four sub-indices. The Capacity sub-index quantifies the existing stock of education across generations; the Deployment sub-index covers skill application and accumulation of skills through work; the Development sub-index reflects current efforts to educate, skill and upskill the student body and the working age population; and the Know-how sub-index captures the breadth and depth of specialised skills use at work. The index also uses five distinct age groups or generations—0–14 years; 15–24 years; 25–54 years; 55–64 years; and 65 years and over—to capture the full human capital potential profile of a country (WEF 2017). Bangladesh has scored 51.75 in the HCI 2017 ranking 111th out of 130 countries (Table 5.4). Bangladesh has scored at the middle level in all four sub-indices. Most importantly, 45.2 is the score of the know-how sub-indicator which depicts the low skilled labour force of the country.

Share of youth not in employment, education or training (NEET) of the total population was 31% in 2005 (Table 5.5). Over twelve years,

Table 5.4 Human Capital Index of Bangladesh 2017

Percentage of population	*Score*	*Rank*
Capacity	51.4	104
Deployment	57.2	105
Development	53.2	100
Know-how	45.2	104
Overall	51.75	111

Source World Economic Forum (2017)

Table 5.5 Share of youth not in employment, education or training (NEET) as percentage

Percentage of population	*Year*					
	2005	*2006*	*2010*	*2013*	*2016*	*2017*
Male	6.7	7.3	14.5	8.8	10	9.8
Female	56.9	58.9	44.9	30.7	47	44.6
Total	31	32.3	30.1	20.2	28.9	27.4

Source ILO (2020)

the share has decreased by only 3.6% hitting 27.4% in 2017. Despite an increase in the number of graduates and enrolment in the education, more than a quarter of the total population of the youth are in the NEET population. The share of females in NEET population was more than half of the female youth population in 2005 standing at 56.9%. The share however is declining as more young women are entering the labour force. In 2017, the share of female youth in NEET population stood at 44.6% indicating 12.3% decrease in twelve years. This brings hope as well as concern since a significant number of the youths continue to remain in the NEET population.

The Global Innovation Index (GII) ranks countries based on particular variables. Bangladesh stands 116th out of 129 countries, according to the GII 2019 report. According to the report, the lower rank is mainly attributed to weaknesses in human capital and research. The dearth of quality of education and research puts the country in the poorer position. Bangladesh also exhibited weakness in the indicator for institutions, implying the political and regulatory environment impede the innovation process in the country.

Waning Citizenship Education

Citizenship is a status that is bestowed on the members of a community who possess equal rights and responsibilities (Marshall 1950). Each community or society has their own form of citizenship based on the institutions of that community and the citizens forgo certain rights for state formation.

Citizenship education has been defined by UNESCO as educating children, from early childhood to become clear-thinking and enlightened citizens participating in decisions concerning society. 'Society' here is understood in the special sense of a nation with a circumscribed territory, which is recognised as a state. Government expenditure on education has been reasoned because of the externalities or spill overs of education. Another important rationale for spending on education is the intrinsic value of education in the form of citizenship formation in a state.

Citizenship education is a contested topic. While to some, citizenship education is about instilling patriotism, love for country and internalisation of the institutions of the nation state and to others, it is about recognising the basic rights of all persons, irrespective of their membership in particular states. It is an education for cosmopolitanism, for egalitarian cosmopolitanism (Appiah 1998).

The rationale for citizenship education stems from the idea of creating a just society where men and women are both an individual and a citizen. The distinction of citizenship from individualism is that citizenship attributes to the rights and duties towards the state bonding by the very social contract that formed the state. The rights include civic and political rights and thus there is great importance of education in terms of elucidating the citizens about these rights which in turn are broadly part of human rights. Educating the citizens about the human rights thus creates citizenship among the population. When the government fails to provide citizens fundamental rights— equality, human dignity and social justice, they may pressurise the government. The people's struggle is the yardstick to make the state accountable to its citizens. Peoples' aspiration for a citizen state is the key to balance between the monopoly power of the state and the struggle of the masses. For the purpose of building a citizen state, education is considered as a fundamental right for every citizen. Education may build a skilled workforce which boosts the economy, but the primary concern of education is to provide the citizens an opportunity to lead a dignified life.

Access to primary and secondary education creates a working middle class who resist being controlled by the political elite and this, in turn, leads to economic growth (McMahon 2002). Sen (1999) argues that primary education allowed the formation of human capabilities. He also argues that the social transformation of China and East Asian countries was caused more by education and literacy rates than trade liberalisation.

Bangladesh scored negatively in the Human Rights Watch index of 2018 (Fig. 5.6a), along with its South Asian counterparts India and Pakistan. Only Pakistan had a lower score than Bangladesh in this index.

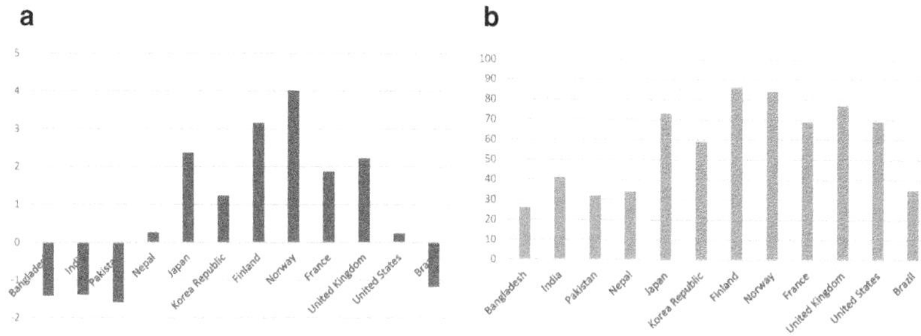

Fig. 5.6 **a** Human Rights Watch Score (*Source* HRW Report 2018). **b** Corruption Perceptions Index 2019

Whilst developed countries scored positively in the index in comparison, Japan and welfare states such as Finland and Norway fared significantly better. Bangladesh is also positioned in the lowest rungs in the Corruption Perceptions Index of 2019, with Pakistan, Nepal and India in not significantly better rankings either. East Asian countries such as Japan score better in comparison in the Corruption Perceptions Index 2019 too, aligning with Sen's (1999) argument of formation of human capabilities in contributing to social transformation in these countries.

The significance of citizenship education had been evidenced by the lack of accord for following state directives for maintaining self-isolation and physical distancing in adapting to the new normal imposed by the pandemic.

Disruptions Caused by the COVID-19 Pandemic

The pandemic has stalled the activities in the education sector in Bangladesh. Owing to the closure of the educational institutions and uncertainty of reopening dates, students have been alienated from their academic curricula for the year. There are around 38.6 million students in Bangladesh. Among them, 3.6 million students are in pre-primary, 18 million in primary, 13 million in secondary, and 4 million in tertiary education (BANBEIS 2019). The government-initiated distance learning through Sangsad TV to continue teaching and learning for all students during the lockdown. It was initially targeted at students of class 6–10 and gradually for the students of primary schools and madrasas. Some schools in urban areas, especially the English medium schools, initiated alternative mechanisms including online classes using video conferencing applications (BRAC 2020).

The impacts of distance learning through television and video conferencing on different populations are however disproportionate. There are children with no access to mobile phones or televisions, let alone internet connectivity. Televisions are available in 50.6% of households, with 4.1% without a single mobile phone (UNICEF 2020). In most cases, owning a mobile phone is not useful for distance learning, as only 37.6% of the households have access to the internet, which is even lower in rural areas. The lack of access erects a digital divide between populations, working as an obstacle to distance learning. Owing to the economic slowdown, households have faced income erosion and loss of employment rendering families unable to afford tuition fees. As a result, private educational institutions encountered financial hardships as they ran out of funds to keep their operation running. A few schools have also announced dissolution due to insolvency, putting students and teachers in grave uncertainties and peril (*The Independent* 2020).

Around 30 million students in all categories of institutions and close to a million teachers and education personnel in Bangladesh have suffered the ills of the shutdown induced by the covid-19 pandemic (Barua 2020). The impacts of prolonged closures of schools and institutions are not limited to hindering academic progress; students also experienced a deterioration in their mental well-being. Students in remote rural areas face disproportionately greater hindrances in attending virtual classes and finishing coursework due to a lack of high-speed internet connectivity and other facilities. Considering the stalemate, public universities may encounter session jams due to examinations not being held in due time (Barua 2020).

The current pandemic has unveiled the necessity of public health education. Fighting against this public bad would be easier if there was proper awareness regarding health and hygiene. Apart from taking dilatory actions, the Government is struggling to raise mass awareness amongst people regarding the fatality of the disease and precautions against it. Most of the people have not taken the pandemic seriously at the preliminary level because of a lack of public health outreach and consciousness. It has become visible that, people seldom know about infectious diseases, how they spread and how they should be tackled. There should be special provisions for public health education in the budget (Unnayan Onneshan 2020).

Transformability Conditions

The transformability conditions focus on three major areas—(i) learning to know, (ii) learning to do and (iii) learning to live together. Learning to know, here, focuses on the need for secondary education in the life of an individual whereas, learning to do focuses on two basic indicators—STEM and the necessity of educational facilities education. STEM is an approach to learning and development that integrates the areas of science, technology, engineering and mathematics. The third condition, learning to live together calls for reforms in the curriculum to accommodate citizenship education in order to transform the education system into a more convenient one to live together in the long-term.

Augmenting Secondary Education

In the beginning, most developed countries spent more on primary and secondary education. This investment resulted in higher percentage of the population having more than secondary education and thus having a relatively higher skilled workforce. Bangladesh lags greatly in terms of adults having secondary education or higher education. Enrolment in primary education in Bangladesh grew faster than secondary education because of the policies by the government. In 2012, the percentage of adults with primary education was 49% and just in five years, the number currently stands at 56% (UNESCO 2020). This shows a significant gap in policies taken by the state in secondary education (Fig. 5.7).

Most developed countries also show a high percentage of population with upper secondary education whereas Bangladesh ranks much lower with only 30% of the population completing upper secondary education.

The state's policy should be focused on first increasing primary and secondary education and gradually move towards tertiary education. This trend is similar for the East Asian countries on their path towards development. The reduction in inequality is strongly associated with secondary education and two-year college access (McMahon 2002). Developing countries or the least developed countries, on the other hand, depict a different picture where there is more emphasis on higher and tertiary education.

Human capital effects on growth are most evident at the primary level in the least developed countries. For the higher income developing countries, it is secondary education and for the developed countries, the key

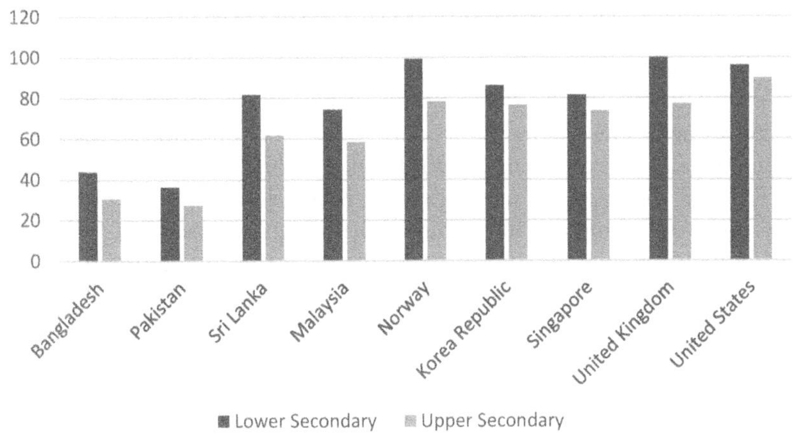

Fig. 5.7 Percentage of population completed secondary education (*Source* UNESCO 2020)

level is the tertiary education for economic growth (Gemmell 1996). Many least developed and developing countries show opposite results in term of funding different levels of education.

Developed countries show almost flat or similar investment in all levels of education whereas in Bangladesh, there is a significant gap in investment between secondary education and tertiary education (Fig. 5.8). Bangladesh, being a least developed country soon to be migrating to middle income status, spends more on per student in tertiary level than the secondary level. South Korea, on the other hand, has emphasised on primary and secondary education level. However, East Asian countries were successful because they appropriately addressed the shortcomings and failures of the market. Their emphasis on high level of primary and secondary education had important payoffs for the economic efficiency and equity. Excess demand that primary education created for secondary and tertiary education was responded by expanding the secondary education through public spending and self-financed system for tertiary education (Green et al 1999).

Similarly, Finland and other Scandinavian countries also successfully corrected the market failures in education by expanding the lower levels of education, mainly primary and lower secondary.

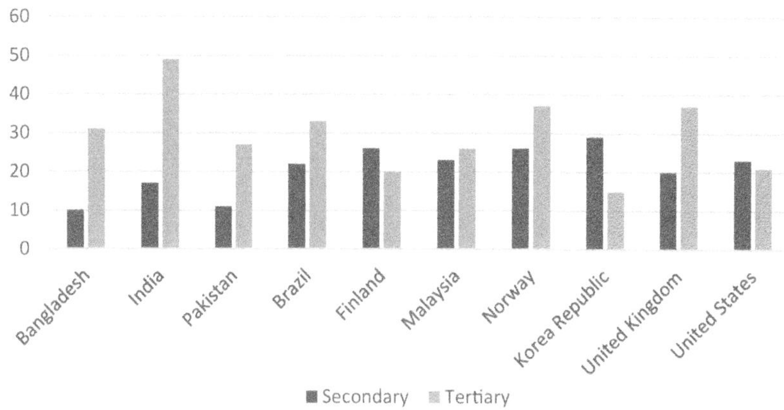

Fig. 5.8 Initial government funding of education per student as a percentage of GDP per capita (*Source* UNESCO 2020)

Vocational and Technical Education for Skilled Workforce

For augmenting the flow of the skilled workforce more emphasis on vocational and technical education is the need of the hour. For example, South Korea has boosted their labour force by specifically focusing on technical and vocational education. Scandinavian countries also have higher number of populations enrolled in vocational education. Almost one-fifth of the students in Scandinavian countries are enrolled in vocational education. In Bangladesh, it is a meagre 1.33%.

In terms of vocational education, Bangladesh stands at a position lower than most of the selected countries (Fig. 5.9). Despite having a large labour force, only 1.33% is enrolled in vocational education. Vocational and technical education can enhance the skills of the workforce. An insignificant government expenditure in vocational education suppresses the growth of this sector. Around 40% of vocational institutes suffered due to a lack of funding (CPD 2018). Such restraints impede the enrolment in this form of education.

Emphasis on Tertiary Education

Low enrolment in tertiary education is inherent in Bangladesh because of lower enrolment in the preceding levels of education. Unless there

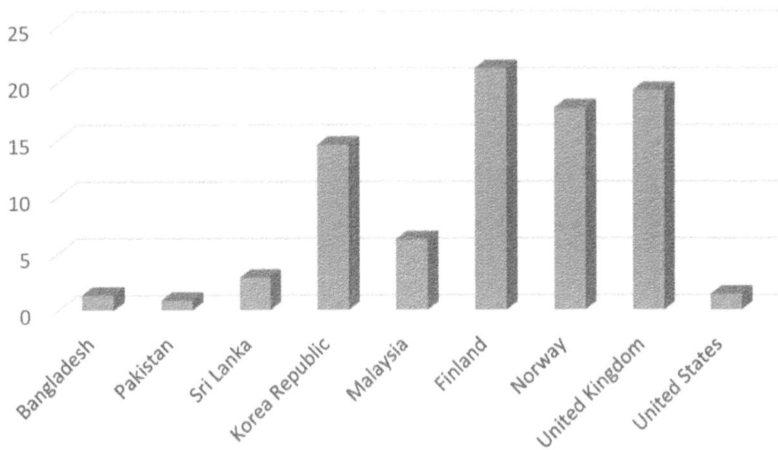

Fig. 5.9 Proportion of 14–24 years-olds enrolled in vocational education (*Source* UNESCO 2020)

is higher enrolment and completion rate in the secondary and upper secondary education, there will always remain a gap in achieving better enrolment in tertiary education. The average school life expectancy in Bangladesh is close to 12 years. The fact is that the theoretical duration of primary and secondary education is 5 and 7 years respectively which adds up to 12, meaning that, on an average, a student in Bangladesh is only expected to complete secondary education since tertiary education starts at the 13th year. The gross entry ratio to first tertiary programmes is much lower in Bangladesh compared to other developed or developing nations.

The number of tertiary graduates has been rising in Bangladesh steadily. The number of tertiary graduates in China and India has seen a growth in recent years (Fig. 5.10).

An important factor in measuring innovation is the human resources of a country and particularly, in subjects related to science. Graduates from Science, Engineering, Technology and Mathematics, are also known as STEM. These subjects act as a global measure for innovation and used in calculating the GII.

In developed countries, around a quarter of the students graduate from STEM subjects (Fig. 5.11). East Asian countries have shown great

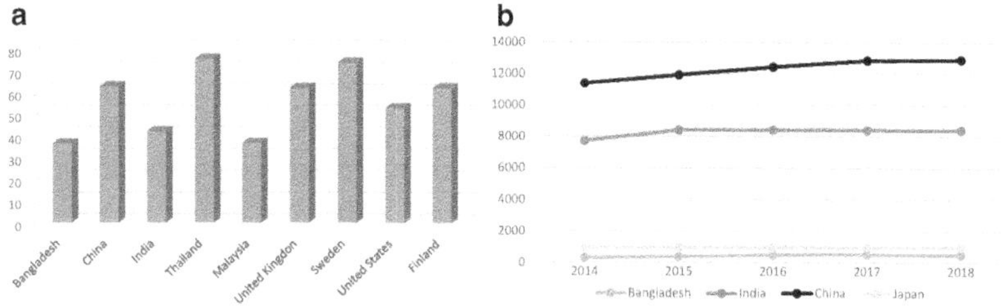

Fig. 5.10 a Gross entry ratio to first tertiary programs. b Number of tertiary graduate (*Source* UNESCO 2020)

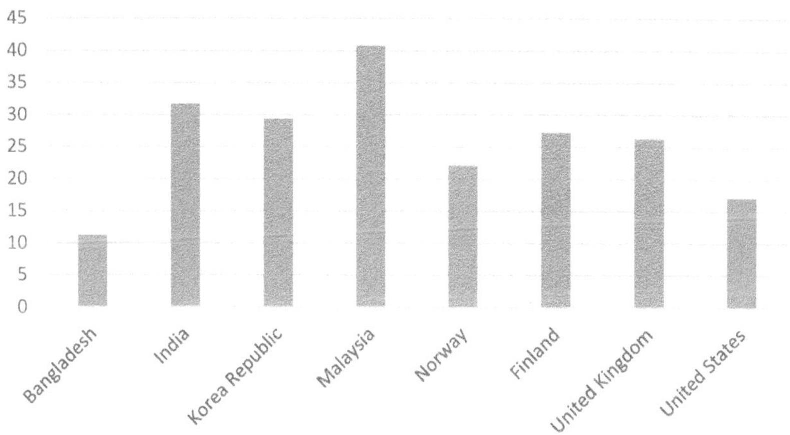

Fig. 5.11 Percentage of graduates from Science, Engineering, Technology, and Mathematics in tertiary education (*Source* UNESCO 2020)

progress in terms of economic growth and technology, and have higher percentage of graduates from the STEM subjects, thereby increasing their ability to foster innovation. Of these countries, Republic of Korea and Malaysia rank 11 and 35 respectively in the Global Innovation Index. India also has much higher percentage of graduates from STEM, and ranks 52nd on the index.

Quality Provisioning

Quality infrastructure enables better quality of education. Pupil-teacher ratio is a measure that strongly depicts the classroom scenario in a country. Higher pupil-teacher ratio means there are fewer opportunities for students for interactions in a classroom. A large number of students in a class at any level of education dampens the quality of education.

Bangladesh has a pupil-teacher ratio of 30 to 1 in tertiary education, much higher than the OECD and East Asian countries (Fig. 5.12). For Bangladesh, the ratio is highest in secondary education and has deteriorated in recent times. There is one teacher for every 45 students in 2019 from a teacher per 34 students in 2008 (UNESCO 2020). The average teacher-student ratio in public universities is 1:40 which is 1:27 in private universities. The situation is even more severe in colleges and polytechnic institutes. In colleges, the teacher-student ratio is 1:77 while polytechnics have a ratio of 1:61 (World Bank 2019).

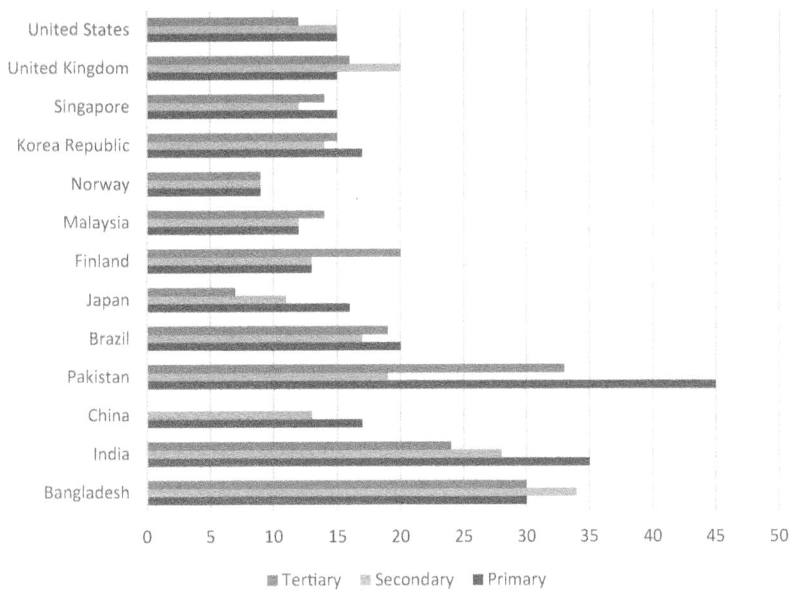

Fig. 5.12 Pupil teacher ratio (*Source* UNESCO 2020)

There is gradual deterioration in the quality of education. National Student Assessment (NSA) 2015 demonstrates that mean scores for Bangla and Mathematics across Grade 3 and Grade 5 declined in 2015 from those of 2013. In 2015, the mean scores achieved by Grade 3 and Grade 5 in Mathematics were 41% and 10% respectively while in 2013, Grade 3 students had scored 58% and Grade 5 scored 25% in the two subjects (MoPME 2017). In primary school grade 2 and 3, only 34% students achieve proficiency in mathematics. However, 84% of Sri Lankan students achieve proficiency, more than double of Bangladesh. East Asian countries all have percentage well over 80%, a stark contrast between Bangladesh and these countries (ESCAP 2020). A number of factors including high student-teacher ratio (STR) and a lack of qualified teachers can explain this.

On the other hand, Scandinavian countries and the East Asian countries have developed a successful education sector. For instance, Finland became a success story by imparting the highest quality of education through providing better teaching facilities (Sahlberg 2007).

Access to Educational Infrastructure

Much of the academic performance and successes in rural and urban communities can be attributed to the availability of physical infrastructure of educational institutions. Infrastructure directly affects quality of education, which is worsening in areas facing inadequate physical infrastructure and depreciation, affecting the quality of teaching offered at these institutions. Thousands of primary schools were flooded and multi-storied buildings of schools were submerged under water due to widespread flooding and waterlogging. There are physical infrastructural lapses and problems specific to the urban and rural contexts the schools are in as well as a result of lack of support from the Ministry of Primary and Mass education.

Dependence on private markets can undermine educational equity and universal access. Private financing relies on a strong demand and ability to pay. Even minimal school fees can harm equity in countries where schooling has high opportunity costs from children's wage labour and domestic work. This effect can fall disproportionately on the poor children from rural areas, and girls. In most cases, private educational institutions are likely to offer better physical infrastructure with top-tier facilities which is reflected in the tuition fees. When public school capacity can accommodate all students, private schools will have to become more competitive by offering either higher quality education or charging lower fees. When public school capacity is low, private schools fill the gap but with no competitive incentive to improve quality. Most of the students of private universities spend more money on tuition fees, housing and better living conditions whereas the students of public universities live in government allocated residence for free and pay significantly lower tuition fees (Barman et al. 2012).

During the pandemic period, different modes and strategies of learning by different countries have resulted in an almost balanced continuation of the learning process but has not been fruitful for all levels of students. The most popular e-learning methods have been adopted by almost every nation and at times considered to be successful. Though the e-learning boom is here to stay, the process also exacerbates the growing divides between the rich and poor receiving education through online platforms. The economic recession heavily impacted students all over the world as well. According to the UNICEF, almost 430 million children in South Asia are affected by school closures and are at risk of dropping out of the education system due to the economic impact on their families. Individuals with psychosocial challenges, mental health issues, hindrance in personal growth and development, unequal access to education materials, economic impact on family incomes are acting as barriers that need to be overcome with the help of short- and long-term approaches in Bangladesh (Barua 2020).

Sustainability Conditions

Sustainability conditions require increased expenditure in education and expanded R&D, with education rooted in rights and responsibilities. The share of GDP spent on education is very low in Bangladesh compared to the neighbouring and the developed nations. For the last ten years the government spending in education has barely exceeded 2% of the GDP (Fig. 5.13).

Lower public spending on education results in inferior quality and limited access to free education as this does not leave any scope to enhance the quality of education by setting up necessary the physical infrastructure (e.g., laboratories, libraries etc.), providing training to teachers, by improving the curriculum or by enlarging the size of classroom and thus it cannot provide access to all citizens (especially the disadvantaged groups)

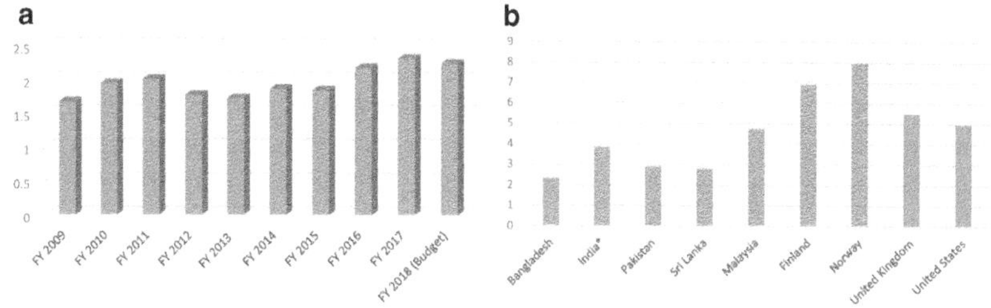

Fig. 5.13 **a** Bangladesh government spending on education as a percentage of GDP. **b** Government spending on education as a percentage of GDP of different countries (*Source* CPD UNESCO (2020). *Spending data for India is for the FY 2013 and for others it is 2017)

to free public education. Unequal access to education and low quality creates a state of inequality and social division of labour as people lag behind in terms of developing their human capital. Low human capital leads to unemployment and underemployment and thus people cannot afford a decent salary and standard of living.

A primary factor why public spending on education, health and social protection are so low in Bangladesh is the low levels of revenues due to low tax effort. The European countries have revenue to GDP ratios in the range of 35–45%. In Bangladesh it is a mere 12% of GDP which is one of the lowest revenue mobilisation efforts even among developing countries. A major reason for low government revenue is low tax collection from personal income taxes. Bangladesh collects a mere 1% of GDP from personal income taxes, while the top 10% of the population owns 36% of the total national income. This yields an effective income tax rate of 3%, which is very low. While efforts are underway to improve income tax collection, the effort is concentrated on fixed income earners. Personal income from business, capital gains, stocks and the like tend to escape substantially their fair share of taxation. Similarly, there is minimal tax effort at the local government level. Remarkably, there is no effective property tax collection system. Capital gains from land transactions and stock ownership mostly escapes taxation with a nominal levy. At the present time, the absence of a modern universal personal income tax is a major contributor to the ineffectiveness of fiscal policy to lower income redistribution (Ahmed 2012).

This low tax-GDP ratio contributes to low spending on the public sector including education and health. In many cases, it has been observed that the state-run educational institutes have scored better in providing quality education but their number is so low that many students do not get the opportunity to enrol in those. The private sector steps into fulfil this unmet demand. Hence, low budget allocation on the education sector is to be blamed according to many studies. As the national budget is expanding every year, the budgetary allocation to the education sector also rises. However, in reality the sector's share in the national budget has declined over the years. In contrast, the OECD countries have invested more than 5% of the GDP. Countries like Pakistan and Sri Lanka have also increased their spending in the education sector (Table 5.6).

The more the teachers' status is ensured, the better the children perform resulting in accelerated economic growth. China, Singapore, South Korea and some other countries are glaring examples of this. The situation in Bangladesh is unfortunately quite the opposite. The outcomes are appalling: the low quality of education is producing a low and semi-skilled workforce, causing enormous detrimental impact on the economy (Liton 2020).

Citizenship education can only be provided through government provisions of the education system. East Asian countries acquired higher

Table 5.6 Government expenditure on education on most recent years

Countries	*Most recent year*	*Value (% of GDP)*
Sweden	2018	6.9
Bhutan	2018	6.6
Finland	2018	5.5
Norway	2018	5.4
Nepal	2018	5.2
United States	2014	5
United Kingdom	2018	4.8
South Korea	2016	4.6
China	2018	4.1
Japan	2016	3.5
India	2018-19	3
Bangladesh	2019-20	2.46
Sri Lanka	2018	2.1
OECD Members	2016	5

Source UNESCO (2020)

Table 5.7 Summary table of the major indicators of education

Indicators	*State of Bangladesh*
Access to education	Access to primary education is at par with international standards. Enrolment in secondary education is still quite low. The dropout rates are high. Access to education in tertiary level is mostly occupied by high income groups
Quality of education	Quality of education is low. All assessments indicate a gradual decline
Skill formation and innovation	More than half the labour force are unskilled. Only 8 percent of labour are highly skilled. Bangladesh ranks 116th among 129 countries in Skills. In the Human Capital Index of 2017 Bangladesh ranked 111th
Employment	Unemployment has increased. Youth unemployment is high. The share of youth not in education, employment or training (NEET) has increased. Graduate unemployment is on the rise
Infrastructure	Pupil-teacher ratio is higher than the East Asian and OECD countries. Still, there are not enough teachers at the primary schools in the rural areas
Government spending	Government spending in education as share of GDP is low and has remained stagnant and less than those of neighbours, East Asian and OECD countries
Technical education	Only 1.33% of the labour force are enrolled in technical and vocational education which denotes a lack of emphasis in creating a skilled workforce

social returns from education because of the unified education system allowing them to formulate new policies and curriculums. Bangladesh has a centralised education system with a national curriculum which has to be followed by all the educational institutions from primary to secondary levels. Such a scenario, however, is absent in reality. As progress continues, it would make sense to try to get focused on the goal of educating for tolerance, human rights and global civility (Reimers 2006).

Concluding Remarks

Education is a right, a vehicle for productive employment, and a mean of unleashing human potentials for a public society. These aspirations are exhibited by the citizens of Bangladesh in their glorious traditions of struggles for establishing such rights for the society in general, and in the sphere of the education system, in particular.

Bangladesh has made remarkable strides in primary education enrolment, but the dropout rates at the later stages are high. The system lags behind in developing a skilled labour force. Citizenship education, on the other hand, has not been institutionalised, which results in unwarranted norms, customs and values, impeding the processes of development.

The transformability conditions have focused on three distinct features of learning through a subset of indicators. The net enrolment in secondary education is exhibiting an increasing trend, but the high dropout rate implies lack of motivation and the right environment for learning to know as well as economic compulsions to join the labour force due to poverty. The enrolment into vocational education is still truncated. Most importantly, assessments imply deterioration in quality, including a sheer absence in mobility in the fields of STEM. The covid-19 pandemic has called for augmentation of technological infrastructure in the education system.

In order to establish a sustainable education system in the country, policy reforms are essential. To maximise the social returns from education, higher emphasis and increased budget allocation are required. The primary target of education is to create a skilled workforce which can be increased through higher spending in secondary and vocational education where the rate of return is the highest. Nevertheless, technology and innovation transform the economies to a sustainable growth path.

Currently, the country is in the midst of a demographic transition. For reaping the benefits of the transition, there must be higher and systematic investment along with necessary reforms in the education sector, enabling the country to move towards a transformative and sustainable development pathway.

References

Ahmed, S. 2012. *Addressing the Challenge of Income Inequality in Bangladesh*. Dhaka: Policy Research Institute of Bangladesh.

Appiah, K.A. 1998. Cosmopolitan patriots. *Cultural Politics* 14: 91–116.

BANBEIS. 2019. Bangladesh Education Statistics 2019. Bangladesh Bureau of Educational Information and Statistics (BANBEIS).

Barman, D.B., I. Sharmin, and D. Dey. 2012. A Comparative Study of the Cost of the Higher Education in Private and Public Universities in Bangladesh. *East West Journal of Business and Social Studies* 3: 47–67.

BBS. 2018. *Labour Force Survey 2016–17*. Bangladesh Bureau of Statitstics.

Barua, A. 2020. The Impact of COVID-19 Pandemic: Education Sector of Bangladesh. https://bipss.org.bd/the-impact-of-covid-19-pandemic-education-sector-of-bangladesh/. Accessed on 1 October 2020.

BIGD. 2020. Coronavirus Outbreak, Schooling and Learning: Study on Secondary School Students in Bangladesh. *BRAC Institute of Governance and Development*. https://www.poverty-action.org/recovr-study/coronavirus-outbreak-schooling-and-learning-study-secondary-school-students-bangladesh. Accessed on 1 October 2020.

Birdsall, N., D. Ross, and R. Sabot. 1995. Inequality and Growth Reconsidered: Lessons from East Asia. *The World Bank Economic Review* 9 (3): 477–508.

BRAC. 2020. A Rapid Assessment Impact of COVID-19 on Education in Bangladesh. *Advocacy for Social Change (ASC), BRAC.*

CPD. 2018. Bangladesh Economy in FY2017–18: Interim Review of Macroeconomic Performance.

Delors, J. 2013. The Treasure Within: Learning to Know, Learning to Do, Learning to Live Together and Learning to Be. What Is the Value of That Treasure 15 Years After Its Publication? *International Review of Education* 59 (3): 319–330.

ESCAP. 2020. *Asia and the Pacific SDG Progress Report 2020*. Bangkok, Thailand: Economic and Social Commission for Asia Pacific.

Gemmell, N. 1996. Evaluating the Impacts of Human Capital Stocks and Accumulation on Economic Growth: Some New Evidence. *Oxford Bulletin of Economics and Statistics* 58 (1): 9–28.

GII. 2019. *Global Innovation Report 2019*. Global Innovation Index.

Green, A., T. Leney, and A. Wolf. 1999. *Convergence and Divergence in European Education and Training Systems*. Institute of Education.

ILO. 2020. *ILOStat*. International Labour Organisation.

Liton, S. 2020. Want More Economic Growth? Ensure Teachers' Status. *The Business Standard*. https://tbsnews.net/analysis/want-more-economic-growth-ensure-teachers-status-141271?fbclid=IwAR1V2fwiCrzZqx7VgodiixV9-JPoIIfKUUe0-XbnDZ-OaI9SQHea25DgtvfY. Accessed on 8 October 2020.

Marshall, T.H. 1950. *Citizenship and Social Class*, vol. 11, pp. 28–29. Cambridge.

McMahon, W.W. 2002. *Education and Development: Measuring the Social Benefits*. Oxford: Oxford University Press.

MoPME. 2017. *Annual Primary School Report 2015*. Ministry of Primary and Mass Education. Bangladesh.

Reimers, F. 2006. Citizenship, Identity and Education: Examining the Public Purposes of Schools in an Age of Globalization. *Prospects* 36 (3): 275–294.

Sahlberg, P. 2007. Education Policies for Raising Student Learning: The Finnish Approach. *Journal of Education Policy* 22 (2): 147–171.

Sen, A. 1999. *Development as Freedom*. Oxford: Oxford University Press.

Smith, A. 1822. *The Theory of Moral Sentiments*, vol. 5.
The Independent. 2020. Impact of Covid-19 on Education. http://www.theindependentbd.com/post/250457. Accessed on 1 October 2020.
Thomas, A.M. 2018. Adam Smith on the Philosophy and Provision of Education. *Journal of Interdisciplinary Economics* 30 (1): 105–116.
Tikly, L., and A.M. Barrett. 2011. Social Justice, Capabilities and the Quality of Education in Low Income Countries. *International Journal of Educational Development* 31 (1): 3–14.
UNDP. 2020. Global Knowledge Index 2020. https://www.undp.org/content/undp/en/home/librarypage/capacity-building/Global-Knowledge-Index-2020.html. Accessed on 11 December 2020.
Unnayan Onneshan. 2020. *Whither Bending the Curves for Life and Livelihoods: A Rapid Assesment of National Budget 2020–21.*
UNESCO. 2020. UNESCO Statistics. Accessed from data.uis.unesco.org. Accessed on 20 January 2020.
UNICEF. 2020. UNICEF Dataset. Accessed from https://data.unicef.org/resources/resource-type/datasets/.
WEF. 2017. *Global Human Capital Report 2017*. Geneva, Switzerland: World Economic Forum.
World Bank. 2019. *Bangladesh Tertiary Education Sector Review: Skills and Innovation for Growth*. World Bank: Washington, DC.

CHAPTER 6

Health in Bangladesh

Introduction

This chapter analyses the access to and provision of universal and equitable healthcare from the standpoint that health is a human right, as per the Universal Declaration of Human Rights (1948). This received a renewed momentum with the adoption of the third goal of SDGs, which aims to ensure healthy lives and promote wellbeing for all at all ages. It also speaks of universal health coverage (UHC), including financial risk protection, access to quality essential healthcare services and access to safe, effective, quality and affordable essential medicines and vaccines for all.

Bangladesh is experiencing low service coverage and absence of quality care amidst a highly unregulated health system. This has resulted in growing health inequality, despite the fact that key health indicators such as life expectancy and coverage of immunisation have improved notably, whilst infant mortality, maternal mortality and fertility rates have dropped significantly over the last decades.

The country has a pluralistic healthcare system, which is highly unregulated and consists mainly of four key actors: government, for-profit private sector, not-for-profit private sector (mainly nongovernmental organisations), and the international development organisations (Ahmed et al. 2015). While the government hospitals often come under scrutiny, the situation in private clinics and diagnostic centres outside the capital is

R. A. M. Titumir, *Numbers and Narratives in Bangladesh's Economic Development*,
https://doi.org/10.1007/978-981-16-0658-8_6

found to be even worse due to the absence of proper equipment, qualified physicians, nurses, emergency services, ambulances and authorised blood banks required for full-fledged operations. The quality of services provided in these health facilities is dire. This has been due to a lack of capacity to regulate the providers of the private healthcare while there has been a mushrooming growth of the clinics, hospitals, blood banks, and diagnostic centres in the private sector. More than 40% of private facilities are not registered with the regulatory agency.

The private sector comprises both formal and informal healthcare services. Informal healthcare in the private sector is largely dominated by untrained medical providers. The informal healthcare is mostly based in the rural areas whereas the formal services provide healthcare largely in the urban areas. A majority of the country's populations still seek their first line of care from informal healthcare providers that is traditional healers, faith healers and community health workers.

Health financing is underfunded. Only 2.48% of GDP is spent on health, which is the lowest in South Asia. Health financial coverage is so sparse that nine percent of households face catastrophic healthcare payments, 5.6% face impoverishment, and seven percent face distress financing, which is met through either borrowing or selling household assets (Islam et al. 2017).

The health system is fraught with inequality as the system frequently proves to be ineffective in reaching the poor, generating less benefit to the poor than the rich, and imposing repressive cost burdens on poor households. Affluent people have little faith in local healthcare services, going abroad for treatment being a regular phenomenon, and drain a substantial amount of foreign currency.

Out-of-pocket (OOP) contributions to health expenditure, one of the most inequitable sources of healthcare financing, in Bangladesh, are among the highest in the world with 74%. Health expenditure in private health facilities is almost exclusively from OOP payments.

The review of Bangladesh's Demographic and Health Survey 2014 reveals inequity in most of the health indicators in terms of economic status, level of education, gender, location and geography (NIPORT 2015). For example, infant mortality rate is 35 per 1000 live births among the people of lowest income quintile, compared to only 14 among the highest income group. Antenatal care (ANC) coverage rate is highly inequitable in terms of all types of stratifications; for example, there are 14.7, 25.7, 37.6, and 37.8 percentage point differences between urban vs.

rural, Khulna division vs. Sylhet division, completing secondary or higher education vs. no education, and highest vs. lowest income quintiles, respectively (NIPORT 2015).

Among fertility and family planning indicators, for example, marital age of first marriage is only 15.3 years in the lowest income quintile versus 17.6 years in the highest (national average 16.1 years). Mean ideal number of children is 2.4 among women with no education versus among those with secondary or higher level of education (national average 2.2). Contraceptive prevalence rate (any method) is only 47.8% in Sylhet Division versus 69.8% in Rangpur (national average 62.4%). Unmet needs for family planning is 17.7 in the Sylhet Division versus 6.7 in Rangpur (national average 12.0).

One of most critical challenges faced by the health systems in Bangladesh is in the arena of human resources for health. The health workforce crisis manifests, amongst others, in terms of absolute shortage, under performance, skill-mix imbalance, difficulty in rural retention, lack of responsiveness (Ahmed et al. 2011; Rawal et al. 2015; Joarder et al. 2017). While private medical institutions are also being set up at random, there is still a dearth of qualified teachers to produce qualified doctors. This also points towards lax regulations.

The pandemic has exposed the fragility of the healthcare in Bangladesh. Doctors, nurses and technicians are dealing with the newly emerged pandemic whereas non-communicable disease could not be handled with optimum care. Fighting against this public bad would have been easier if there was a universal public health system. The health sector had been in shambles because of trivial budget allocation, inadequate equipment, deficient infrastructure, low-quality services and high OOP expenditure. Along with supply side constraints, there are demand-side barriers in this sector as well, pertaining to less responsive healthcare seeking behaviour, sociocultural barriers and a lack of empowerment (Joarder et al. 2019). Consequently, the whole health structure had been plunged into crisis.

The chapter is divided in three sections. Stability conditions investigate into the status of expenditure and quality of healthcare system through two major indicators—access to healthcare and out of pocket expenditure (Fig. 6.1). The transformability conditions capture the measures needed to uplift the healthcare system. Thus, the section focuses on creating a Universal Health Care (UHC) system along with the matched public expenditure in health. Sustainability conditions comprise factors to ensure

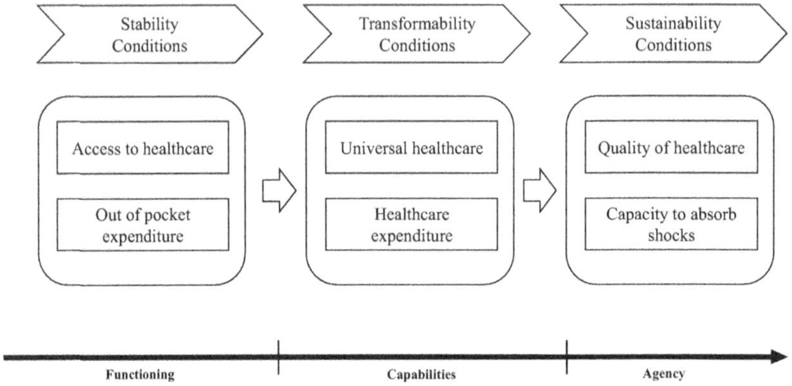

Fig. 6.1 Conceptual framework (*Source* Prepared by Author)

equitable and quality healthcare to the population. In light of the covid-19 pandemic, an important sustainability condition is maintaining the capacity of the healthcare system in sustaining shocks.

Stability Conditions

Since health is human right, it is imperative to ascertain that people from all sections get health benefits irrespective of their socio-economic status, religion, class, race and other categories. Many developed countries have been successful in providing health services universally. As a result, these countries assured good quality service at an affordable cost for mass people. Low and middle-income countries have been struggling with policy experimentations, such as the privatisation of health services, targeted approach to provide treatment facilities and social safety net programmes etc. Since this is a policy choice, the goal of universal health coverage is deeply embedded in politics, ethics and international law (Sachs 2012).

According to Article 25 of the 1948 Universal Declaration of Human rights, everyone has the right to an adequate standard of living, medical care and the right to security in case of illness or disability. In the same year, the constitution of the World Health Organisation published and noted that "the enjoyment of the highest attainable standard of health is one of the fundamental rights of every human being without distinction of race, religion, and political belief, economic or social condition." Universal health coverage has substantial commitments; yet access to health care facility depends on social and economic conditions (Sachs 2012). Privatisation of health care in many countries have been resulting in failure due to profit motive over services, absence of regulatory regimes, poor governance, rampant corruption, malpractice and manipulation by the companies.

Low Public Expenditure

Constant upward motion of OOP expenditure has created mass inequality. Private expenditure has increased more than the public expenditure. Because of the high cost of treatment facilities and inadequate services many people are deprived of equal access to health service due to their socio-economic status.

For the last two decades, there is limited growth in health expenditure made by the government. Despite health being a basic need of the population, only 2.48% of the GDP on average is being spent on the health sector in the period 2009–2016. In fact, this figure is only 0.27% higher than that of the average of the decade prior to this period (Table 6.1). At the same time, the OOP of the population is gradually increasing over time. During the period of 2000–2008, the OOP expenditure as a share of current health expenditure was 64.03% which increased to 68.92% in the following period (2009–2016). Instead of getting maximum support from the government in health spending, people are spending out of their pocket more. During the period of 2009–2016, the domestic government health expenditure was 19.64% of the current health expenditure. The domestic private health expenditure has increased over the two periods by 4.54%, implying that the private sector invested more in the health sector than the government. As a result, the general population has to access the services at a high OOP expenditure. A quite large part of the population cannot even access these health services.

The budget allocation in the health sector is not up to the mark. Domestic general government health expenditure has declined. Bangladesh has done well in reducing maternal and infant mortality rates. Still, areas outside the capital are suffering from inefficient health services due to the lack of modern equipment and logistical support. People who struggle hard to make their ends meet each day tend to take traditional treatment very often, which further adds miseries. Affluent

Table 6.1 Performance of key health indicators

Indicators	*Period*	
	2000–2008	*2009–2016*
Current health expenditure (% of GDP)	2.21	2.48
Current health expenditure per capita (current US$)	10.95	25.40
Domestic general government health expenditure (% of current health expenditure)	23.82	19.64
Domestic general government health expenditure (% of GDP)	0.52	0.48
Domestic private health expenditure (% of current health expenditure)	66.99	71.54
Out-of-pocket expenditure (% of current health expenditure)	64.03	68.92
External health expenditure (% of current health expenditure)	9.18	8.81
Mortality rate, adult, female (per 1,000 female adults)	145.09	116.43
Mortality rate, adult, male (per 1,000 male adults)	168.59	154.915
Mortality rate, infant (per 1,000 live births)	53.14	34.18

Source Author's calculation World Bank

sections prefer to have their treatment overseas, such as India, Thailand and other countries, draining foreign currency reserves. In such unequal circumstances, Bangladesh has to embrace the challenge of ameliorating its health services for all at affordable prices.

Inequality in Health Outcomes and Access

The methods of treatment in Bangladesh indicate a great deal of variation, with inequality at its core. Most people rely on non-qualified medics and compounders at pharmacies and dispensaries to reduce OOP expenditure (Table 6.2). The patients prefer private practices than government facilities due to easy access and better outcomes at the private chambers, despite high OOP expenditure. Another noticeable health care seeking behaviour is that a large section of the population seeks care from traditional practitioners such as ***kabiraj/hakim/ayurbed***, more than those of NGO health workers or doctors, who are professional and generally provide quality services. Moreover, the percentage of people relying on traditional healers such as ***peers, fakirs, tantrics, ojhas*** and ***baidyas*** is similar in percentage seeking help from the NGOs. This is serious cause of

Table 6.2 Methods of medical treatment in national level (%)

Method of treatment	*National*	*Urban*	*Rural*
Govt. health worker	2.41	1.70	2.57
NGO health worker	0.37	0.64	0.31
Homeopathic doctor	3.44	3.26	3.49
Kabiraj/hekim/ayurbed	1.00	0.41	1.13
Peer/fakir/tantric/ojha/baidya	0.36	0.56	0.31
Govt. doctor (govt. institution)	9.28	12.53	8.52
Govt. doctor (private practice)	14.34	19.57	13.11
NGO doctor	0.20	0.13	0.22
Private doctor	24.46	22.00	25.04
Pharmacy/dispensary/compounder	40.21	36.05	41.20
Family treatment	0.88	0.78	0.90
Self-treatment	0.61	0.74	0.58
Others	2.43	1.63	2.62

Source BBS (2019)

concern for the wellbeing of Bangladeshis as these traditional providers do not have licenses and cannot be held accountable for the care they provide, compounding potential threats to the remedy seekers.

The percentage of services rendered by traditional practitioners and healers ***kabiraji/hekim/ayurbed*** or ***peer/fakir/tantric/ojha/baidya*** is lower in urban areas than that of rural settings. Literacy is a key variable as there are more educated people in urban areas, who seek professional health care providers. In rural areas, people are easily diverted and entangled into the traps. Due to limited employment opportunities in rural areas, people cannot afford better health services in their region or are hard pressed to receive services from the cities. Income inequality drives many people to choose quacks and other traditional forms of health services without considering the dangerous outcomes this may lead to. Thus, a vicious cycle of inequality persists.

While Bangladesh lacks in providing quality care, India has successfully been able to institute health tourism. India has become the preferred destination of Bangladeshis health tourism (Table 6.3). Although OOP expenditure is quite high, India has made services cheaper than many other countries.

Table 6.3 Patients visiting different countries from Bangladesh

Country	*Percentage*
India	77
Thailand	4
Singapore	13
Malaysia	2
Other countries	4

Source Adopted from Hasan and Hassan (2013)

High Out of Pocket Expenditure (OOP)

Out of pocket expenditure—which is directly paid by a patient during service use and not reimbursed by any insurance coverage—in Bangladesh is increasing over time. This was 67% of total health expenditure in 2014, the highest among all SAARC countries (Table 6.4). This has increased to 74% in 2017, compared to the global average (18%) and many neighbouring countries (62% in India, 58% in Nepal, and 50% in Sri Lanka).

Government hospitals provide at an affordable price and, in some cases, free of cost health services, but there is an acute problem of accommodation, adequate equipment and proper management systems. Although many private hospitals have burgeoned, it is much dearer.

Job opportunities have shrunken more severely than before. The informalisation of the economy is also taking place, reducing the scope for

Table 6.4 Household OOP expenditure as percentage of Total Health Expenditure by SAARC nations

Country	*2005*	*2006*	*2007*	*2008*	*2009*	*2010*	*2011*	*2012*	*2013*	*2014*
Afghanistan	90	85	92	83	72	69	73	65	67	64
Bangladesh	60	59	61	60	61	61	61	63	67	67
Bhutan	21	18	13	15	18	11	12	26	25	25
India	66	66	65	64	63	63	64	65	64	62
Maldives	18	21	23	18	21	27	25	24	22	18
Nepal	53	47	50	48	45	45	41	46	49	48
Pakistan	66	69	68	66	64	61	61	55	55	56
Sri Lanka	45	43	42	44	44	45	48	49	41	42

Source Bangladesh National Health Accounts 1997–2015 (2017)

Table 6.5 OOP as a share of current health expenditure in some East Asian and OECD countries

Country	*2011*	*2012*	*2013*	*2014*	*2015*	*2016*
China	40.3	39.2	38.2	36.6	35.1	35.9
Japan	13.1	13	12.7	12.9	12.9	13.5
South Korea	34.6	35	34.6	34.3	34	33.3
Canada	14.7	14.6	14.5	14.5	14.5	14.6
Turkey	15.9	15.9	16.9	17.7	16.9	16.5
Germany	13.9	13.9	13	12.6	12.7	12.4

Source World Bank (2020b)

decent jobs. Due to reduction in real wages and the incessant price hikes, the consumption and savings capabilities of low- and middle-income groups have declined. In such milieu, high OOP brings in another layer of fiasco. People from rural areas and the poor are the worst sufferers.

East Asian and OECD countries have tolerable and less OOP than that of Bangladesh (Table 6.5). East Asian and OECD countries have successfully curtailed their OOP for general people through the generation of people-oriented policies, health schemes and insurances which assure permanent sustainable health care provision for all. Even many low-income and developing countries surge ahead of Bangladesh in reducing their health expenditures.

Life expectancy has increased over time in Bangladesh and the number is now well above that of India and Pakistan. Such a number has come at the cost of high OOP expenditure rather than that of government expenditures in health services. OECD and East Asian countries have lower OOP expenditure and, at the same time, have higher life expectancies (Fig. 6.2).

Transformability Conditions

Stability conditions lay the foundation of the healthcare system whereas, transformability conditions provide a doorway to transform the system into a developed one to cater to everyone with quality care. Two basic indicators, namely healthcare expenditure and universal healthcare are discussed as transformability conditions.

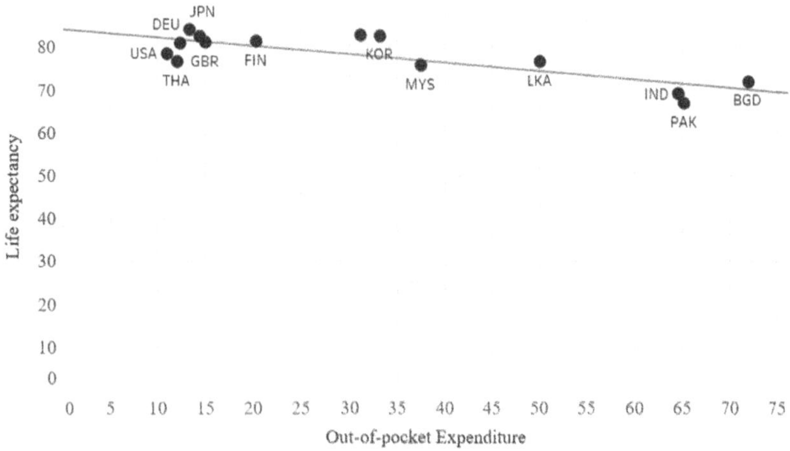

Fig. 6.2 Life expectancy versus out-of-pocket expenditure (*Source* Prepared by Author, based on World Bank 2020b)

Budget Allocation for Universal Healthcare

There are several factors in the health sector in Bangladesh which are obstacles to achieve universal health care in Bangladesh. Besides, inadequacy and skewed distribution of the healthcare workforce, there is a dearth of modern equipment, particularly in rural areas, with which treatment could be easier and resilient. Both require a high allocation than the current meagre budgetary spending.

According to the Bangladesh Health Facility Survey 2017, only 28% of health facilities have all six basic equipment—a stethoscope, thermometer, blood pressure apparatus, adult scale, child or infant scale, and light source—while 80% of Upazila (sub-district) Health Complexes do not have functioning X-ray machines (NIPORT 2017). It is therefore not surprising that these public hospitals are not equipped with oxygen and ventilators, which have been crucial for covid-19 management.

Severe shortages in the workforce is another core issue in the health system that requires immediate attention. For every 1,581 people, there is only one physician—in a country with a population of over 164 million. The number of medical technologists is 0.32 per 10,000, and the number of community and domiciliary health workers is 2.13 per 10,000, according to the 2018 Bangladesh Health Bulletin. The government facilities lack all types of health professionals including medical technologists, nurses and other support staff. The shortage of the health workforce with non-functioning equipment has always been a challenge for providing quality care at government facilities. During this pandemic, where people of all ages are affected, hospitals faced difficulties in providing required services with reasonable quality. Compared to other countries of the world, the ratios are quite at the bottom (Table 6.6).

In relation to SDG indicator 1.3.1 on effective coverage for mothers with new-borns, in Asia and the Pacific, 33.4% of women giving birth received maternity cash benefits (ILO 2017). On the other hand, in 81.4% of women received the benefit in Europe and Central Asia (ILO 2017).

Moreover, an increasing number of the elderly population due to demographic transition, combined with the dual burden of communicable and non-communicable disease, will create huge pressures on the health system in the future.

For many years, the government's budget allocation to the Ministry of Health and Family Welfare (MOHFW) has been hovering around the 5% mark. In 2017, health expenditure was 2.3% of GDP, substantially

Table 6.6 Health facilities per 10,000 population

Country	*Density of medical doctors 2009–2018*	*Density of nursing and midwifery personnel 2009–2018*	*Hospital beds*
Bangladesh	5.3	3.1	8
India	7.8	21.1	7
Pakistan	9.8	5.0	6
Nepal	6.5	26.9	50
Japan	24.1	115.2	134
Thailand	8.1	29.6	21
Singapore	23.1	72.1	24
Republic of Korea	23.7	69.7	103
Finland	38.1	147.2	44
Germany	42.1	132.0	83
Norway	46.3	181.2	39
United Kingdom	28.1	82.9	28
United States	25.9	85.5	29

Source WHO (2020)

lower than the South Asian and Lower Middle Income Country (LMIC) average at 5.3 and 5.4% of GDP (World Bank 2020a).

The health sector definitely needs a much higher allocation, but increasing budgetary allocation alone will not be able to transform the system. The government needs to move from the current incremental, norm-based allocation system to a "needs-based" allocation model. The first step is to assess the health needs of the population, their demographic status, disease patterns, and service utilisation—and allocate resources according to "need."

Ensuring Universal Healthcare System

Universal Health Care (UHC) ensures that people have access to needed quality health care services without any financial hardship. Bangladesh has made some remarkable progress in health indicators and extended health care services to its citizens. There are however inadequacies and disparities in access to services by low-income, marginalised groups. In this regard, the financial barrier is a major concern. This financial barrier is raised when the cost of health care is met by individual's regular income irrespective of their affordability. OOP payments for accessing healthcare is one of the most regressive ways of financing healthcare and is responsible for pushing a substantial number of households into poverty annually in Bangladesh (Bangladesh Health Watch 2011).

Rising OOP health expenditure increases poverty. The increase in the poverty gap, due to OOP health expenditure, expressed as a proportion of the 1.90 USD a day poverty line, was 2.69 in 2016 in Bangladesh from 0.81 in 2010 and 0.59 in 2005 (WHO 2019). This poverty gap increase is the highest in rural areas. In addition, higher government spending in the health sector can significantly decrease the poverty in the country. 24.67% of the household spend more than 10% of the income towards health. 9.53% of the population recorded their share of household expenditure on health that is greater than 25% (WHO 2019).

Two basic aspects of poverty are often neglected in health policy making; in developing countries, most of the people are poor and cannot afford to buy health services. The other aspect is governments in less developed countries have budget constraints. The question therefore is whether a nation should focus on health services provided by public provision or a combination of public, private and NGOs. Many may argue for private sector health provision through public financing but there is a strong incentive for the private sector to show inflated cost of the services. Besides, there may arise pressure from lobbyists to provide for the needs of middle and upper class rather than the poor. Therefore, the last hope for the poor people is government clinics and hospitals. The private provision therefore cannot be a solution to reach the poor with health care services. Rather, the public sector should come up with these services even though they have revenue deficits and organisational shortcomings. For extremely poor countries, aid by donor agencies can be a good source of the budget allocation (Sachs 2017).

Ensuring a UHC system in Bangladesh needs a massive infrastructural change in the current system, starting from local to the national level. A change in the management system has to be brought on through instituting the independent National Health Commission at the centre as well as the local health authorities at the delivery level, which will be directly elected to ensure accountability. The independent commission will be responsible for the implementation of the system. Secondly, a national health database has to be prepared with vital statistics, building upon National Identity Cards. Each citizen will be registered with a general physician and access to the specialist hospitals will be through a referral system.

Sustainability Conditions

The constitution of the country pledges to ensure basic healthcare to its citizens by the state. Only a sustainable healthcare system can ensure the fulfilment of this pledge. This section discusses two basic concepts for ensuring sustainability in the healthcare system- i) quality health service and ii) capacity to absorb shocks.

The WHO defines quality of care as "the extent to which health care services provided to individuals and patient populations improve desired health outcomes. In order to achieve this, health care must be safe, effective, timely, efficient, equitable and people-centred." A safe healthcare means delivering health care that minimises risks and harm to service users, including avoiding preventable injuries and reducing medical errors. An effective healthcare system focuses on providing services based on scientific knowledge and evidence-based guidelines. Reducing delays in providing and receiving health care opts for a timely system. Effective and equitable health system delivers health care in a manner that maximises resource use and avoids waste and does not differ in quality according to personal characteristics such as gender, race, ethnicity, geographical location or socioeconomic status. Providing care that takes into account the preferences and aspirations of individual service users and the culture of their community, finally, make the health care system a people-centred one (WHO 2018).

At the same time, capacity to absorb shocks can be termed as the health management capacity. Building resilience in order to mitigate the stresses and impacts of a shock is essential for the sustainability of the health care system. For proper functioning of an important basic need like health, a strong capacity to absorb the impacts of a shock is mandatory. The covid-19 pandemic has brought out the core importance of building resilience in the health sector despite the pre-existing instabilities. Capacity building in the health sector requires infrastructure development as well as regulatory reforms in order to establish a sustainable health sector.

Moving Towards Quality Health Service

Quality health service is a prerequisite in the pathway of sustainability. Quality of care is also a key component of the right to health, and the route to equity and dignity for women and children. WHO identifies six elements to measure quality of care, namely, safe, effective, timely, efficient, equitable and people-centred.

The prevailing healthcare in Bangladesh is far from reaching those standards. One way is to measure the standard by the patients is to look at the problem-solving capacity, which is quite dissatisfactory. Even 53.8% of mild problems remain unsolved (Table 6.7). This scenario puts a big question mark on the effectiveness of the health system. OOP is ever increasing but quality remains doubtful. Low quality health service affects general people multi-dimensionally. Due to the absence of desired and appropriate health services, people are also losing their productivity. Low

Table 6.7 Complaint outcomes across different complaint types (% of total complaints)

Types of problems	*Problems unsolved*	*Problems solved*
Mild	53.8	46.2
Moderate	82.7	17.3
Serious	97.1	2.9

Source World Bank (2012)

productivity results in low return on labour. People who can afford to seek treatment abroad are the winners. This is another reason of the persisting high inequality.

Capacity to Absorb Shocks: Healthcare During the COVID-19 Pandemic

Bangladesh has been entangled in fighting covid-19 for seven months now. As of December 14, 2020, there are 490,533 confirmed cases and 7,052 deaths. Bangladesh's response suffered from a lack of inter-sectoral coordination. If Bangladesh had carried out the public health response planning based on a worst-case scenario, it might have started dealing with covid-19 earlier and more effectively (UNDP 2020). Based on a review of Bangladesh Doctors Foundation (BDF), doctors now make up 6.5% of total cases (UNDP 2020).

Allocation to the health sector stands at 5.14% of the total fiscal year 2021 budget and is less than one percent of GDP amid the pandemic. In light of the impacts of the covid-19 pandemic, building a resilient healthcare system is essential for the sustainable development of the country.

Concluding Remarks

The major hindrances to the stability of the health sector of Bangladesh are the unequal access to health services and a high out of pocket expenditure. Health services are marred by low service quality, inequalities between rural and urban areas, and immense dependency on traditional and controversial health services propound that the healthcare sector itself is diseased. Of all the risks that poor households are facing, health risks probably pose the greatest threat to their lives and livelihoods in Bangladesh.

Considerable challenges remain at the forefront in the efforts to improve the health status of the population, reduce health inequalities, improve the quality of care and public satisfaction with healthcare, and to increase the efficiency and sustainability of service-delivery agencies.

Equity in access to, and utilisation of, healthcare is an important goal for any health system and an essential prerequisite for achieving Universal Health Coverage for any country. At the same time, in order to transform the healthcare system into a Universal Health Care system, an appropriate

Table 6.8 Summary table of the major indicators of health

Indicators	*State of Bangladesh*
Access to healthcare	The sector is ridden with inequality in access and outcomes. Affluent section goes abroad to access health services. The doctor patient and medical workforce population ratios are very low
Out of pocket expenditure	Out of pocket expenditure is increasing and has become 74% of total health expenditure which is more than that of other South Asian, East Asian and OECD countries
Budget allocation	Allocation in health sector as share of total budget has declined in the last decade, despite poor infrastructure, shortages of staff and changing disease burden
Universal health care	Inadequacy and disparities in access to services along with financial barriers are can be overcome through UHC. For every individual having a GP (general physician), institutional, structural and fiscal systems have to transform
Quality of health service	Quality of care in terms of safety, effectiveness, timeliness, efficiency, equity and people-centred are at low rung
Capacity to absorb shocks	In light of the impacts of COVID-19 pandemic, building a resilient healthcare system is essential for the sustainable development of the country

need-based budgetary allocation is essential. It also needs to overcome health workforce crisis manifesting, amongst others, in terms of absolute shortage, under performance, skill-mix imbalance, difficulty in rural retention, lack of responsiveness. Infrastructure developments are necessary along with the focus on health education and health research. A UHC system refers to a system having equal access to health services for all.

The outbreak of the covid-19 pandemic on the health sector has opened up a new opportunity for reforms in the sector. For Bangladesh's ailing sector to be repaired, the Government could take lessons from the successes of neighbouring countries like Thailand and other developing and developed countries to make lasting changes in the healthcare sector. A change in the management system has to be brought on through instituting the independent National Health Commission at the centre as well as the local health authorities at the delivery level, which will be directly elected to ensure accountability. The independent commission will be responsible for the implementation of the system. Each citizen has to be registered with a general physician and access to the specialist hospitals will be through a referral system. The country's healthcare system needs drastic reform to better suit to the requirements of the common people.

References

Ahmed, S.M., B.B. Alam, I. Anwar, T. Begum, R. Huque, and J.A.M. Khan. 2015. *Bangladesh Health System Review*, ed. A. Naheed and K. Hort. Dhaka, Bangladesh: World Health Organization.

Ahmed, S.M., M.A. Hossain, A.M. RajaChowdhury, and A.U. Bhuiya. 2011. The Health Workforce Crisis in Bangladesh: Shortage, Inappropriate Skill-Mix and Inequitable Distribution. *Human Resources for Health* 9 (3).

Bangladesh Health Watch. 2011. *Bangladesh Health Watch Report 2011: Moving Towards Universal Health Coverage*. BRAC.

BBS. 2019. Report on Household Income and Expenditure Survey 2016. Bangladesh Bureau of Statistics.

Hasan, S.R., and M. K. Hassan. 2013. Health Tourism: A Demographic Study on the Outbound Health Tourists from Bangladesh. *Journal of Business* 34(2).

ILO. 2017. World Social Protection Report 2017–19: Universal Social Protection to Achieve the Sustainable Development Goals.

Islam, M.R., M.S. Rahman, Z. Islam, C.Z. Nurs, P. Sultana, and M.M. Rahman. 2017. Inequalities in Financial Risk Protection in Bangladesh: An Assessment of Universal Health Coverage. *International Journal for Equity in Health* 16 (59).

Joarder, Taufique, Tahrim Z. Chaudhury, and Ishtiaq Mannan. 2019. Universal Health Coverage in Bangladesh: Activities, Challenges, and Suggestions. *Advances in Public Health* 2019, Article ID 4954095, 12 pages. https://doi.org/10.1155/2019/4954095.

Joarder, T., A. George, M. Sarker, S. Ahmed, and D. H. Peters. 2017. Who Are More Responsive? Mixed-Methods Comparison of Public and Private Sector Physicians in Rural Bangladesh. *Health Policy and Planning* 32: iii14–iii24.

NIPORT, Mitra and Associates, and ICF International. 2015. *Bangladesh Demographic and Health Survey 2014: Key Indicators*. Dhaka, Bangladesh, and Rockville, MD.

NIPORT, Mitra and Associates, and ICF International. 2017. Bangladesh Health Facility Survey 2017. Dhaka, Bangladesh, and Rockville, MD.

Rawal, L.B., T. Joarder, and K. Mahmud. 2015. *The Assessment of Rural Retention Policies for Human Resources for Health in Bangladesh [Internet]*. Dhaka, Bangladesh. http://www.coe-uhc.org/index.php/publications/category/9-working-paper-series.

Sachs, J.D. 2012. Achieving Universal Health Coverage in Low-Income Settings. *The Lancet* 380 (9845): 944–947.

Sachs, R.E. 2017. Administering Health Innovation. *Cardozo Law Review* 39: 1991.
UNDP. 2020. Covid-19: A Reality Check for Bangladesh's Healthcare System: UNDP in Bangladesh. United Nations Development Programme https://www.bd.undp.org/content/bangladesh/en/home/stories/a-reality-check-for-bangladesh-s-healthcare-system.html. Accessed on 1 October 2020.
WHO. 2018. *Handbook for National Quality Policy and Strategy*. World Health Organisation.
WHO. 2019. *World Health Statistics 2019*. World Health Organisation.
WHO. 2020. *World Health Statistics 2020*. World Health Organisation.
World Bank. 2012. Bangladesh Health Facility Survey 2011. World Bank. Washington D.C.
World Bank. 2020a. A Case for Building a Stronger Health Care System in Bangladesh. https://blogs.worldbank.org/endpovertyinsouthasia/case-building-stronger-health-care-system-bangladesh. Accessed on 1 October 2020.
World Bank. 2020b. World Development Indicators. World Bank. Washington D.C.

CHAPTER 7

Poverty and Inequality in Bangladesh

Introduction

The advent of the covid-19 crisis in Bangladesh has manifested itself, not only in healthcare, but also aggravated income, expenditure and unemployment. Widespread erosion in incomes, return of migrant workers, soaring unemployment, decrease in food expenditure, distress sale of agricultural produce by farmers and other adverse consequences have intensified the setbacks facing communities at different levels. Economic inactivity of workers in the informal sector, the lack of coping mechanisms and the inadequacy of fiscal support effectively reaching vulnerable communities imply that a considerable portion of the population including also the non-poor households remains vulnerable to financial hardship and impoverishment, and eventual pauperisation. A new poor population is therefore emerging as vulnerable non-poor households lose income, livelihoods and future earning potential.

Examining the state of poverty and inequality in Bangladesh, this chapter ushers that the rate of poverty reduction exhibits a slowing down trend during the pre-covid-19 era, which is not compatible with the story of the 'high' rate of growth of GDP. At the same time, inequality has been mounting at a high pace. Resources are concentrated in the pockets of a few at the expense of many. In spite of acquiring an acclaimed high GDP rate, the gap between the bottom 40% poorest people and top 10% richest

R. A. M. Titumir, *Numbers and Narratives in Bangladesh's Economic Development*,
https://doi.org/10.1007/978-981-16-0658-8_7

people has deepened (BBS 2019). Access to resources has concentrated to a particular group of people. On the backdrop of ongoing discrimination in terms of wealth, income and consumption provision, a large section of people is becoming peripheral and deprived.

The poverty rate has declined in the last decade but the rate of reduction has slowed down in the pre-covid era. The spectrum of regional poverty indicates that some belts have fallen into the vicious hole of poverty again. Access to employment, education, health and social security programmes is still out of the reach of a large class of poor people. Real wage is declining. On the other hand, due to the lack of skilled labour, productivity is on the downward direction. In addition, slower growth of real wage relative to labour productivity has moved the functional distribution of income against labour and in favour of the owners of non-labour factors of production, such as land and capital (Osmani 2015).

The Covid-19 pandemic has severely impacted the life and livelihoods of the marginalised section of the society—particularly the low-income people, women, children, the elderly, the unemployed, the informal sector workers, lower-middle and middle classes. Income erosion resulting from the losses in various sectors from the shutdown will create new poor in the country. The poverty situation may plunge into a deeper valley of uncertainty due to the repatriations of large number of migrant workers. Almost two million migrant workers are expected to come back to the homeland, creating the possibility of an increase in the number of vulnerable families who are solely dependent on their income (Unnayan Onneshan 2020).

The on-going development process of the country has failed to generate outcomes that are compatible with the aspirations of an equitable and democratic society. Admittedly, the existing system has created a pernicious cycle that perpetuates the various forms of inequality in subtle and not-so-obvious ways permeated by the concentration of wealth, misuse of resources, power, and public institutions along with serious violations of human rights. Rising economic inequality and widening disparities across all aspects of people's lives largely belie the spirit of the Liberation War that mobilised the countrymen to fight against the concentration of power, discrimination and violation of democratic rights.

Considering the global changes in conceptualising and measuring inequality, there is need for an indigenous approach to understand and frame the discussion on inequality in the context of Bangladesh, which can be guided by the three principles of the Liberation War namely equality, human dignity and social justice. This realisation necessitates a perspective to explore the major aspects of inequality and its underlying processes for a more nuanced and context-specific understanding of the case of Bangladesh.

Largely, Bangladesh displays a stark economic inequality and a high degree of disparity in different socio-economic aspects of people's lives including inequality in access, outcomes and quality of education, health, judicial and public services. These are also in tandem with the growing income inequality over the years and the slowing down of the rate of poverty reduction in Bangladesh, despite steady economic growth in recent decades (UNDP 2018). For example, the latest Household Income and Expenditure Survey (HIES) of 2016 by the national statistics agency reveals that the Gini-coefficient of income inequality has increased to 0.483 in 2016 from 0.458 in 2010 while the wealth concentration also explicates worsening inequality over time. The share of income held by the top 5% households has increased to 27.9% in 2016 from 24.6% in 2010. On the other hand, the income share of the lowest 5% households has decreased substantially from 0.78% in 2010 to 0.23% in 2016 (BBS 2019).

The crisis of the pandemic has also exposed the deep divide in the society. Income cuts will disproportionately affect those living in a mediocre standard of living, and extraction of liquidity from powerful elites being neglected as a source of revenue is likely to worsen the pre-existing income inequality. Inequality will further aggravate in the absence of rights-based universal social security, depriving the poor and vulnerable population. Accordingly, the inequality will deepen, with further differentiated return on labour and capital due to erosion of income given the preponderance of most of the labour force engaged in the informal sector and the loss of employment in both formal and informal sectors (Unnayan Onneshan 2020).

Indubitably, the discussion on inequality nowadays occupies a central place in both academic and policy circles, even though the concept is quite old and nuanced as it may be reflected in the evolution of thinking on inequality. Classical economists like Ricardo and Marx talked about growing inequality inherent in the capitalist system; Ricardo mainly talked about rent and Marx talked about profit from capital (Ricardo 1817; Marx 1867). Kuznets' inverted U hypothesis shows that the income inequality will rise with economic growth; however, after a certain period the inequality will start to fall (Kuznets 1955). The reason is the transition of workers from the lower income agriculture sector to the higher income industrial sector during economic growth. With this, the debate of inequality shifted toward inequality in opportunity. Some researchers even tried to prove that income inequality is good for GDP growth of a country (Sahota et al. 1993; Cook 1995). However, the empirical data of 82 countries, where 20 countries are industrial, and 62 countries are developing, suggest that the relationship is ambiguous (Schmidt-Hebbel and Servén 2000; Dynan et al. 2004; Bunting 2015).

The debate of inequality then turned towards inequality of opportunities and intergenerational mobility along with new measures of inequality (Stiglitz 1973a). Sen's capability approach, which mainly analyses poverty, is used to find the dimensions of inequality that extend beyond the narrow income-based measures. Research was also done to show how education helped to persist inequality contrary to popular belief that education reduced inequality (Stiglitz 1973b). The debate of income inequality came to more prominence with Piketty's new findings that show if $r > g$ (rate of return to capital exceeding rate of income growth) persists for a long time, then inequality increases (Piketty 2003). Piketty directly criticises Kuznets's study and mentions that besides statistical data, it is politically influenced (Piketty 2014). In addition to exploring multidimensional aspects of inequality, a globally rights-based approach to inequality has drawn much attention in recent years that goes beyond the traditional measures based on income or wealth.

The chapter highlights the stability conditions of poverty and inequality (Fig. 7.1). The transformability conditions lay out the necessary and sufficient conditions required to meet in order to cover the gaps in the trend of these indicators. Lastly the sustainability conditions highlight the policy provisions required for building resilience, for curbing the worsening of inequality in the post pandemic context and the measures for climate shock adaptability and preventing pauperisation of vulnerable populations. The two-pronged thematic framework therefore illustrates the conditions such as income augmentation and provision of social security for the vulnerable populations will render gains in poverty reduction stable, while transformability conditions such as the policies of active restraint will lead to lower deterioration in inequality. Sustainability conditions such as a strengthening of the social contract will ensure the

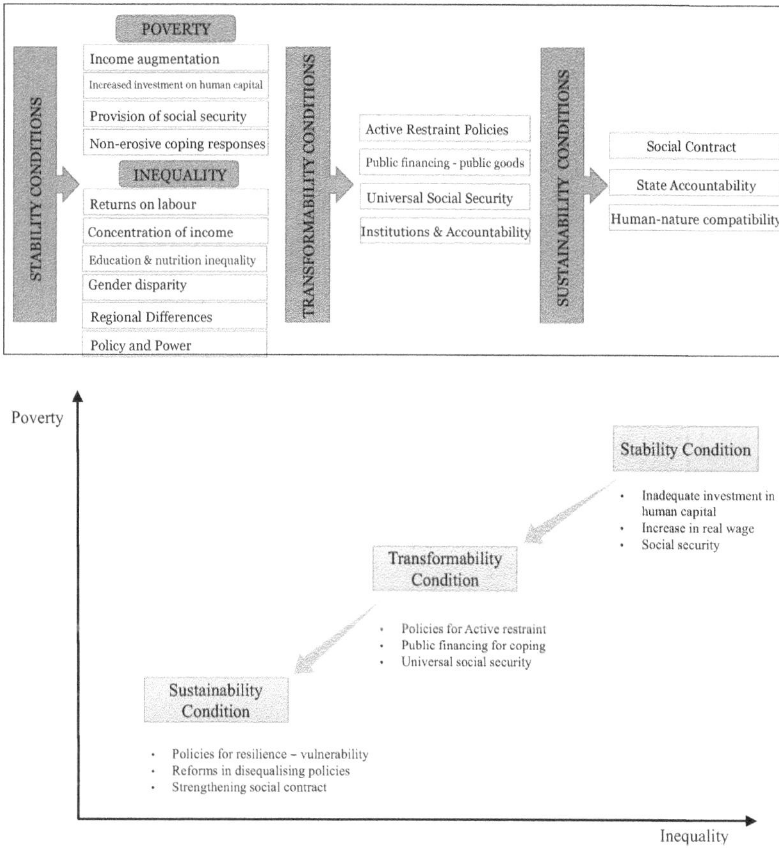

Fig. 7.1 Systematic thematic framework (*Source* Prepared by author)

longevity of the progress in poverty and inequality over time. A coordinated achievement of the conditions will therefore lead to a steady and sustained decline in both poverty and inequality.

Stability Conditions

The section highlights the reasons behind the visible improvements in poverty. In addition, it also explores whether the advances in the indicators are consistent with other indicators. Conditions such as real wage growth, regional differences in poverty, investment on merit goods are analysed to decipher the stability of the gains in poverty reduction and curbing inequality.

Slow Reduction

The pre-covid-19 state of poverty seems to be quite satisfactory. The rate of poverty has declined considerably (Table 7.1). The incidence of poverty decreased from 48.9% in 2000 to 20.5% in 2018–2019 while the incidence of extreme poverty stood 10.5% in 2018–2019 from 34.3% in 2000 (BBS 2019). It appears that the pace of poverty reduction has become slower from 2010 when the poverty rate was 31.5%. In 2016, the poverty rate became 24.3% which reached 20.5% in the 2018–2019 period. From 2005 to 2010, the poverty rate reduced by 8.5%. Between 2010 and 2016, the poverty rate reduced by 7.2% and during 2016 and the 2018–2019 period, it reduced by 3.8%. The situation of extreme poverty is not better than that of the poverty rate. During the 2005–2010 period, the extreme poverty rate decreased by 7.5%. During 2010–2016 and 2016 to 2018–2019, the extreme poverty declined by 4.7% and 2.4% respectively. It is clear that both poverty and extreme poverty rates are decreasing but at a much slower pace than before, putting a question mark on the current national growth spectrum.

This pace of the rate of the poverty reduction does not recognise the story of the high GDP growth of the country. In 2000–2005 and 2005–2010, the upper poverty reduction rate was 1.8% and 1.7% respectively, which slowed further in 2010–2016 (1.2%) (Table 7.2).

Income elasticity of poverty, which measures the magnitude of the effect of per capita income growth in reducing the rate of poverty in percentage terms, provides crucial information about the role of economic

Table 7.1 Poverty incidence

	HIES 2000	*HIES 2005*	*HIES 2010*	*HIES 2016*	*2016–2017 (estimated)*	*2017–2018 (estimated)*	*2018–2019 (estimated)*
Poverty	48.9	40	31.5	24.3	23.1	21.8	20.5
Extreme poverty	34.3	25.1	17.6	12.9	12.1	11.3	10.5

Source BBS (2019)

Table 7.2 Rate of reduction in poverty incidence

	2000–2005	*2005–2010*	*2010–2016*
Upper poverty	1.8	1.7	1.2
Lower poverty	1.8	1.5	0.8

Source BBS (2019)

growth in poverty alleviation. The annual rates of decline in poverty rates and rates of increase in real GDP per capita during the broad period 2005–2015 and the estimated value of income elasticity of poverty for South Asian countries provide some revealing insights (Table 7.3).

Bhutan, Sri Lanka, Nepal, and Pakistan have achieved the largest reduction in poverty at a rate around 15% annually with India's rate of decline to be around 9%, whereas the rate of decline for Bangladesh is the lowest at about 5% annually. Considering the relative rates of annual change in average income and poverty rates, countries such as Bhutan, Sri Lanka

Table 7.3 Income elasticities of poverty (using international poverty line) for South Asian countries, 2005–2015

Country	*$1.90 poverty rate, 2005 (%)*	*$1.90 poverty rate, 2016 (%)*	*Annual rate of poverty decline, (DP), %*	*Annual growth rate of GDP per capita, (GY), %*	*Elasticity (DP/GY) (-)*
Bangladesh	25.7 (2005)	14.8 (2016)	−4.89	4.82	1.01
Bhutan	17.6 (2003)	1.5 (2017)	−16.13	5.25	3.07
India	38.2 (2004)	13.4 (2015)	−9.08	5.06	1.79
Nepal	46.1 (2003)	15 (2010)	−14.82	3.06	4.84
Pakistan	16.5 (2005)	3.9 (2015)	−13.43	1.20	11.19
Sri Lanka	8.3 (2002)	0.8 (2016)	−15.39	5.38	2.86

Note 1. Poverty rates are taken from World Bank Poverty and Equity Data Portal (2019b) and following Ram (2011, p. 2436), annual rate of decline is calculated as $[\{(P2/P1)\exp(1/n)\} - 1]$ where P2 and P1 are the poverty rates for the last and first years and n is the number of years. The rate is then multiplied by 100 to convert it in percentage points

2. Annual rate of growth of GDP per capita (G) is calculated by taking constant-price GDP per capita in local currency from World Development Indicators for 2017, and estimating the expression for exponential growth $\text{Ln}(Y) = a + G(t) + u$, where t takes values equal to number of time periods for each country

Source Unnayan Onneshan (2019) and Rahman and Ram (2020)

and India experienced higher rates of growth in income along with higher rates of decline in poverty. However, countries, such as Bangladesh and Pakistan, experienced lower rate of decline in poverty despite higher rates of growth in income.

Clearly, significant variability is observed in the estimated elasticity rates among this small group of neighbouring countries. The highest elasticity is exhibited in Pakistan (11.19) and the lowest in Bangladesh (1.01). The income elasticity of poverty for rest of the four countries in South Asia are 4.84, 3.07, 2.86 and 1.79 for Nepal, Bhutan, Sri Lanka and India respectively (Table 7.4).

Compared to the 1990–2005 period, poverty rates have declined substantially in the recent decade and poverty's responsiveness to income growth has increased substantially in the recent period. However, income elasticity of poverty declines as one raises the cut-off point of the poverty line. This suggests that the role of income growth is much smaller (almost half or lower than that of USD 1.90 estimates) when the USD 3.20 poverty rate is used. Since most of the countries in the group are in the lower middle-income category, elasticity estimates with USD 3.20 poverty line is considered more reasonable than they were with the USD 1.90 poverty estimates.

Table 7.4 Income elasticities of poverty for South Asian countries using three different poverty measures

Country	Reference period	*Income elasticity of poverty (DP/GY) (-)*			*Elasticity using $1.25 poverty rate, 1990–2005*
		$1.90 poverty rate (%)	*$3.20 poverty rate (%)*	*$5.50 poverty rate (%)*	
Bangladesh	2005–2016	1.01	0.43	0.10	0
Bhutan	2003–2017	3.07	1.80	0.86	0.91
India	2004–2015	1.79	0.72	0.21	0.35
Nepal	2003–2010	4.84	1.85	0.36	1.19
Pakistan	2005–2015	11.19	4.48	1.27	4.67
Sri Lanka	2002–2016	2.86	1.69	0.69	0.67

Note 1. $3.20 and $5.50 Poverty rates are taken from World Bank Poverty and Equity Data Portal (2019b) and elasticities are calculated by Rahman (2020) following the same procedure as the previous table
2. Elasticity estimates using $1.25 poverty rate for the period 1990–2005 are taken from Ram (2015)
Source Unnayan Onneshan (2019) and Rahman and Ram (2020)

Notably, the observed variability shows the highest elasticity is in the case of Pakistan and lowest in Bangladesh with Nepal, Bhutan, Sri Lanka and India taking second to fourth positions. The pattern of variability in elasticity estimates among this small group of countries implies that cross-country factors other than income play a more significant role in reducing poverty. Targeted policies besides economic growth matter much since the similar rates of income growth are found to be have considerably varied effects on poverty reduction. However, unusually high estimates for a few countries should be read with caution since there might be some issues with poverty data which are reported by each country. For example, a high elasticity in the case of Pakistan despite the lowest economic growth in the group may be inflated by data discrepancy.

Persistent Regional Differences

Albeit both urban and rural poverty and extreme poverty rates have lessened throughout the years, 26.7% rural people emerged as poor in 2016 whereas 19.3% people in urban areas have remained poor. The urban poverty rate has not decreased satisfactorily from 2010 (21.3%) to 2016 (19.3%). The situation of extreme poverty rate is worse in urban areas. In 2010, the extreme poverty rate was 7.7% in urban areas which increased to 8% in 2016 (Table 7.5). This implies that more people have fallen into the poverty trap.

The regional poverty situation has not been same in recent years. On the circumstance of the acclaimed achievement of minimum poverty and the extreme poverty rate, the regional picture makes for a different illustration. In fact, the poverty rate has increased in Rangpur reversely. In 2010, the poverty rate in Rangpur division was 42.3%, which increased to 47.3% in 2016 and extreme poverty rate has increased to 30.6% in

Table 7.5 Urban and rural poverty incidence

	Poverty (%)				*Extreme poverty (%)*			
	2000	*2005*	*2010*	*2016*	*2000*	*2005*	*2010*	*2016*
Rural	52.3	43.8	35.2	26.7	37.9	28.6	21.1	15
Urban	35.1	28.4	21.3	19.3	19.9	14.6	7.7	8.0

Source World Bank (2019a)

Table 7.6 Poverty reduction across divisions (2010–2016)

	Poverty (in %)		*Extreme poverty (in %)*	
	2010	*2016*	*2010*	*2016*
Barisal	39.4 (3.3)	26.4 (1.5)	26.7 (3.2)	14.4 (1.3)
Chittagong	26.2 (2)	18.3 (1.2)	13.1 (1.4)	9 (0.9)
Dhaka	30.5 (1.6)	20.5 (1.1)	15.6 (1.1)	9.9 (0.7)
Khulna	32.1 (2.3)	27.7 (1.3)	15.4 (1.6)	12.1 (0.8)
Rajshahi	29.7 (2.1)	29 (1.5)	16 (1.6)	14.3 (1)
Rangpur	42.3 (3.2)	47.3 (1.3)	27.7 (2.9)	30.6 (1.2)
Sylhet	28.1 (3)	16.2 (1.7)	20.7 (2.5)	11.5 (1.4)

Note Standard error in the parentheses
Source World Bank (2019a)

2016 from 27.7% in 2010 (Table 7.6). The condition of the Rajshahi division is not satisfactory either. The poverty rate reduced slightly from 2010 (29.7%) to 2016 (29%). Reduction pattern of extreme poverty is worse than that of upper poverty.

The disparity exists within urban areas as well. In Dhaka and Chittagong, two main cities of the country, only 27.86% household has any savings compared to 51.54% in other cities. Metropolitan cities have worse medical condition as well. Only 27% of the household visits hospitals compared to 76% in other cities. In terms of nutrition, households in metropolitan cities consume less milk and beef but consumes more rice than other cities, though spend higher in food consumption (BBS 2020).

New Poor Due to COVID-19

The economic shutdown put in place to curb the contagion of COVID-19 also halted businesses and economic activity in the physically interactive sector. Jobs in the informal sector such as construction workers, rickshaw pullers, day labourers, petty vendors and domestic aid workers temporarily faced economic inactivity. So, for those living hand-to-mouth, loss of daily wages prolonged over a period of time. Small, informal enterprises found themselves devoid of a targeted fiscal stimulus or short-term financial support for being unregistered and unlisted with the formal authorities. The rural economy was jolted by a shutdown of the transportation industry, which barred their agricultural produce from reaching the main markets in urban cities, leading to a distress sale by farmers.

The influx of returnee migrant workers added to the plight of the rural economy, as most of these workers were newly unemployed, and a lack of relevant skills and employment opportunities during a contraction of the national economy would thus push the unemployment rate almost 3% higher (Unnayan Onneshan 2020). The widespread income erosion of low income-earners with minimal savings would therefore push non-poor households under the poverty line. Rapid surveys suggest that around 77% of the recognised vulnerable non-poor population had fallen back into poverty due to the COVID-19 crisis, leading to the emergence of the new poor (BIGD and PRRC 2020).

Inadequate Investment in Education and Health

The education budget has, in fact, decreased as a share of total budget. The allocation of education as a share of GDP remains stagnant (2.1%) in fiscal years of 2019–2019 and 2019–2020. The figures remained below the standards set by seven five-year plan (7FYP), which was 3% of GDP and Education 2030 Framework for Action of UNESCO (4–6% of GDP). Moreover, the implementation of the overall education budget in 2017–2018 (85.8%) was the lowest in the last decade, which expresses concern about the incentives for investment in human capital (Ministry of Finance 2018). A similar scenario prevails in the health sector. Allocation for health as a share of total budget has fallen (from 5.1% in 2018–2019 to 4.9% in 2019–2020). Since 2017, the health budget as a share of GDP remained constantly at 0.9% level only. The government budget for health as a share of GDP is considerably lower than the targets stipulated in the 7FYP and World Health Organisation (WHO) benchmark where the 7FYP target was 1.12% of GDP, whilst the WHO target was set at 5% of GDP. Per capita allocation for health sector (in nominal terms) has slightly increased (from Tk.1349 in 2018–2019 to Tk.1537 in 2019–2020) but the rise is much lower in real terms. The utilisation of the overall health budget has been decelerating in recent years and stood lowest in 2017–2018 (83.7%) during the last ten fiscal years.

Greater inequality reduces the rate of overall economic growth that can be realised from a given rate of skill-biased technical progress. Productivity growth accrues to human capital because physical capital is elastically supplied at a constant return. When technological progress or other economic fundamentals favour skilled labour—which has evidently been the case—the induced growth rate of overall productivity is proportional to the labour income share of skilled workers. Other things equal, greater earnings inequality reduces this share because the relative demand for skilled labour is price elastic—the elasticity of substitution between skilled and unskilled labour exceeds 1.0. This means that factors causing greater inequality lower the rate of economic growth associated with a given rate of skill-based technology transfer, because employers substitute away from relatively expensive skilled labour. Public social expenditure (excluding health) on people of working age is only 0.7% of total GDP (ILO 2017). In Southern Asia, non-health public social expenditure for older persons is 5.5% of total GDP, which is lower than other Asian regions (ILO 2017).

Bangladesh had an unemployment rate of 4.3 in 2018 and 4.2 in 2019 (ILO 2020). Unemployment rate in South Asian countries was 5.3% and 5.4% respectively during 2018 and 2019. India, Bangladesh, Bhutan and Nepal have stayed somewhat stable in 2020, albeit Bhutan and Nepal have rates of 1.47 and 2.39 in 2020, compared to 4.15 in Bangladesh (ILO 2020). The number of unemployed people was 37 million and 37.7 million respectively in 2018 and 2019 in South Asian region (ILO 2020). This number is projected to reach 39 million in 2021. Labour underutilisation rate was 10.9% in South Asian regions. At the same time, the percentage was 10.3%, 10% and 9.8% in Asia and the Pacific, East Asia and South-East Asia and the Pacific regions (ILO 2020).

Declining Real Wage and Rising Inequality

The discrepancy, demonstrated by an increasing income per capita and decreasing rate of poverty reduction points to explaining how the substantial growth in developing countries, may have contributed to poverty reduction through the significant role of inequality in the growth–poverty nexus (Bourguignon 2003; Epaulard 2003; Fosu 2009; Kalwij and Verschoor 2007; Ravallion 1997; World Bank 2006).

GDP growth stood at 8.13% in fiscal year of 2018–2019, given by provisional estimates of BBS, which was 7.86% in the previous fiscal year. However, at the same time, the Gini coefficient, which is the economic measure of equality, stood at 0.482 in 2016, up from 0.458 in 2010. The income held by the poorest 40% of the population in Bangladesh declined from 17.41% in 1991 to 13.01% in 2016, whilst income held by the richest 10% and 20% of the population in Bangladesh increased from 23.3% and 37.4% in 1991 to 26.8% and 41.4% in 2016. These figures indicate that inequality has worsened over the span of time, despite higher growth of GDP per capita, raising questions over the nature of economic growth that only serves the rich, at the expense of the well-being of the poor. Even in China, which has achieved remarkable poverty reduction, further reduction could have possibly occurred in the absence of the amassing income inequality associated with growth (Chen and Ravallion 2008).

Remarkably, the high economic growth in Bangladesh has been accompanied by increasing income inequality in the labour force. The return on labour has declined over the recent years, making inequality an inevitable outcome of the process. A careful analysis reveals that during the decade of 1985/1986 to 1995/1996, the real wage increased at an average rate of 1.26% annually whereas the growth in labour productivity was 2.88%, while the real wage growth rate and labour productivity growth rates were 1.16% and 2.42% respectively (Table 7.7).

Quite significantly, this trend has reversed during the most recent decade since 2005/2006 to 2015/2016 when the real wage increased only at a rate close to zero (0.03%) despite further boost in the labour productivity growing at rate of 3.59% on average (Fig. 7.2). This indicates that due to declining real wages, in spite of increasing labour productivity, the situation of income distribution is exacerbating, further disfavouring the working class. Since the mid-1980s, the growth rate of real wage increasingly lagged behind the growth rate of labour productivity, and this

Table 7.7 Annual average growth rate of GDP, employment, labour productivity and real wage (%)

Period	*1985/1986–1995/1996*	*1995/1996–2005/2006*	*2005/2006–2015/2016*
Real GDP growth	4.21	5.56	5.89
Employment growth	1.33	3.14	2.3
Labour productivity growth	2.88	2.42	3.59
Real wage growth	1.26	1.16	0.03

Source Osmani (2018)

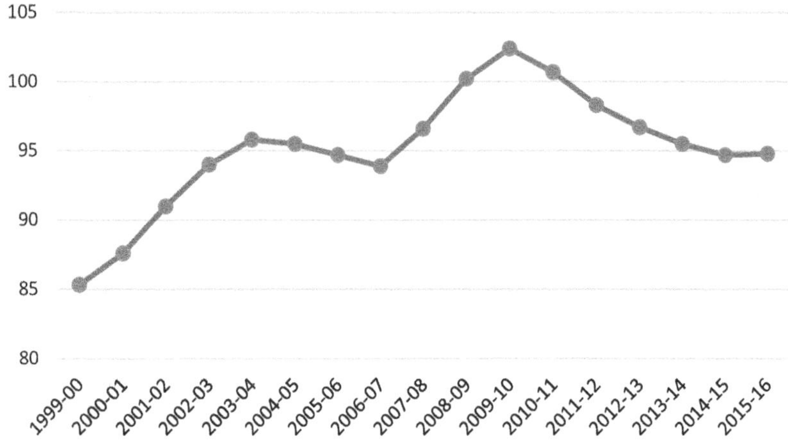

Fig. 7.2 Trend in real wages of unskilled workers (2010/2011 = 100), 1999–2016 (*Source* Osmani 2018)

implies the share of labour in the national income is decreasing consistently. This explains the trend of rising inequality as captured by other traditional measures like the Gini-coefficient and the Palma ratio.

Absence of Universal Social Security

The covid-19 crisis points out public goods provision failure in health, social security, etc. because of underfunding in value generating public provisioning. On the contrary, capital or exchange value generating was prioritised. This originates from a misconstrued ideology that the market is the organising principle and society is equivalent to the market. Rather, the market is subordinated to social, political and cultural norms. The use-value producing public goods is indispensable for augmenting capabilities of citizens to transform economic structure, political settlement and organisation of society. Under such circumstances, fulfilling the basic needs of citizens must be the foundation of the policy framework in any legitimate state. For instance, it is high time the private sector dependent healthcare system was extensively modified to create a universal national healthcare system.

A large population still remains without earnings, in hunger and without security. The initiatives existing under social safety nets are however ineffective, low coverage and marred with corruption. Social protection provisions are marred by problems of fragmentation, errors of inclusion and political patronage-based targeting (Razzaque 2020). Mismanagement and poor governance lead to error in selecting the beneficiaries. When the emerging new poor population is taken into consideration, the intended number of beneficiaries for these safety net programmes is inconsequential and results in an exclusion error. The lack of inclusive social safety nets has given rise to shortcomings in constructing the list of recipients, allowing a leeway for ineffective management of resources, extortion and abuse of power. Inclusion error comes into play when non-eligible recipients are selected for a programme (Fig. 7.3).

Conditions had deteriorated well ahead of the onset of the pandemic. The rate of poverty reduction had slowed down; in 2000–2010, the rate of decline was about 1.8 percentage points, which dropped to 1.2 percentage points in 2010–2016 (BBS 2019). Furthermore, a pre-covid-19 estimate by the World Bank suggests that the vulnerable population at risk of falling into poverty increased to 55% of the total population. The prevailing social protection and social safety nets are ineffectual. Those nominated as beneficiaries for the schemes, in many cases, are selected in terms of political affiliation, leaving the deserving unserved, with plenty of

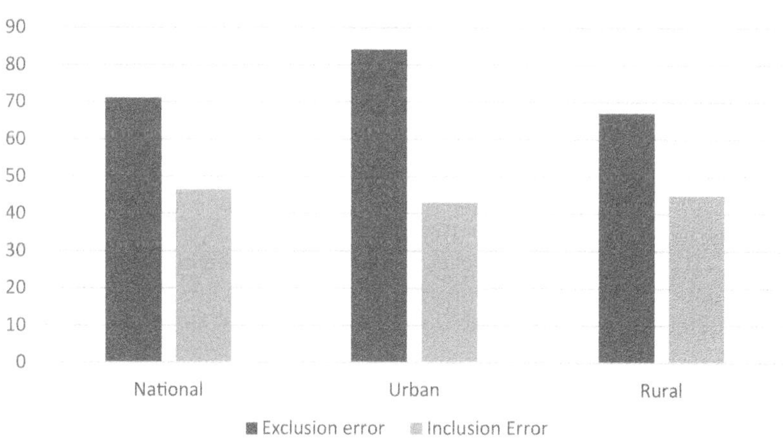

Fig. 7.3 Targeting error in social security system in Bangladesh (%) (*Source* Razzaque 2020)

cases of leakage and maladministration. Moreover, the aggregate figures presented in the budgets are misrepresentative. For example, the total earmarked in the 2019–2020 financial year is BDT 743.64 billion, of which pension for the 0.63 million retired government employees of is BDT 230.1 billion, a significant share (*New Age* 2020). These imply that the current approach of social safety net and protection schemes lack prudential planning and targeting of beneficiaries, and are inadequate to ensure a decent standard of living for all in a complete life cycle, in terms of consumption, safety, healthcare and allowances for vulnerability.

The government has announced BDT 321.66 billion in the proposed budget of 2020–2021 to the social security purpose. This accounts for a real change of 2.5% on the budget of the previous fiscal year. Under the circumstances of the economic crisis, this low social security budget will be difficult to distribute to the increased number of vulnerable groups (Unnayan Onneshan 2020).

Budget allocation in the social safety net sector is going to increase to BDT 955.74 billion which is 3.01% of GDP (Ministry of Finance 2019). However, a striking observation has been made which posits that this allocation also includes unrelated expenditures such as pensions and stipends, excluding which the real value reveals a fall from 9% to 7.6% share in the budget compared to fiscal year of 2019–2020 (*The Business Standard* 2020). The existing social protection and social safety nets are ineffective. Those selected as beneficiaries for the schemes, in many cases, are chosen politically, leaving the deserving unserved, with plenty of cases of leakage and mishandling. Moreover, the aggregate figures shown in the budgets are misleading.

Rising Trend in Income Inequality

In Bangladesh, the disparity between rich and poor, despite the economic growth, is growing over the years, leading to increased concentration and centralisation of wealth among the richest groups. In 1991–1992, the Gini coefficient in rural areas was 0.36, which reached 0.45 in 2016. Therefore, income inequality has risen largely in rural areas, due to the decline in real wages whereas some families gained more money mainly through remittances sent by their relatives. However, not every family can send their wards abroad as capital. Hence, comparatively solvent families get higher incomes and the poor remain unchanged. Besides, agricultural wages are very miniscule in rural regions. Farmers do not receive proper

Table 7.8 Income inequality (Gini coefficient) in Bangladesh 1991–2016

Year	*1991–1992*	*1995–1996*	*2000*	*2005*	*2010*	*2016*
National	0.39	0.43	0.45	0.47	0.46	0.48
Rural	0.36	0.38	0.39	0.43	0.43	0.45
Urban	0.4	0.44	0.5	0.5	0.45	0.5

Sources BBS (2011, 2019)

labour return, causing rural–urban migration. In the urban region, especially in the capital, Dhaka, there has been a large influx of new arrivals from rural regions, many of whom are unskilled and remain jobless, or earn hand to mouth from informal jobs. The inequality in urban areas saw large increases by 11.11% (from 0.45 to 0.5). It has been found that there is a high concentration of households in the richest quintile in the urban areas in Bangladesh (52.4%) as compared to the rural areas (BBS and UNICEF 2015) (Table 7.8).

Although the Gini-coefficient shows the magnitude of inequality at the aggregate level, it does not state much about the nature and dynamics of the concentration of wealth among the top and the bottom of the income groups. One of the notable limitations of the Gini coefficient measurement is that the aggregate index does not show if there is any change in the bottom of the distribution that may adversely affect the poor or raise the disparity between the poorest and the richest income groups. Moreover, the same coefficients in two different years may not indicate similar types of income distribution. For example, inequality in urban areas was 0.5 in all three years in 2000, 2005 and 2016, but it would be unreasonable to think that the nature of distribution remained identical in the whole period. There are alternative measures that provide deeper insights about the changes in the nature of inequality and the concentration of income.

Growing Concentration and Centralisation of Income

It is evident that the share of income has concentrated and centralised over the years in Bangladesh. The rich are getting richer in a system that makes the poor even poorer. Two measures provide vivid illustrations; one is the income share for different quintiles and the other is the Palma ratio. Decile distribution of income is the most commonly used measure to assess the pattern of distribution of percentage share of household income among ten decile groups.

First, the share of income by decile groups demonstrates that the distribution of income is becoming unequal in every year. The percentage share of household income for the first three deciles (group consisting of one tenth of population ranked by income share with Decile-1 at the bottom) has decreased from 2005 to 2016 at the national level for populations in both rural and urban areas. For instance, the income shares of the bottom 5% at the national level declined from 0.77% in 2005 and 0.78% in 2010 to 0.23% in 2016. (from 0.88 in 2005 to 0.25 in 2016 for rural areas and from 0.67 in 2005 to 0.27 in 2016 for the urban areas). On the contrary, the percentage share of the top income groups (i.e., the upper 5%) has increased from 2005 to 2016 at the national level for both rural and urban areas (for the rural area 24.25 from 22.93 and for the urban area 32.12 from 23.39) (Table 7.9).

Second, the Palma ratio, which measures the ratio of income share of the top 10% and the bottom 40% of the population in the income distribution, vividly shows the concentration of income in the country. The Palma ratio grew from 1.73 in 1985–1986 to 2.93 in 2016 and the ratio was 2.23 in 1995–1996 and 2.62 in 2005. This implies that the concentration of income has increased by 69.36% in the last three decades (Table 7.10).

Overall, inequality in the country is growing at an alarming rate, widening the gap between the richest and poorest sections of the society due to increasing income concentration by the top 10% of the population at the expense of the bottom 40% when the income shares of the middle 50% remained almost stagnated (decreased by 3.06%). While the income shares of the bottom 40% declined by 28.40% during the period from 1985–1986 to 2016, the income share captured by the top 10% increased by 21.30%.

Consumption and Nutritional Inequality

The inequality of consumption is considered with respect to individual's access to and affordability of minimum food requirements. Whether an individual has sufficient monetary capability or purchasing power to access and afford the specified amount of food determines the status of his/her wellbeing at the very basic level. Nutrition gap is mostly a reflection of income inequality and altogether it marginalises a large section

Table 7.9 Percentage share of income of households by decile groups and rural–urban regions

Household Income Group	*2005*			*2010*			*2016*		
	National	*Rural*	*Urban*	*National*	*Rural*	*Urban*	*National*	*Rural*	*Urban*
Bottom 5%	0.77	0.88	0.67	0.78	0.88	0.76	0.23	0.25	0.27
Decile-1	2.00	2.25	1.80	2.00	2.23	1.98	1.02	1.06	1.17
Decile-2	3.26	3.63	3.02	3.22	3.53	3.09	2.83	2.99	3.04
Decile-3	4.10	4.54	3.87	4.10	4.49	3.95	4.05	4.36	4.10
Decile-4	5.00	5.42	4.61	5.00	5.43	5.01	5.13	5.52	5.00
Decile-5	5.96	6.43	5.66	6.01	6.43	6.31	6.24	6.58	6.15
Decile-6	7.17	7.63	6.78	7.32	7.65	7.64	7.48	7.89	6.88
Decile-7	8.73	9.27	8.53	9.06	9.31	9.30	9.06	9.52	8.44
Decile-8	11.06	11.49	10.18	11.50	11.50	11.87	11.25	11.80	10.40
Decile-9	15.07	15.43	14.48	15.94	15.54	16.08	14.86	15.51	13.47
Decile-10	37.64	33.92	41.08	35.85	33.89	34.77	38.09	34.78	41.37
Top 5%	26.93	23.03	30.37	24.61	22.93	23.39	27.89	24.25	32.12

Source BBS (2011, 2019)

Table 7.10 The Palma ratio: a measure of concentration of income

Percentage share of income	*1985–1986*	*1995–1996*	*2005*	*2016*
Income share of bottom 40%	18.17	15.54	14.36	13.01
Income share of middle 50%	50.37	49.78	48.00	48.83
Income share of top 10%	31.46	34.68	37.64	38.16
Total	100.00	100.00	100.00	100.00
Palma ratio	1.73	2.23	2.62	2.93

Source Based on Osmani (2018)

Table 7.11 Trend of consumption inequality (Gini coefficient), 1995–2016

Year	*1995–1996*	*2000*	*2005*	*2010*	*2016*
National	0.302	0.307	0.310	0.320	0.324
Rural	0.265	0.271	0.278	0.275	0.300
Urban	0.363	0.368	0.353	0.338	0.330

Source BBS (2011, 2019)

of population in the country. The consumption inequality as measured by the Gini-coefficient shows a long-run increasing trend during the last two decades when inequality increased from 0.302 in 1995–1996 to 0.324 in 2016 (Table 7.11).

Similar to income inequality, the consumption Gini-coefficient is higher for urban residents compared to their rural counterparts. But during the most recent period since 2010, consumption inequality in urban areas declined by 2.37% whereas inequality in rural areas increased by 9.1% (from 0.275 in 2010 to 0.300 in 2016). In fact, since 1995–1996, the rise of inequality on a national level is entirely driven by increases in consumption inequality in the rural areas against a declining trend in urban areas.

Inequality in Food and Nutrition Intakes

Household survey data on food intake (grams) by the types of residence from 1995–1996 to 2016 indicates some variations based on rural urban divides (Table 7.12). In 2016, the estimated average amount of food consumed was 975.5 g per day at the national level, while the average

Table 7.12 Average per capita food intake (grams)

Year	*1995–1996*	*2000*	*2005*	*2010*	*2016*
National	913.8	893.1	947.8	1000.0	975.53
Rural	910.5	898.7	946.3	1005.2	974.32
Urban	930.8	870.7	952.1	985.5	978.74

Source BBS (2011, 2019)

amounts for rural and urban areas were 974.32 g and 978.74 g respectively. The most striking aspect observed from the data shows a decline in the food intake in the recent period since 2010 at the national level and for both rural and urban areas (a reduction of 24.47 g or −2.45% for national, 30.88 g or −3.07% for rural and 6.76 g or −0.67% for urban areas). It is observed that the average food intake (grams) in urban areas is higher than rural areas except in 2010 and 2000. Nevertheless, the data do not show any persistent pattern over the years.

Gender Inequality in Literacy and Education

Prevailing disparity between male and female in terms of literacy rates shows no sign of decline in recent years in Bangladesh. The trend of the literacy rate from the education household survey shows that the literacy rate of males is higher than it is for females (73% for male and 68.9% for female). The male literacy rate has increased from 59.3% to 73% during the period from 2011 to 2016, displaying a continuous rising trend. The female literacy rate also indicates the same trend, increasing from 55.1% to 68.9% during the same period (Fig. 7.4). However, the female literacy rate is still lower compared to that of male.

Bangladesh has performed well in advancing girls' education. The female enrolment rate in the primary and secondary levels of education has increased over the last decades due to certain initiatives taken by the government including the introduction of conditional cash transfer schemes (Al-Samarrai 2008). The enrolment of females in the tertiary level, however, has not increased at the same pace. Both enrolment and completion rates in primary education are higher for girls. In the secondary level, despite higher enrolment rate, the completion rate for girls is lower and the drop-out rate is higher (Shilpi et al. 2017). For example, the drop-out rates in grade 6 and 7 are lower for girls than for

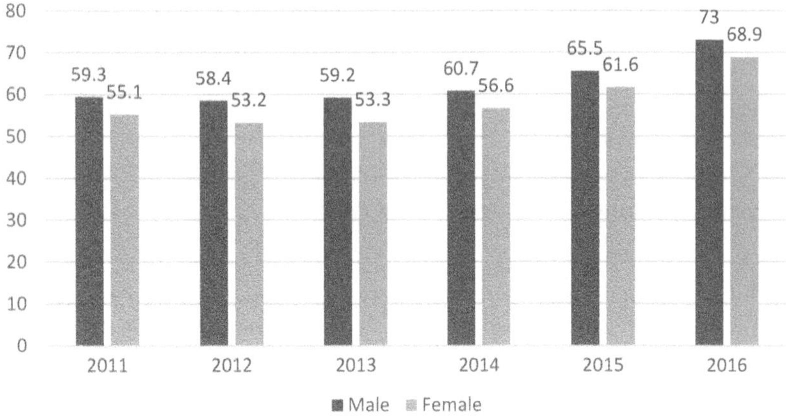

Fig. 7.4 Literacy rate (sex) for proportion of population aged 7 or above (*Source* BBS 2015)

boys, but the rate of drop-outs in grade 8 to grade 10 is much higher for girls (i.e., at grade 10, drop-out rate for girls is 18.52% against 8.78% for boys) (Table 7.13).

Gender disparity is more visible at the university level in the country. Only 33.94% of university students, including both public and private universities, are female while the proportion of female university teachers is 26.46% (BANBEIS 2019). The percentage of males with graduate and equivalent level of education is 2.35% against 1.00% for female. Further, the percentage of postgraduate and diploma/vocational degree holders is 1.19% and 0.44% for males against 0.41% and 0.22% for females respectively.

Table 7.13 Grade wise drop-out rate for boys and girls at secondary level in 2015

	Grade 6		*Grade 7*		*Grade 8*		*Grade 9*		*Grade 10*	
	Boys	*Girls*	*Boys*	*Girls*	*Boys*	*Girls*	*Boys*	*Girls*	*Boys*	*Girls*
2015	6.64	5.49	1.85	6.41	16.83	21.07	4.64	4.76	8.78	18.52

Source BANBEIS (2016)

Gender Disparity in Participation and Earnings

The labour force is defined by the population aged 15 years or older who contribute or are available to contribute to the production of goods and services in the country (BBS 2018). In Bangladesh, the female participation rate is significantly lower than the male participation rate in the labour market. In 2016–2017, the female labour force participation rate was 36.3% and the male labour force participation rate of 80.5% (Fig. 7.5). While labour force participation rate for males is declining gradually over the years, the rate for females has increased slightly in 2016–2017 compared to 2010 level.

A segregation by gender and education reveals higher participation rates for females with tertiary levels of education which is 56.9% (89.4% for male with same level of education) compared to the rates for females with no primary education which is 38.1% in 2016–2017 (Fig. 7.6). This implies increasing level of education for females might offset gender disparity in the labour market participation rates.

Turning to the issue of gender disparity in income, the trends of average monthly incomes by sex from the various labour force surveys show that the male average income is higher than the average income earned by females in the survey years 2013, 2015–2016 and 2016–2017

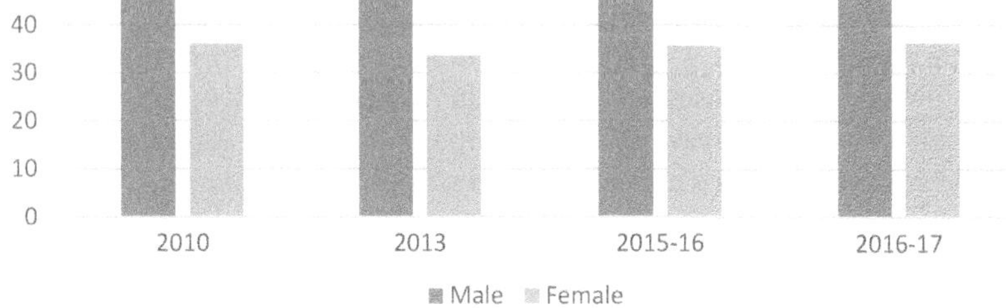

Fig. 7.5 Labour force participation rate by gender 2010–2017 (*Source* BBS, Various Labour Force Surveys 2010, 2013, 2015–2016, 2016–2017)

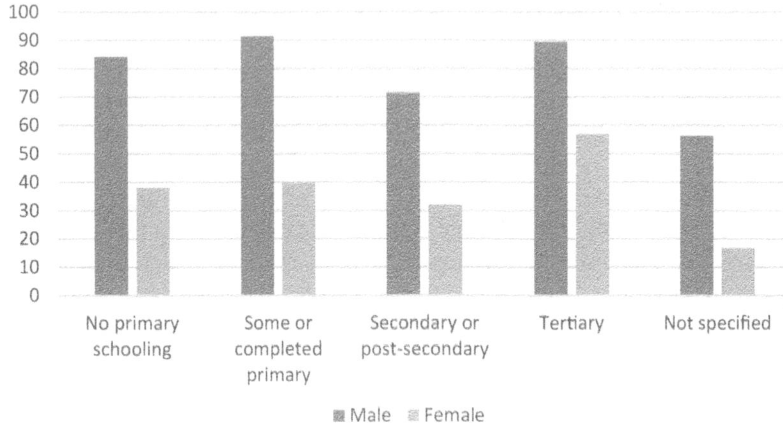

Fig. 7.6 Labour force participation rate by gender and education level, 2016–2017 (*Source* BBS 2018)

respectively. In 2016–2017, average monthly incomes for females was BDT 12,3000 compared to BDT 13,600 for males. Quite strikingly, the gap between males and females in terms of average monthly earnings has been growing over the recent years. In 2013, females on average earned 4.31% less income per month than their male counterparts, whereas in 2015–2016 and 2016–2017, average income for females was 7.63% and 9.56% lower than males (Fig. 7.7).

In Bangladesh, there is a noticeable wage gap between rural and urban areas. Average monthly income in rural areas is lower for the same profession (Table 7.14). Urban areas are developed in terms of infrastructure and opportunities than the rural areas of Bangladesh. As a result, the gross income of urban areas is higher than rural areas. Therefore, the average monthly income increases at a higher rate in urban areas.

Regardless of the areas, male counterparts get higher wages than their female counterparts in similar types and roles of employment.

Fiscal Policy—Dependence on Regressive Taxes

An integral part of the fiscal policy, tax structure and revenue mobilisation, decides how various types of taxes are collected and then disbursed as benefits to the marginalised and deprived communities in order to

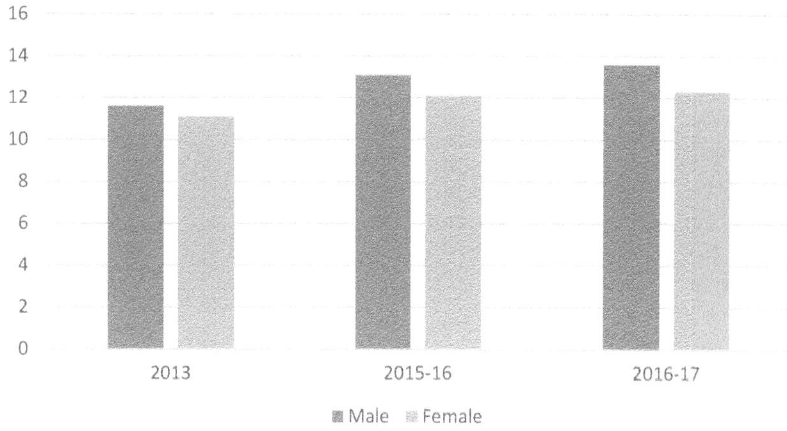

Fig. 7.7 Trend in average monthly income (in thousand BDT), 2013–2017 (*Source* BBS (2017, 2018), Various Labour Force Surveys 2013, 2015–2016, 2016–2017)

Table 7.14 Wage gap in a different area for different occupation (average monthly income)

Year	*2013*		*2015*		*2016–2017*	
Location	*Rural*	*Urban*	*Rural*	*Urban*	*Rural*	*Urban*
Monthly income	10,294	13,605	11,527	15,066	11,608	15,912

Source: BBS (2016) (Household Income and Expenditure Survey)

redistribute income. Around 89.5% of the total revenue earned by the government is sourced from tax revenue (Ministry of Finance 2018). Taxes primarily include direct taxes and indirect taxes- the former include taxes on personal and corporate income, and the later includes customs duties and value added taxes that are levied on expenditure regardless of the individual's income.

During 2009–2017, the Government's revenue was 76% of the total Government expenditure in Bangladesh (UNCTAD 2020). During 2002–2008, it was 77% Least developed countries like Afghanistan (98%), Angola (95%), Bhutan (99%), and Cambodia (86%) are ahead of Bangladesh with respect to revenue as a share of government expenditure

Table 7.15 Tax and non-tax revenue

Year	*Tax revenue*	*Non-tax revenue*
2010–2011	79,052	16,135
2011–2012	94,754	22,279
2012–2013	116,824	22,846
2013–2014	130,178	26,493
2014–2015	140,676	22,695
2015–2016	155,399	22,000
2016–2017	192,261	26,239
2017–2018	232,202	27,252

Source Ministry of Finance (2018)

during 2009–2017 period (UNCTAD 2020). The low revenue collection results in low public spending in the productive sector (Table 7.15).

The manner in which taxation is structured may have implications on the level of inequality in the economy. The concept of 'optimal taxation' was introduced in economics to derive the equity/efficiency trade-off that a policymaker may encounter when designing a 'direct redistribution system' that concentrates on providing a high level of subsidies to the poorest while 'charging the financial cost to the richest' (Bargain and Spadaro 2008). This is due to the fact that taxes may be progressive or regressive in nature; progressive taxes become more incident as the individual or firm's income increases. On the other hand, regressive taxes are more incident for lower levels of incomes as it constitutes a bigger proportion of income. Hence, regressive taxes are more incident on individuals with lower incomes. Therefore, in order to identify whether the tax policy may in fact contribute to inequality, it is necessary to determine the nature of the tax structure i.e. if the taxes are primarily sourced from regressive taxes, the structure is not equitable or fair (Table 7.16).

Similarly, another fiscal instrument is the national budget, which may also have implications on the level of inequality. Progressive taxes are mostly used with the intent of redistribution of income from the rich to the poor through the provision of various benefits and financial assistances to deprived populations. If the tax revenue is not effectively mobilised in order to ensure transmission of redistributive income to the poorer populations, much of the intent of tax collection becomes futile. If redistribution is not taking place, incomes remain unequal and markets remain inequitable. Apart from the self-financed projects of autonomous groups, the total size of the Revised Annual Development Programme (RADP)

Table 7.16 Tax revenue

Year	*VAT (local)*	*VAT (import)*	*Total indirect tax*	*Income tax*	*Total direct tax*
2012–2013	26,367.26	14,815.16	71,441.27	37,120.65	37,710.46
2013–2014	29,252.11	15,291.31	76,971.33	43,207.27	43,848.52
2014–2015	32,290.13	17,690.47	87,346.90	47,477.40	48,353.80
2015–2016	34,862.82	20,587.14	101,279.67	51,328.92	52,347.29
2016–2017	38,287.76	25,561.09	117,844.29	52,754.93	53,812.15
2017–2018	47,171.80	29,367.76	140,711.06	64,548.26	65,695.19

Source National Board of Revenue

of 2017–2018 is BDT 1483.81 billion, compared to BDT 571.2 billion in 2012–2013 (Planning Commission 2019). In 2017–2018, income tax revenue stood at BDT 645.48 billion, compared to BDT 371.2 billion in 2012–2013. Therefore, a key stability issues arises as, over the years, RADP increased by 160% whilst income tax grew only by 73.9%, implying that despite a significant increase in development expenditure, it was not entirely matched by an increase in income tax, indicating that the redistribution of income has been relatively low.

The tax structure may lead to inequality in other ways as well, apart from its regressive nature. Bangladesh has a narrow tax base that hinders revenue mobilisation, and a low tax to GDP ratio compared to neighbouring countries. Lower tax revenue further hinders the ability of the government expenditure budget to implement a comprehensive and far-reaching welfare benefit scheme. Wealth inequality, alongside income inequality, worsens as wealth is inherited by future generations, leading to humongous accumulation of wealth over the years by a small affluent population. To make matters worse, the small affluent group is not adequately taxed, thus creating a concentration of wealth in the hands of a few—the rich get richer, the poor become poorer.

Low Tax-GDP Ratio

Bangladesh has one of the lowest tax-to-GDP ratios in the region. In fiscal 2017–2018, the tax-to-GDP ratio was 10.9% (Ministry of Finance 2018), which is far below the developing country average (Table 7.17).

Total revenue collection is estimated at BDT. 3780 billion in the proposed national budget for fiscal year 2019–2020. Of the total estimated revenue for the next fiscal year, BDT 3300 billion will be

Table 7.17 Tax to GDP ratio

Year	*Tax to GDP ratio (%)*
2010–2011	8.63
2011–2012	9.12
2012–2013	9.74
2013–2014	9.69
2014–2015	9.28
2015–2016	8.97
2016–2017	10.28
2017–2018	10.90

Source Ministry of Finance (2018)

collected through the National Board of Revenue (NBR) (Ministry of Finance 2020). On the contrary, total direct tax revenue, which primarily consisted of income tax, stood at BDT 656.95 billion in 2017–2018. The promise to make an almost 400% leap in collecting income tax revenue poses severe stability issues, especially in the absence of significant expansion of the tax base, stronger tax compliance or other tax structure reforms.

New Poor Driven by Covid-19

Being a longstanding development challenge in Bangladesh, the rate of reduction in poverty had reached a slowdown prior to the onset of the pandemic, exposing an inefficacy of existing poverty eradication policies. This highlights the incongruences in the poverty reduction trajectory of the country. In addition, for the first time since 1992, the country is expected to experience an upward movement in the poverty rate owing to the contraction of the economy due to shutdown of economic activities causing income erosion for many, increased economically inactive population in the informal sector, distress in the rural economy and an influx of returnee migrant workers facing unemployment. Several communities are expected to face the effects of dispossession, leading to pauperisation for the marginalised, vulnerable sections of the population. The process of dispossession affects vulnerable populations disproportionately which is often not reflected in national, simple ratio indicators such as national poverty headcount; an inquiry into the trends of how sectorial and regional poverty has changed over the years, and at the onset of the pandemic, is more likely to reveal the intricacies required for a rethinking in poverty dynamics.

The disproportionate effects on communities without entitlements in the post-pandemic context indicate a shift in the thinking and discourse of poverty as a development challenge. Income erosion and uncertainty of livelihoods has affected the working population not limited to the informal sector—those employed in the formal sector faced income cuts or were sent on furlough with no subsequent financial support from the government. The population living closely above the poverty line, also predominantly involved in the informal sector leaving them at risk of unexpected income loss or unfair dismissals, faced shocks to income and livelihood, along with health crises posed by the virus, because of the economic shutdown, causing them to fall back into poverty. Thus, emerged the new poor population, leading to an upward movement in the poverty rate. The inclusion of the new poor represents an evident pauperisation of communities, and will hence require a paradigm shift in policy thinking regarding poverty and targeted interventions for eradication.

An aggravation of the inequalities is more evident in the policies undertaken to combat the economic ills of the pandemic such as stimulus for large businesses and financial benefits for government officials, which is likely to result in greater accumulation of wealth by elitist networks, while lower income groups lose out even further. Small businesses find it difficult to meet the terms and conditions of drawing out loans provided for them in the stimulus package, while the informal sector remains deprived of any fiscal stimulus at all for being unregistered. The mounting inequalities in the economy were largely led by the differentiation between classes being aggravated leading to polarisation between communities. In circumstances where incomes were decreasing for the existing low-income population, they were increasing for the affluent classes. Vulnerable non-poor households are falling back under poverty, fragmenting the middle class into a new poor population, which is likely to worsen the Gini coefficient, crossing the fault line of 0.5 (Unnayan Onneshan 2020).

Inequality Propelled by Covid-19

As discussed in earlier chapters, return on labour has been decreasing due to the prevailing low level of skill and productivity of labour and a declining real wage growth over the years, whilst return on capital has experienced increments at the same time. This has led to greater accumulation of capital by the wealthy, and the decline in real wages has worsened the impoverishment of low-income populations. Inequality had already been mounting in the pre-pandemic context, and it has only been aggravated due to disproportionate ramifications on different communities of the pandemic and economic shutdown. Pauperisation, or the emergence of the new poor, has been discussed in the stability conditions. This section focuses on the later stages of the dispossession—differentiation and polarisation.

Differentiation is the mechanism through which the pauperisation is taking place—presumably through impacts of policy or systemic reasons on vertical and horizontal inequality. Vertical inequality refers to the differences between individuals and households that may be aggravated by ill-designed policies that produce lop-sided ramifications for different income groups, often preferentially serving the elite networks. Horizontal inequality refers to the feature of unequal societies that discriminate against certain groups based on distinct characteristics such as gender, class or race. The differential impact of the pandemic-induced ills is likely to lead to polarisation between the classes. Widespread income erosion and unemployment owing to the contraction of the economy is likely to push down returns on labour even lower, compared to its pre-pandemic level, whilst capitalists who were equipped to utilise the gap in the market and expand their businesses in the physically disjointed sector have experienced greater revenues. The apparent divergence between the trends in income of the two groups are likely to take form in the K-shaped growth path (Fig. 7.8).

A power imbalance is evident between the groups as stimulus packages were largely designed in favour of large industries and clientelist networks, as many small businesses find themselves unable to avail the bank loan support intended for SMEs. The lack of job security and social protection for the informal sector which employs almost 87% of the employed population in the country is deteriorating the conditions for the labour force. A prognosis of the stakeholders in the state-provided financial stimulus packages exhibits a possible imbalance in the powers exercised by different groups yielding largely non-equalising results (Table 7.18).

The decision-making in this regard is the state provided stimulus package—how the power relations influenced the preferences in allocation. Each of the stakeholders ideally has different positions of power i.e. from above, lateral or from below. Poor and low-income households

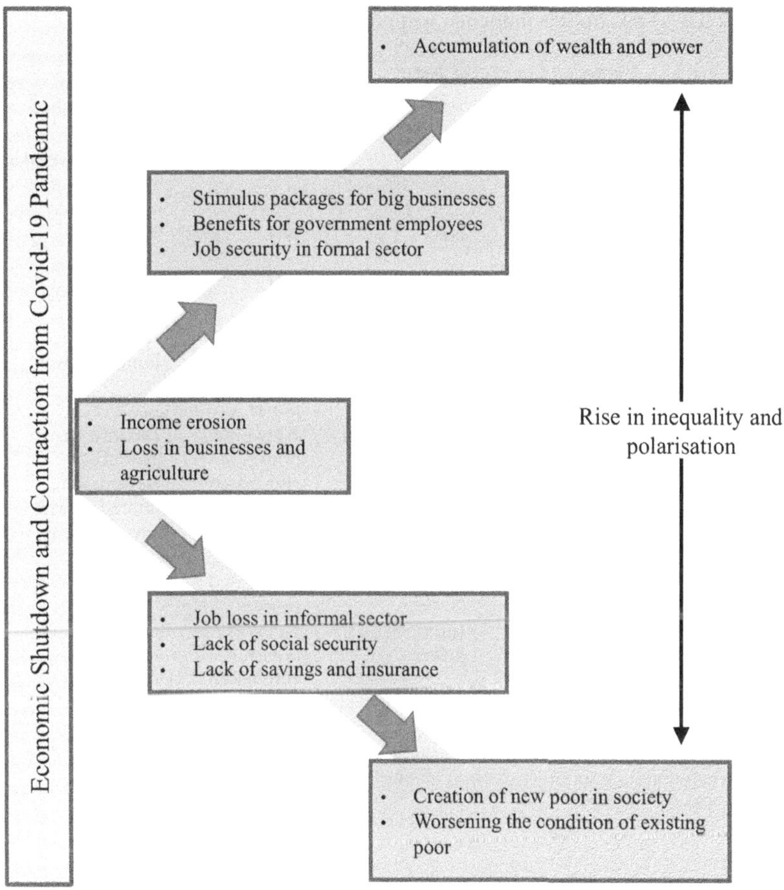

Fig. 7.8 K-shaped growth path (*Source* Prepared by author)

generally are characterised as having power from below, among which they have a dearth in the most forms of power. On the other hand, stakeholders such as large industries or clientelist groups hold more lateral sources of power, whilst public service officials and the government may exercise more power from above. Stimulus packages were designed for groups with political leverage, or the powerful elites, and often did not reach the employees at the lower tiers.

Table 7.18 Stakeholder influence mapping

Stakeholder	*Forms and sources of power*			
	Power over	*Power to*	*Power with*	*Power within*
Low-income households	Counter hegemonic power	NIL	NIL	Self-empowerment and voice
Households in poverty	NIL	NIL	NIL	NIL
Farmers	NIL	NIL	NIL	NIL
Informal sector	NIL	NIL	NIL	NIL
Large industries	Coercive power	Collaborative power	Networked power, elite-based power	Accountable, limited power
Public service officials	Centralised or despotic power	Infrastructural power	Networked power, elite-based power	Identity based power, accountable, limited power
Clientelist networks	Coercive power	Collaborative power, Infrastructural power	Networked power, elite-based power	Identity based power
Government	Centralised or despotic power	Infrastructural power	Networked power, elite-based power	Identity based power

Note Power over = to influence actions of others; Power to = to have agency; Power with = to use collective action; Power within = sense of dignity and empowerment
Source Prepared by author

The tainted focus of the stimulus packages serves as an example of how the power dynamics mediate differentiation and eventually polarisation. The combination of collaborative and infrastructural power of clientelist groups allows them to influence decision-making to a large extent. Collaborative power refers to the power of using collective action to realise a shared goal between groups, with or without the state. Infrastructural power refers to the power of the state or political authorities to influence the actions of others for a definite objective or interest. At the same time, a shortcoming of power networked at grassroots of, say, farmers, renders them feeble in the face of meddling by intermediaries.

Table 7.19 Summary table of risks and fragility

Indicators	*Risks and fragility*
Income and consumption	Decline in real wage has reduced income and consumption over time Lack of universal basic income for shock absorption capacity Sudden job loss or unfair dismissal in informal sector during the pandemic has caused income erosion Increasing food prices has waned the real income for people Lack of non-erosive coping responses will likely decrease future income earning potential and consumption Pandemic-induced income erosion has caused impoverishment for vulnerable non-poor households Returnee migrant workers will negatively affect consumption behaviour in rural areas as remittance helped increase consumption Contraction of economy will dampen income generating potential
Return on labour	There is a decline in productivity in agricultural sector and hence return on labour decreased Low level of skills results in lower return from labour Low private investment is likely to decrease productivity of labour Increased return on capital increases illicit capital outflow, whilst little is reinvested in business
Human capital	High out-of-pocket expenditure on health indicates the lack of affordable and accessible healthcare Unexpected health crises may lead to catastrophic health expenditure for uninsured populations Under-nutrition, stunted growth dampens future productivity of the labour force Lack of quality education results in lower level of skills in the labour force Gender disparity in education and earnings result in disproportionate income generating potential
Policy and power	Absence of social security, and inadequate social safety nets are inconsequential to bringing real improvement in wellbeing Lack of access to formal financial services leaves a large population without access to credit, and dependent on informal borrowing sources Greater accumulation of wealth by the few, especially in the post-pandemic context, as larger firms were able to innovate and take advantage of the unsaturated physically disjointed sectors Stimulus packages were designed to serve mainly clientelist networks Imbalance of power in stakeholders' influence on the allocation of fiscal support and financial stimulus packages has skewed focus towards the needs of large industries at the expense of smaller businesses and marginalised communities Short-sighted nature of policies, particularly the dependence on regressive taxes, affect the lower income groups more disproportionately, eroding future earning potential

(continued)

Table 7.19 (continued)

Indicators	*Risks and fragility*
Recovery	New poor population is likely to emerge as non-poor households fall back into poverty due to shutdown and contraction of the economy Inequality will worsen due to income erosion and lack of shock mitigating measures for low-income groups, particularly in the informal sector Lack of focus on small and medium enterprises is likely to lead to greater loss-making and unemployment Climate shocks and displacement for uninsured population will lead to overturning decades of improvement in standard of living if impacts of shock exposure are not minimised Idiosyncratic shocks such as health crises for uninsured population may lead to adopting erosive coping responses, causing impoverishment, owing to a lack of universal healthcare Prolonged systemic shocks (e.g. COVID-19) are a combination of idiosyncratic and covariate shocks which can shudder the structures of economy and society if protective measures are not put in place Deficit in governance and accountability lead to a weak social contract and active citizenship, making compliance and recovery a bigger challenge

Transformability Conditions

Achievement of significant advances in the indicators of poverty and inequality may be ensured through transforming the stability conditions to be better able to withstand in the face of systemic shocks. The transformability conditions for poverty and inequality constitute policies of active restraint consisting of public goods provision, redistributive actions, macro-financial interventions and structural policy reforms; institutional provisioning for labour skill enhancement; and policies for aiding coping mechanisms for poor and vulnerable non-poor households.

Policies of Active Restraint

The economic shutdown provided a leeway for businesses to modify their models to adapt to the conditions of the new normal. The shift was observed through an expansion of business in physically disjointed sectors. The capacity to adapt to the new normal has favoured the capitalist, who could utilise new avenues of profits during a contraction in the economy, further heightening returns to capital vis-a-vis to labour, leading to a greater concentration of wealth. During the period of 1991–2006 the country experienced a form of competitive clientelism that was favourable for increasing labour returns. From 2006 onwards however the state has been evidently moving towards a relatively more authoritarian clientelism, that has increased returns to capital proportionately more than labour returns. Real wage growth has in fact decreased in the wake of the pandemic, from 6.56% in January to 5.82% in July (BBS 2020). A more authoritarian clientelist atmosphere combined with a conducive environment for expansion of larger industries reflects an increase in losses for smaller businesses, the informal sector and labour returns in general. The phenomenon indicates a worsening of inequality between higher and lower income groups in society, as high-income groups accumulate greater wealth, whilst low-income households lose out due to inadequate social security and coping mechanisms.

The recovery path of the economy from the fallouts of the pandemic is therefore likely to assume a *K*-shaped path, as income cohorts diverge while clientelist networks exploit the imbalance of power between the groups. The impacts of dispossession on the low-income population and the middle class inherently centralises the possession of power around the clientelist networks. Resources or the forms of capital are concentrated in the hands of a few by design. Inequality is increasing due to systemic reasons induced by the pandemic.

The business-as-usual policies act as a form of active inaction which accelerates the rise in inequality, and hence polarisation, whilst a paradigm shift by design could act as active restraint that curbs the degree of aggravation of inequality and polarisation. In order to hold the reins over inequality in the long run, it is imperative for the state to adopt policies of active restraint which will help curtail the inevitable deterioration in inequality.

Institutional Provisioning for Skilled Labour

The declining real wage growth discussed in the earlier sections indicates towards disproportionate impacts on unskilled labour particularly. The level of skill prevailing in Bangladesh is largely of primary standard, as discussed in Chapter 6. Most of the labour force is of the lowest skill level category, owing to a large deficiency of investment and policy focus on vocational education and skill-development training programmes. A significant portion of the national budget on education and training is spent behind payment of staff salaries and infrastructure development, leaving little for improvement of quality of education.

Labour remains trapped in a lower tier of skills thus resulting in a vicious cycle of low wages and thus lower potential for future earnings. The vicious cycle of the dearth of skills sets poor and vulnerable non-poor households into a vicious cycle of lower income, lower social opportunities, lower nutrition and productivity and eventually lower standard of living. Therefore, in order for the conditions of poverty and inequality to be transformable, it is crucial for transformation in policies for skill enhancement—strengthening institutions focused primarily on training and vocational education will lead to the development of youth capabilities, augmenting future potential for earning and higher real wage growth.

Public Financing for Coping

Transforming dynamics in poverty and inequality will also necessitate a shift in conventional policy measures. The economic shutdown has revealed the extent of vulnerability of low-income populations in the country as many such households have been pushed back into poverty.

A negative shock is a risk that materialises as a manifestation of pre-existing vulnerability to the particular risk. Low-income households with minimal savings and assets to fall back on, often may have to resort to coping mechanisms that are erosive for future sustenance. Erosive coping responses such as borrowing from informal sources at exorbitantly high interest rates or sale of productive assets may be adopted by households for immediate liquidity to cover shortfall in expenses, but these responses may be responsible for eroding future disposable incomes. This is because the high interest rates will need to be paid from future income, and the sale of productive assets will diminish potential future earnings from the asset. Unless income generating capabilities are widely expanded for these households, they may face a permanent decrease in income, and even pauperisation.

The capability of vulnerable households to absorb these shocks largely depend on available choices of coping responses. Better shock absorption against uninsured shocks is facilitated by dissaving, sale of buffer stock, sale of non-productive liquid assets, borrowing from formal sources with reasonable interest rates. On the other hand, responses such as decreasing food consumption will hamper nutrition and health security, producing gendered differentiation as women will likely absorb more of the shortfall in consumption; informal borrowing and sale of livestock will dampen future consumption and earnings, despite temporary relief. This section discusses the inequalities in these indicators to depict how the consequences of earlier shocks have manifested in inequalities other than income. It is evident that the necessary conditions for survival of households such as income or health are insubstantial and susceptible to unprecedented shocks, implying that the economic development of the low-income population is brittle to support the households against unforeseen calamities.

Strengthening Coping Mechanisms for Climate Displaced Communities

Areas in Bangladesh, particularly coastal regions, remain more vulnerable to climate shocks such as cyclones, tidal waves, river erosion, salinity intrusion, crop failure, landslides and flooding. These together constitute as covariate shocks that affect all households in the community as a whole, whilst idiosyncratic shocks such as health crises or death of livestock affects a single household. As most of these communities remain uninsured against climate shocks, exposure to a natural calamity therefore results in widespread loss of assets, resources and shelter, displacing entire communities from their habitat. The lack of restorative measures for shelter and income-generating opportunities compels most households to migrate to other regions in search of life and livelihood.

Resilience stemming from the community is often weak as well. The effectiveness of the ability to cope with shocks also depend on geographical location, socio-economic status and access to microfinance (Santos et al. 2011). Households may often pursue coping responses such as informal borrowing, dissaving or reduction in consumption for idiosyncratic shocks. However, for covariate shocks, risk pooling for coping is not viable because all households will require the pool of funds at once. Poorer households are more prone to facing covariate shocks such as natural disasters which implies that coping without external cash support may not be possible (Santos et al. 2011).

Government intervention is primarily required in regions that experience natural calamities, impoverishment and displacement for rehabilitation and revival of employment opportunities in the area. For regions particularly vulnerable to climate shocks, policies may be put in place for greater adaptability and state provided allowances that build resilience of these population allowing them to self-insure against such risks. The recurrence of certain climate shocks and subsequent adverse impacts are also the precursor to underlying issues in structural capability in climate change adaptability and protection. For these populations to be able to smoothen their consumption over time, and therefore sustainably maintain their household and livelihoods will require policies aimed at risk reduction and insurance.

Social Security in the Post-pandemic Era

Bangladesh performs very poorly in terms of providing social protection to its people, ranked 78th out of 82 countries in a new Social Mobility Index (WEF 2020). Social protection provisions are currently stained by problems of fragmentation, errors of inclusion and political patronage-based targeting (Razzaque 2020).

The unsettled issue is, in case of rising official figures of people living below poverty which may increase to new heights after repatriation of more migrant workers, coverage and scope of social security may require reconsideration. Will the social safety net scheme be able to help the new poor to come out of poverty due to the covid-19 pandemic? Stimulus packages were designed for groups with political leverage, or the powerful elites, and often did not reach the employees at the grassroots. Poor and low-income households generally are characterised as having power from below, among which they have a dearth in the most forms of power. On the other hand, stakeholders such as large industries or clientelist groups hold more lateral sources of power, whilst public service officials and the government may exercise more power from above. The imbalance in power may lead to the needs of the new poor population to be left unaddressed in formulating social security interventions in the post pandemic context.

A permanent life cycle based, household-centred fully-fledged social security programme should include allowances for new mothers, women, elderly, and the differently-abled, along with benefits for child education, healthcare, basic income grants and climate-risk adaptation. Nevertheless, the allocated proportion of GDP for the recent budget proves that a fully-fledged social security programme is indeed financially feasible for public provision in Bangladesh, if unrelated expenditures are minimised and life-cycle based allowances are introduced. Social security in Thailand caters to old age, disability and survivors through social insurance and a national savings fund, sickness and maternity through universal coverage and social insurance, unemployment and family allowances through social insurance systems, funded by the government, employers and social insurance. In Germany, old age allowances are provided through social insurance and need-based social assistance, healthcare is insured by a statutory sickness insurance system and family insurance, with long term care benefits (Social Security Administration 2018). In the budget of 2020–2021 in Bangladesh, the state proposed a bolstered social security allocation which amounts to 9% of GDP (Ministry of Finance 2019). This allocation however also includes unrelated expenditures such as pensions and stipends, excluding which the real value reveals a fall from 9% to 7.6% share in the budget compared to 2019–2020 (Hussain 2020).

Sustainability Conditions

The stability and transformability conditions for poverty and inequality highlight the gaps in improvement of the performance of policies in each regard and the factors that required strengthening in order to curb fragility of the advances in the poverty and inequality due to exposure to unfavourable circumstances. The sustainability conditions further stress on the requirements of the economy in this regard in order to ensure that the improvements in poverty and inequality are long-standing and will continue favourably in the foreseeable future. In this section, the chapter focuses on the policies for resilience, reforms in non-equalising policies, the social contract and living in harmony with nature that are required for sustaining the achievements of poverty eradication policies, and active restraint policies for curbing inequality.

Policies for Resilience

The onset of a pandemic has served as a reminder and also a lens to view the discrepancies in the economy particularly in state provision of public goods for every citizen. The economic shutdown led to grave uncertainties for vulnerable households, facing income erosion, lack of fiscal support and thus an absence of coping responses, leaving households in turmoil and a fight for survival. Prior to the pandemic, public goods provision had been tainted with inadequate budgetary allocation over the years particularly on education, healthcare and social security, while the provision of these turned more market-centric, depriving lower income groups of access.

The state of public good provisions acts as the precursor to the discussion on resilience of citizens in absorbing an unforeseen systemic shock. Resilience refers to the capability of individuals or households to recuperate from or adapt to the disrupting effects of shocks in terms of income and consumption. Even prior to the pandemic, social safety nets were meagre in comparison to the needs of the people. While around 87% of the labour force is employed in the informal sector, they remain excluded from labour protection laws and minimum wage legislations. Combined with a lack of social security allotments, credit and financial assistance, the capability of households to recover from the ills of an exogenous shock is curbed owing to the dearth of social protection policies.

Much of the adaptability, hence resilience, of vulnerable households in Bangladesh stems from their own practice and experiences of dealing with earlier shocks. Coping responses largely range between decreasing food expenditure and informal borrowing from friends or relatives for idiosyncratic shocks such as health crises or sudden loss of income. These coping mechanisms reflect an initiative of individuals or households to recover from the shock exposure, rather than being policy-led mechanisms such as social security allowances, basic income grants or a fiscal stimulus. During the shutdown, only around 14% of low-income households received government cash support, while 5% received support from NGOs (Rahman and Matin 2020).

Policies for creating resilience addressing systemic shocks should not be focussed solely on efficiency and short-term profitability, but rather on the groups most affected by the shock, how policies targeted at these groups will affect others and in the long run, the origins and underlying incongruences of the systemic shock (Hynes et al. 2020). For vulnerable populations in Bangladesh, resilience towards systemic shocks was built on their own efforts in the absence of state directed policies for strengthening and equipping the population to cope with exposure to shocks. However, for the tendency of erosive coping responses to curtail future earning potential and for resilience to be longstanding in the face of future systemic shocks, a shift in policy focus is required. A move from short-term policies for damage control to more long-term policies for building system resilience, by effectively putting into place institutions that can withstand and recover from inevitable future shocks is necessary.

Accountable and Equalising State

A crucial marker of the well-being of most citizens is the state of a country's macro economy, often told by the level of unemployment and inflation. When macroeconomic policies fail to control unemployment or inflation, it is usually the population with the lowest incomes who suffer the most, implying that policies may indeed have inequitable consequences for the population. Both fiscal and monetary policies may, therefore, have destabilising consequences on the economy leading to inequality. This section focuses on the fiscal policy, specifically the stability issues in the tax structure, tax collection and revenue mobilisation through public expenditure, the conditions required for the variables to be transformable and hence promote sustainability.

The real challenges facing today are that incomes are eroding, jobs are insecure, poverty is mounting, inequality is escalating, unemployment is worsening, and control over life is weakening, amidst the uncertainties posed by the economic slowdown. The untold anxieties probing through the minds of the people revolve around motivations larger than economic growth itself; the pandemic has brought to the forefront the inquiries into the nature of growth, the mode of achieving growth and whom the growth will cater for.

The covid-19 crisis has pinpointed the fractures in the structures of economy, politics and society in functioning in coordination with the others. Citizens are thus more likely to expect accountability from the state in ensuring taxpayers' money is allocated in providing benefits with a focus on equalisation.

Strengthening Social Contract

Many countries with high rates of taxes and social contribution burden as well as a relatively weak legal frameworks encourage a sizeable informal economy. This is particularly worse in developing countries where business can be more profitable if they remain informal. In Bangladesh, the total corporate tax rate as a percentage of profit is 32.5% (Schwab and Sala-i-Martín 2015) and the personal income tax is around 10–25% based on level of income (NBR Bangladesh). It is evident from research conducted by Schneider (2002) that a high level of tax and social security burden induce people to operate in the informal sector. Large and medium enterprises of Bangladesh generally keep a portion of their operations informal due to high tax rates, complex procedure of paying tax liability and often a weak legal enforcement (Hassan 2017).

Tax evasion in Bangladesh has been a perennial problem for fiscal policy implementation. Income tax is one of the major components of tax revenue. Tax revenue is largely utilised for development expenditure and investment on education, infrastructure and public welfare programmes such as public healthcare, social safety nets, unemployment benefits, special allowances, and public housing. Other non-development expenditure using tax revenue involves transfer payments to government employees and debt payments. Since the revenue generated from income taxes is regarded as the means of redistributing income, it can act as a sustainable and stable source for financing development in the country and reduce inequalities.

As of June 2018, there are approximately 3.5 million tax identification number (TIN) holders, of which only 1.95 million submitted tax returns, showing a significant curtailing of the government's capacity to redistribute income equitably (National Board of Revenue 2019). Moreover, the problem does not end here. It does not certify that those who have paid tax have not evaded it. In fact, tax evasion may occur in various forms, such as under-reporting of VAT by firms, and under-invoicing by importers. Therefore, tax compliance itself is a key challenge here in generating adequate tax revenue for financing development.

The fiscal social contract refers to the procedure where citizens are required to pay a certain amount in tax, which is later utilised by the government to finance welfare programs for all citizens. Contemporary scholars have recognised an association between the states' ability to generate taxes and their levels of development (Besley and Persson 2014; Burgess and Stern 1993; Ivanyna and Haldenwang 2013), implying that government-citizen relationships are key in ensuring tax compliance and collecting adequate tax revenue to fund development expenditure.

Given the low tax to GDP ratio in Bangladesh, it is apparent that Bangladesh's tax compliance is relatively lower than neighbouring countries and thus, the fiscal social contract between the government and citizens is weak and distrusting. When citizens believe that the services they receive from the government are not in accordance with what they pay for, i.e. the social contract is not honoured, they are more likely to reduce their tax compliance by evading or avoiding paying income taxes (Haider 2018).

A higher tax to GDP ratio may be achieved by strengthening the social contract between the government and citizens by improving transparency, accountability and participation in the policy-making and budgetary processes. An increase in the current tax base in Bangladesh is likely to lead to a higher tax to GDP ratio, which may be brought about by curtailing the size of informal sector by easing the procedures to incentivise the formalising of informal enterprises. Incentives such as lucrative non-cash benefits for taxpayers may assist in decreasing tax avoidance. Altogether a reform in agenda for the improvement in tax compliance will likely reduce the reliance on regressive taxes and enable greater redistribution of income and curb the mounting inequalities in the economy.

A Human-Nature Compatibility

Poorer households often inhabit areas that are more prone to climate shocks such as cyclones, tidal waves and landslides, and seasonal calamities such as salinity intrusion, river erosion, floods and waterlogging. As they remain perpetually vulnerable to natural disasters, resilience is formed in these communities using indigenous tools and knowledge, buttressed by the public provision of shelters, food and income support at times of crises. Any government intervention in these areas therefore needs to be careful of preserving the balance in the human-nature relationship that has intrinsically evolved in these communities over generations. A policy or intervention devoid of consideration of the impacts on the environment and subsequently the people will likely harm the compatibility between the communities and nature, leaving them more vulnerable, and less resilient, to unforeseen disasters.

Protection of the ecological balance is thus an immutable concern for policy focus and design in meeting development challenges. For improvements in poverty and inequality to be sustainable and longstanding, a compatibility between humans and nature that allows for mutually evolving processes of improvement in well-being is the precursor. In ambitions of achieving high growth rates in the economy, the environmental impact of, for instance, coal fired power plants has been disregarded by policy-makers for the Rampal power plant, a joint venture between Bangladesh and India, being constructed very near the Sundarbans, the largest mangrove forest which has been protecting the coasts from natural disasters.

A lack of harmonising of the needs of the environment leaves coastal populations in greater vulnerability to climate shocks and displacement, with the capacity to overturn the achievements in stability conditions. Use of fossil fuels should be lessened massively and solar and wind-based plants should be established extensively by regaining the control of the power sector through renegotiating the coal and LNG based power plants. Where most of the nations have been abandoning fossil fuels and nuclear power, dependence on such sources does not look future-proof.

Concluding Remarks

The chapter sets out to critically assess the stability, transformability and sustainability issues regarding the trend of poverty and inequality in Bangladesh over the years. The covid-19 pandemic has severely impacted the life and livelihoods of the marginalised sections of the society—particularly the low-income people, women, children, the elderly, the unemployed, the informal sector workers, lower-middle class and middle-class group. Income erosion resulting from the losses in various sectors from the shutdown will create a new poor population in the country, leading to an upward movement in poverty rate for the first time since

1992. Coronavirus has also exposed the deep divide in the society. Income cuts will disproportionately affect those living in a mediocre standard of living, and extraction of liquidity from powerful elites being neglected as a source of revenue is likely to worsen the pre-existing income inequality. Accordingly, the inequality will deepen, with further differentiated return on labour and capital due to erosion of income given the preponderance of most of the labour force engaged in the informal sector and the loss of employment in both formal and informal sectors.

The key stability issues facing the state of poverty in the country is the slowdown in poverty reduction in recent years, insufficient investment on human capital, e.g. education and health, which increase productivity and well-being, absence of social security, and absence of government aided coping mechanisms from shock exposure. The slow reduction in poverty indicates towards a stalemate in the effectiveness of existing poverty eradication policies, combined with a declining real wage particularly for low-skilled labour owing to a lack of human capital development. The meagreness of current social safety nets for the vulnerable population is inconsequential to produce a real impact on the standard of living.

Stability issues in inequality include the concerns of decreasing return on labour vis-à-vis return on capital, which has been aggravated in the post-pandemic context, regional differences in gains in poverty reduction, inequality of education and nutrition, gender disparities in education and earnings, policy and power in taxation, and greater inequality driven by the covid-19 crisis.

In order to be transformable, it is crucial for the economy to undertake a four-pronged approach in ensuring that the achievements in stability are buttressed against systemic shocks. Transformability of the economy will be brought about through policies of active restraint which focus on public goods provision, redistributive actions, macro-financial interventions and structural policy reforms. In addition, an economy's capability of being transformable will depend on the level of public financing for promoting non-erosive coping responses for vulnerable populations as shock exposure cannot be entirely mitigated, and providing a fully-fledged life-cycle based universal social security programme.

Finally, sustainability entails a strengthening of the social contract through active citizenship and building higher trust between the state and citizens so as to inculcate compliance to state directives in the population. The dearth of compliance to state directives was particularly evident in recent times during the imposition of the economic shutdown induced by the pandemic, as workers, particularly in the informal sector, had been at a loss due to a complete erosion of income and livelihood for a prolonged period of time. Simultaneously, the state must also ensure accountability towards citizens and also establish a culture of compatibility between nature and humankind, so as to limit the destruction caused by future climate shocks, and conserve energy resources for production.

References

Al-Samarrai, S. 2008. Governance and Education Inequality in Bangladesh.

Bargain, O., and A. Spadaro. 2008. Optimal Taxation, Social Contract and the Four Worlds of Welfare Capitalism. *Flora* 33 (July): 1–31.

BANBEIS. 2016. Bangladesh Education Statistics 2015. Dhaka: Bangladesh Bureau of Educational Information and Statistics.

BANBEIS. 2019. Bangladesh Education Statistics 2018.

BBS. 2011. Report on Household Income and Expenditure Survey 2010. Dhaka, Bangladesh: Bangladesh Bureau of Statistics.

BBS. 2015. Education Household Survey 2014. Dhaka, Bangladesh: Bangladesh Bureau of Statistics.

BBS. 2016. Report of the Household Income & Expenditure 2016. *Ministry of Planning* 1: 1–5. https://doi.org/10.1007/s13398-014-0173-7.2.

BBS. 2017. Report on Quarterly Labour Force Survey (QLFS) 2015–16. Dhaka.

BBS. 2018. Bangladesh Labour Force Survey 2016–17. Bangladesh Bureau of Statistics.

BBS. 2019. Report on Education Household Survey 2019. Dhaka, Bangladesh: Bangladesh Bureau of Statistics, Statistics and Informatics Division (SID), Ministry of Planning, Government of the People's Republic of Bangladesh.

BBS. 2020. Urban Socioeconomic Assessment Survey 2019. Bangladesh Bureau of Statistics.

BBS and UNICEF. 2015. Multiple Indicator Cluster Survey 2012–13. Dhaka: Bangladesh Bureau of Statistics. New York City: United Nations Children's Fund.

Besley, T., and T. Persson. 2014. Why Do Developing Countries Tax So Little? *Journal of Economic Perspectives* 28 (4): 99–120.

BIGD and PPRC. 2020. PPRC-BIGD Rapid Response Research Livelihoods, Coping and Support During Covid-19 Crisis. BRAC Institute of Governance and Development (BIGD). Power and Participation Research Centre (PPRC).

Bourguignon, F. 2003. The Growth Elasticity of Poverty Reduction: Explaining Heterogeneity Across Countries and Time Periods. In *Inequality and Growth: Theory and Policy Implications*, 1(1). Cambridge: MIT Press.

Bunting, D. 2015. Savings and the Distribution of Income. *Journal of Post Keynesian Economics*. https://doi.org/10.1080/01603477.1991.11489873.

Burgess, R., and N. Stern. 1993. Taxation and Development. *Journal of Economic Literature* 31 (2): 762–830.

Chen, S., and M. Ravallion. 2008. The Developing World Is Poorer Than We Thought, but No Less Successful in the Fight Against Poverty. World Bank Policy Research Working Paper 4703.

Cook, C.J. 1995. Savings Rates and Income Distribution: Further Evidence from LDCs. *Applied Economics*. https://doi.org/10.1080/00036849500000009.

Dynan, K.E., J. Skinner, and S.P. Zeldes. 2004. Do the Rich Save More? *Journal of Political Economy*. https://doi.org/10.1086/381475.

Epaulard, A. 2003. Growth, Income Inequality and Poverty Reduction in Namibia. Poverty Income Inequality and Economic Development in Namibia. Windhoek: Bank of Namibia.

Fosu, A.K. 2009. Inequality and the Impact of Growth on Poverty: Comparative Evidence for Sub-Saharan Africa. *The Journal of Development Studies* 45 (5): 726–745.

Haider, A.A. 2018. The Problem with Our Tax System. *The Daily Star*. Available at: https://www.thedailystar.net/opinion/governance/news/the-problem-our-tax-system-1661620. Accessed 14 December 2019.

Hassan, M.H. 2017. Determinants and Effects of the Informal Economy: Bangladesh Perspective. *SSRN Electronic Journal* (March). https://doi.org/10.2139/ssrn.2777694.

Hussain, Zahid. 2020. The Social Protection Budget Continue to Elude. *The Business Standard*, June 20. https://tbsnews.net/analysis/social-protection-budget-continues-elude-95905#:~:text=It's%20not%20just%20that%20the,in%20the%20outgoing%20fiscal%20year!. Accessed 26 October 2020.

Hynes, W., B. Trump, P. Love, and I. Linkov. 2020. Bouncing Forward: A Resilience Approach to Dealing with COVID-19 and Future Systemic Shocks. *Environment Systems and Decisions* 25: 1–11.

ILO. 2017. World Social Protection Report 2017–19: Universal Social Protection to Achieve the Sustainable Development Goals.

ILO. 2020. ILOStat. International Labor Organization.

Ivanyna, M., and C. Haldenwang. 2013. Assessing the Tax Performance of Developing Countries. Bonn: German Development Institute.

Kalwij, A., and A. Verschoor. 2007. Not by Growth Alone: The Role of the Distribution of Income in Regional Diversity in Poverty Reduction. *European Economic Review* 51: 805–829.

Kuznets, S. 1955. Economic Growth and Income Inequality. *American Economic Review* 45: 1–28.

Marx, K. 1867. *Das Kapital*.

Ministry of Finance. 2018. Bangladesh Economic Review. Ministry of Finance, Government of Bangladesh.

Ministry of Finance. 2019. Bangladesh Economic Review. Ministry of Finance, Government of Bangladesh.

Ministry of Finance. 2020. Budget at a Glance. Bangladesh: Ministry of Finance.

National Board of Revenue. 2019. Annual Report 2017–18. Dhaka, Bangladesh.

Osmani, S.R. 2015. Linking Equity and Growth in Bangladesh. Background paper prepared for the Seventh Five Year Plan of The Government of Bangladesh.

Osmani, S.R. 2018. Aspects of the Poverty Scenario in Bangladesh During 2010–2016. *Bangladesh Development Studies* XLI (3): 1–31.

Piketty, T. 2003. Income Inequality in France, 1901–1998. *Journal of Political Economy* 111 (5): 1004–1042. https://doi.org/10.1086/376955.

Piketty, T. 2014. Theories of Persistent Inequality and Intergenerational Mobility. *The Business Times* 1: 1–34. https://doi.org/10.1016/S1574-0056(00)80011-1.

Planning Commission. 2019. Revised Annual Development Programme (RADP). Government of the People's Republic of Bangladesh.

Rahman, M.Z. 2020. Income Elasticity of Poverty: Recent Estimates for South Asian Countries. *Economics*: 4. https://ir.library.illinoisstate.edu/urseco/4.

Rahman, M.Z., and R. Ram. 2020. Income Elasticity of Poverty: Recent Estimates for South Asian Countries. *Empirical Economics Review* 10 (3).

Rahman, H.Z., and I. Matin. 2020. *Livelihoods, Coping, and Support During COVID-19 Crisis*. Dhaka: BRAC Institute of Governance and Development.

Ram. R. 2011. Growth Elasticity of Poverty: Direct Estimates from Recent Data. *Applied Economics* 43(19): 2433–2440.

Ram, R. 2015. Income Elasticity of Poverty: Estimates for South Asian Countries. *The Economics and Finance Letters* 2(1): 1–7.

Razzaque, Abdur. 2020. Rethinking Social Protection Responses to the Covid-19 Crisis: Issues and Policy Priorities for Bangladesh. Prepared for the General Economics Division (GED), Planning Commission, Government of Bangladesh.

Ravallion, M. 1997. Can High Inequality Developing Countries Escape Absolute Poverty? *Economics Letters* 56: 51–57.

Ricardo, D. 1817. On the Principles of Political Economy and Taxation. publicado en.

Sahota, G.S., W.A. Darity, and P.J. Taubman. 1993. Saving and Distribution. *The Economics of Saving*. https://doi.org/10.1007/978-94-017-3294-9_5.

Santos, I., I. Sharif, H.Z. Rahman, and H. Zaman. 2011. How Do the Poor Cope with Shocks in Bangladesh? Evidence from Survey Data. The World Bank.

Schmidt-Hebbel, K., and L. Servén. 2000. Does Income Inequality Raise Aggregate Saving? *Journal of Development Economics* 61 (2): 417–446. https://doi.org/10.1016/S0304-3878(00)00063-8.

Schneider, F. 2002. Size and Measurement of the Informal Economy in 110 Countries. In *Workshop of Australian National Tax Centre, ANU, Canberra* (Vol. 17).

Shilpi, M., S. Hasnayen, T. Ilahi, M. Parvin, and K. Sultana. 2017. Education Scenario in Bangladesh: Gender Perspective. Bangladesh Bureau of Statistics, UCEP Bangladesh and Diakonia Bangladesh.

Social Security Administration. 2018. Office of Retirement and Disability Policy, USA.

Stiglitz, J. 1973a. Approaches to the Economics of Discrimination. *American Economic Review*. https://doi.org/10.2307/1817088.

Stiglitz, J.E. 1973b. Education and Inequality. *The ANNALS of the American Academy of Political and Social Science* 409 (1): 135–145. https://doi.org/10.1177/000271627340900115.

Schwab, K., and X.B. Sala-i-Martín. 2015. The Global Competitiveness Report 2013–2014. In World Economic Forum, International Center for Competitiveness.

Titumir, R.A.M. 2020. From Social Solidarity to Economic Solidarity. *New Age*, May 14. https://www.newagebd.net/article/106369/from-social-solidarity-to-economic-solidarity. Accessed 26 October 2020.

UNCTAD. 2020. UNCTADStat. Accessed from https://unctadstat.unctad.org/.

UNDP. 2018. Bangladesh Quarterly Development Update, October–December, 2017. United Nations Development Programme, Bangladesh Country Office, IDB.

Unnayan Onneshan. 2019. Balancing the Imbalances: A Rapid Assessment of National Budget 2019–20. Dhaka. Bangladesh: Unnayan Onneshan.

Unnayan Onneshan. 2020. Whither Bending the Curves for Life and Livelihoods: A Rapid Assesment of National Budget 2020–21.

WEF. 2020. Global Social Mobility Index 2020. https://www.weforum.org/reports/global-social-mobility-index-2020-why-economies-benefit-from-fixing-inequality#:~:text=Denmark%20tops%20the%20rankings%20with,)%20and%20Iceland%20(82.7). Accessed 26 October 2020.

World Bank. 2006. Equity and Development. World Development Report 2006. Washington, DC: World Bank.

World Bank. 2019a. *Bangladesh Poverty Assessment: Facing Old and New Frontiers in Poverty Reduction*. Washington DC: World Bank.

World Bank. 2019b. *Poverty and Equity Data Portal*. https://povertydata.worldbank.org/poverty/home/. Accessed 8 December 2019.

CHAPTER 8

Conclusions: Institutions, Political Settlement and Economic Outcome

The book sets out to analyse the necessary and sufficient conditions of the development of the economy of Bangladesh. The necessary conditions imply the factors of economic growth—land, labour, capital and technology while the sufficient condition is epitomised here by political settlement, which has further been bifurcated into formal and informal institutions (Fig. 8.1). The analysis has hovered around the achievements in growth, the real sector, the financial sector, education, health, poverty and inequality, while focusing on stability, transformability and sustainability conditions.

Political settlement is not a 'common understanding between elites.' Rather it refers to the balance or distribution of power between contending social groups and social classes, on which any state is based (Khan 1995, 2000). In the long line of thinking in the historical political economy, starting with Marx, analysing the balance of power between contending groups and classes has been central in exploring the formation and change of institutions such as the process of democratisation (Moore 1966), the transition from feudalism to capitalism (Brenner 1976), the effectiveness with which industrial policy is implemented (Khan 1995; Kohli 2004), and the closely related effort of historical institutionalists to explain the varied routes to capitalist transformation (Hall and Soskice 2001). Historical sociologists have also deployed the concept in a similar

R. A. M. Titumir, *Numbers and Narratives in Bangladesh's Economic Development*,
https://doi.org/10.1007/978-981-16-0658-8_8

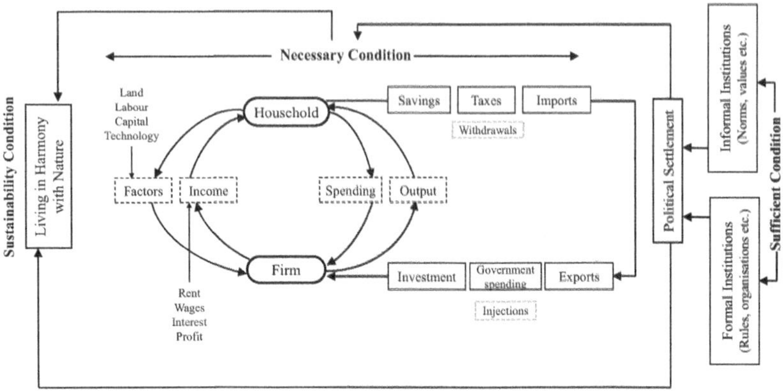

Fig. 8.1 Theoretical framework (*Source* Prepared by Author)

way, for instance Melling's (1991) analysis of industrial capitalism and social insurance in Britain, where he argues that "the social policies of the state formed part of a wider political settlement at key moments of development", stressing the limits of analyses that focus only on economic and state structures (Di John and Putzel 2009).

Both formal and informal institutions have been presumed as the sufficient conditions for development. Institutions determine the structure of economic incentives in the society and the productive allocation of resources. If institutions function well, create an inclusive and competitive political environment and ensure checks and balances, continued growth can be achieved. If sufficient conditions are not accomplished, the quality of growth and development cannot be attained. Absence of meeting the sufficient conditions raises the question of sustainability of the quantitative achievement.

The circular flow of income comprises the necessary conditions for growth by enabling a greater involvement of households and firms in expanding the potential of earnings on each factor of production. Underlying the rapid growth experience, lies an exhaustive labour extraction function, particularly in the RMG sector that uses cheap labour, and a heavy reliance on informal employment and remittance inflows from low and semi-skilled migrant workers. Problems of low diversification, overuse of fertilisers and land fragmentation hamper the growth of the agriculture sector. The manufacturing sector is marred by low expansion of productive capacity, employment generation and technological catching-up. In the time series analyses in the preceding chapters, the discrepancies in the stability over the years of these major sectors have been identified.

The recent ascendency of socio-economic development in Bangladesh instead of poor governance has been lamented as "development surprise" (Devarajan 2005; Asadullah et al. 2014), "development paradox" (Chowdhury et al. 2013) or "Bangladesh conundrum" (Mahmud et al. 2008). These lamentations about the quantitative achievement in terms of different social and economic indicators neither reckon the exact characteristics of the economy of Bangladesh nor describe the causality between political variables and economic factors. Instead tagging such adulations suppresses or fails to capture the intersectionality amongst institutions, economic outcomes and political settlement, which requires serious scrutiny.

Much of the quantifiable changes during 1991–2006 may be attributed to the competitive nature of clientelism. There has however been a dearth of development in qualitative terms during the period, leading to fragilities hindering transformability. Countries failing to observe the sufficient conditions of development along with necessary conditions have been found miscarrying their high growth performance and social development. Stable, transformed and sustained economic outcome requires favourable political settlement and institutional capacity along with necessary economic variables—land, labour, capital and technology. There is, therefore, no reason left to be surprised.

It is nevertheless the nature of the institutions, which shapes the norms and values existing in society. Over the years, accumulation of wealth has become the yardstick of values indoctrinated by informal institutions that consist of resource-dependent networks. The particular form of materialist incentives of primitive accumulation of resources through the use of power and coercion has led to a system of clientelist political networks in Bangladesh. The clientelist resource-dependent networks, for perpetuating their objective of accumulation of wealth and power, are symbiotically connected at the vertical layer (local, regional, and national) and are intrinsically interlinked at the horizontal layer with business, administration, law-enforcing agencies and the judicial system.

The chapter therefore attempts to summarise the relationships between necessary and sufficient conditions in all the sectors discussed in the book. The principal task is to demonstrate as to how institutions—formal and informal—underwritten by political settlement have shaped the outcomes for the stability, transformability and sustainability of the economy and its various sectors.

Power, Institutions and Economy

The confrontational nature of Bangladesh polity is widespread. Yet, there is little attention in framing, let alone unearthing, the causes-drivers-determinants-process of such an outcome. This requires a coherent comprehension of the dynamics of political competition and the accumulation strategies pursued by different political parties in their struggle to capture and sustain power and material benefit in this resource-scarce country.

In the post-military era, there is a newfound belief in the political landscape of the country that the power will shuttle between the two major political parties. The entrepreneurs interested in accumulation of wealth started to venture into political projects, recognising politics as another form of enterprise, and realising that other means of profiteering are either painful or a long-run affair and that maximisation of profit even out of traditional commercial enterprise is directly related to a degree of connection with political processes.

The nature of competition is motivated by usurpations of assets and there is an incentive to compete for accumulation of political power of the state. The cadres of the newly-elected government who were in opposition before the change of the guard take control from the cadres of the outgoing government who wait for their turn and continue to agitate against the government. This cyclical pattern of control, agitation, and return for control perpetuates the reproduction of the politics of confrontation. The material basis of this particular form of accumulation has, thus, given birth to a nexus amongst politicians, members of the administration, the law enforcing agencies and the judicial system in Bangladesh. Such a nexus is cyclical and transient, and always houses with the party/alliance in power.

The reproduction of the networked system lies in the ability to capture resources and consequential distribution, either directly to grassroots, or through creation of provision for central, regional and grassroots leaders. This requires pursuance of 'winners-take-all' strategy and use of power and coercion over administrative, law-enforcing, judicial, and criminal justice systems. In this process the opposition members become totally deprived, waiting with high intent and figured strategies of how to multiply the loss incurred during the period of absence from power. The system thus has been able to create on its own a system of reproduction and welfare system for members belonging to factions of different parties, at the expense of ordinary citizens. The networked system of factions in Bangladesh has given birth and sustained a system of private force, parallel to the apparatus of the state, in order to steer the process of acquiring and maintenance of command over the captured resources, as such process warrants considerable expression of intimidation, coercion, and oppression.

This was true for the period of competitive clientelism during 1991–2006 where the nature of power was cyclical and transient as the change in regime with each election led to a change of hands in power. However, the weakening of opponent parties and a growing invincibility of a single regime gains traction; the existing clientelism adopted a more permanent and subsequently authoritarian stance. The values and norms established through these clientelist networks become longstanding and deeply embedded in the political processes. The recent norms of resource-dependent clientelism and rent-seeking lead not to a capture of power or elite consensus by clientelists, but rather a form of political settlement that enables primitive capital accumulation through coercive power of the state. The nature of clientelism in Bangladesh in recent times therefore cannot be explained in terms of Weber's patrimonialism or Clapham's neo-patrimonialism—it does not remain to be an issue of patrons using resources of the state to serve the interests of the clientelist networks, rather these networks establish an informal channel for transactions involving resources of the state and economy by being embedded with the party/alliance in power.

The clientelist networks are grabbing the economy by dint of state power. The political process in Bangladesh has evolved in a particular direction, corresponding to the characteristics of political activists and the incentive-structure to reproduce the political system. As such, the main pillars of the state, namely a functioning judiciary, an effective parliament and a civil administration to implement the political mandate for the people given by the people to the elected representatives of the people, are getting eroded. The motive of the ruling elite is simply to have a centralised state with concentration of power. The system has become authoritarian and cannot withstand even muted dissent and public scrutiny.

The previous chapters demonstrate that the regulatory discrepancies in macroeconomic management are owing to institutional fragility. For example, the huge amount of default loans in banking sector and the widespread siphoning of capital abroad are direct resultants of clientelism. Public investment and employment creation therefore compromised, results in poor pace of poverty reduction and a rapid rise in inequality. The failure to bring the economy to order, therefore, results in unsustainable economic outcomes, which go to the pockets of few at the expense of many. These unequal and unjust economic outcomes are reflected in every sphere of the economy.

The autonomy and credibility of institutions are at risk. For example, estimation of the rate of growth does not corroborate with other economic data, which raises question against the concerned data collection agencies of the government. The provision of the real sector, health, education, poverty, inequality, banking and finance has been proved failing due to mismanagement and irregularities. The government and other state agencies, however, remain out of public scrutiny and accountability. The reason behind the non-responsiveness of the state lies in the nature of the state. The uneven power distribution of the state has made an exploitative and authoritarian system of governance that only serves the interest of the powerful ruling class, therefore purports widespread anomalies in the state.

The recent spurt in quantitative achievement, however, cannot be transformed and sustained if the institutions and political settlement do not function in an inclusive manner. A key over-riding challenge also remains to develop and enhance productive capacity and provision of public services for a decent living. This would require productive use of technology and infrastructural facilities. Skills—much beyond traditional concept of education—and technology are key elements in the future transformative equation. So are the questions of employment creation and reduction in inequality to establish a fairer society. The sufficient condition for achieving those objectives is an inclusive political system.

The concept of 'human dignity' of the citizens embodies a number of intrinsic meanings, denoting that an individual at least enjoys freedom. Citizenship entails an individual to be an active participant, indicating his or her political, social and economic rights. The liberals have favoured 'negative freedom'—the rights of non-interference, absence of obstacles and no harm to others. Therefore, citizenship and rights go hand in hand,

and are inalienable and sometimes even absolute. The fundamental crisis of the Bangladesh polity is the citizens' disempowerment.

Institutions and the Economy

The story of growth in Bangladesh, therefore, is nothing like a surprise or paradox. The growth of Bangladesh was made possible in large by migration of the underemployed from the countryside to urban cities and flowing out to the world over, mostly concentrating in West Asia. The remittance from home and abroad has fuelled largely consumption-led economic growth. The continual greater-than-before participation of women in the labour market and women's entrepreneurship along with their demonstrated resilience has made inspiring changes. The farmers have continued to work tirelessly in their green croplands, with innovation and intensity, despite distress sale of products, without fair prices, with high input cost, and changing climatic conditions. There has been a creeping rise of entrepreneurship. Despite labour being at the heart of such development, labourers are dispossessed in a number of ways. There is a growing disparity between the rate of growth in employment and unemployment, implying fragility of absorption capacity and vulnerability of labourers to low wages and non-adherence to rights. In this pace, like other successful countries, the state played a significant role either through formulating favourable policies or through providing different incentive structures. The quality of the changes, however, has remained questionable amidst fragile institutions and an extractive political system.

It is observed that the spurt of growth in almost all of the macroeconomic indicators started and was robust during the 1990s. Afterwards, there have been negative trends in most of the provisions, which have emerged as earnest concerns for the economy. It is, therefore, imperative to explore the reasons. The transformability conditions, described in this book, underscore that competitive clientelism was present during the 1990s which created business confidence and a favourable environment for productive expansion of the economy in contrast to authoritarian, uncontested and extractive clientelism. The political and institutional arrangement, therefore, has been seen to significantly affect the economy.

Growth and Real Sectors

Throughout the book, the analysis suggests that the rate of GDP growth is overestimated, which does not corroborate with other data. It is observed that the average rate of export growth was highest during the 1990s. After that it has been gradually declining despite the rise in export volume. Despite an increase in the volume of remittance inflows since the 1980s, the growth rate of remittance has drastically declined during 2010–2018. Despite the increase of gross savings as percent of GDP, the growth rate of savings has also declined during the period of 2010–2018. In addition, though volume of gross savings increased, investment as percent of GDP has not increased accordingly. The gap between savings and investment, therefore, suggests widespread capital flight, which is also supported by many international organisations. The productive expansion has been thwarted, resulted in jobless growth. The private investment demand has been depressed due to a lack of business confidence owing to political uncertainty and inadequate availability of infrastructure primarily due to reduced public investment, as the government has been diverting resources to service non-development expenditure, including payment to employees and debt servicing.

The main two drivers of growth—RMG export and remittance inflows are showing a declining trend of rate of growth (Chapter 1, Growth). Moreover, the method of agriculture has become unsustainable leaving a heavy toll on nature and environment, with overuse of fertilisers and wasteful irrigation (Chapter 2, Agriculture). The declining trend in agricultural productivity has been a serious concern. In terms of food security Bangladesh stood lowest in South Asia.

If the institutions start to fracture in a country, there arise problems in maintaining the rate of development. For example, in Bangladesh, investment picked up to a level and then was caught up in inertia to remain stagnant (Chapter 1, Growth). A conspicuous example is the case of the banking sector and the capital market wherein plundering and breakdown of discipline have led to perpetual fragility.

Institutions are as important a factor in ensuring growth as are sound economic fundamentals. Post-colonial Bangladesh is being run by a continuing legacy of civil and military bureaucrats as well as the nouveau rich, who are thriving through primitive accumulation of capital. For this, they prefer an absolute hold on power. Therefore, the political class, the different shades of bureaucracy, and the businesses, in most cases come together to procure and secure their wealth by using or abusing power. Thus, the drive for primitive accumulation of resources has led to formation of clientelist networks in Bangladesh in every walk of economic activity. The never-ending urge for primitive accumulation of capital has led the ruling elite to justify this comical slogan of "development first, democracy later." A lack of action for political freedom can only multiply human misery and intensify law and order breakdown, leading to the rise of extremism and destabilisation.

Financial Sector

The financial sector has also failed to form capital and productivity up to the marks. The amount of non-performing loan as percent of total loans is higher than neighbouring, East Asian and OECD countries. The frequent scams in the capital market have quashed capital formation over the years.

Of late, crisis in the banking sector has made the financial sector in Bangladesh the worst among the emerging Asian countries reflecting poor risk management ability of the central bank, the Bangladesh Bank (BB). The recent heist again shook the financial system and the economy. The ongoing crisis in the banking sector, mainly due to increased default loans, reflects the institutional weakness of the financial system and causes increased cost of fund and shortfall in bank capital. The government recapitalises the shortfall with taxpayers' money instead of correcting the faults of the institutions, which not only increases the burden on taxpayers but also causes a loss to the economy. Besides being a dysfunctional financial sector, it is also mired in high rates of interest and spreads—the difference between the lending and the deposit rates. The goal of financial inclusion remains rhetorical.

Share market scams in 1996 and 2010 caused a huge loss to the small and medium investors and many became penniless. The gloomy situation has been continuing as investors have lost their confidence in investing in the market. The problems of the capital markets in Bangladesh are structural. There are syndicates colluding with each other to artificially influence the prices resulting in huge profits for them at the expense of the average investors who put in their hard-earned lifetime savings. The Securities and Exchange Commission (SEC), which is supposed to regulate, seems to favour the syndicates, which primarily consist of high-net-worth individuals and the stock exchange members, resulting in an "artificial demand-driven market."

Education and Health

The stability conditions of education can be termed as a functioning stage which consists of three main factors- access, skill formation and innovation and citizenship formation. Access incorporates enrolment, completion, repetition and adult literacy rates. Afterwards, the stability stage conduces transformation, where learning to know, learning to do and learning to live be as well as learning to live together become prime factors.

Since health is a public good, it is imperative to ascertain that people from all sections get health benefits irrespective of their socio-economic status, dignity, religion, class, race and other categories. Low and middle-income countries have been struggling with policy orientation regarding the health sector through experimentation, such as the privatisation of health services, targeted approach to provide treatment facilities, social safety net programmes and others. Health expenditure has increased in Bangladesh in recent years, whilst public provision of healthcare has declined. Bangladesh, a state in which wage inequality has been prevailing insidiously is burdened with high out-of-pocket expenditure to attain health services.

The expenditure in social sectors like education and health has been increasing in nominal terms. The rate of increase, however, has slowed down in the last several years. In addition, these two sectors have been suffering from insufficient budgetary allocation as well as from the slow rate of implementation of the Annual Development programme (ADP). The declaration in allocation is attributed to the diversion of resources to meet up growing payment on account of principal and interest (this has become the largest expenditure item in the revenue budget of the country) and rent-accruing subsidies.

The outcomes in education and health are not satisfactory either, therefore, contributing little to human capital generation and citizenship creation. The quality of education does not match with market demand, creating large number of unskilled graduates. Though life expectancy has improved significantly, the out-of-pocket expenditure is highest compared to neighbouring, East Asian and OECD countries.

Poverty and Inequality

The rate of reduction in poverty has slowed down. As regards equality, inequality in terms of income and access to resources, rural-urban divide, male–female gap is conspicuous and increasing faster than before. The benefit of productivity growth was being enjoyed mostly by the owners of non-labour inputs—the richer segment of the society. The rampant rise in inequality supports this contention that the return to labour is higher that return to capital. Moreover, real wage is declining over the years as well as the rate of poverty reduction has declined since 2010. The dimensions of inequality and deprivation are expanding progressively amidst fragile institutions and an extractive political settlement.

Most strikingly, there is little discussion on the wealth inequality. Thus, advantages of birth, for instance, harbours a culture in which work and effort is discouraged. Lack of institutions has worsened inequality. Bangladesh is being run by intermediate classes, who are interested only in securing wealth by any means. Broadly, the intermediate classes comprise rich and middle-class peasants, urban petty bourgeoisies and educated middle classes, who have greater degree of organisational ability than those of workers, poor peasants and the unemployed illiterates. This also brings home an absence, and crisis in formation, of elite or bourgeoisie.

The political process in Bangladesh has evolved in a particular direction, corresponding to the characteristics of political activists and the incentive-structure to reproduce the political system. The particular form of materialist incentives of primitive accumulation of resources through use of power and coercion has led to a system of clientelist political networks in Bangladesh. The clientelist resource-dependent networks, for perpetuating their objective of accumulation of wealth and power, are symbiotically connected at a vertical layer (local, regional, and national) and are intrinsically interlinked at the horizontal level with business, administration, law-enforcing agencies and the judicial system.

The ever-increasing hunger for accretion of economic rents wants an exclusive political system to spread all over the horizontal and vertical levels, creating a culture of occupying a position—from member of parliament down to the chairman of the Union Parishad—uncontested or without any competition from opposition political parties. The process of fear and exclusivity has created a sense of low business confidence, which has resulted in depressed investment demand, leading to a reduction in job creation. The economic rents also fly out from the country as exhibited through increased capital flight from Bangladesh.

The absence of an inclusive political system has also exerted pressures on the institutions, and as a result, the institutions have been degenerating. In order for economic growth and social development to be sustainable, the sufficient condition is a representational public order.

Only a democratically accountable system of governance can advance the three core principles of the war of independence. All of these lead to the idea of establishing a new social order between the citizens and the state through a new social contract. A new and strengthened social contract should aim for shared prosperity and equal opportunities in creating an egalitarian republic, fulfilling the vision of the struggle for independence. A fairer, more equitable system can be brought about through addressing the multiple vulnerabilities and fragilities of the state that poses a threat to the well-being of its citizens.

Achievement of the sufficient conditions for making social development sustainable should lead to the pursuit of buttressing institutions so as to construct a welfare state that caters to the holistic and equitable well-being of its citizens in terms of economic, political, social and environmental functioning. Bangladesh's hope sits on pluralism and an inclusive political system can infuse actualisation of its unlimited potentials of shared prosperity which is indeed stable, transformable and sustainable.

References

Asadullah, M.N., A. Savoia, and W. Mahmud. 2014. Paths to Development: Is There a Bangladesh Surprise? *World Development* 62: 138–154.

Brenner, R. 1976. The Origins of Capitalist Development: A Critique of Neo-Smithian Marxism. *New Left Review* 104 (July–August): 25–92.

Chowdhury, A.M.R., A. Bhuiya, M.E. Chowdhury, S. Rasheed, Z. Hussain, and L.C. Chen. 2013. The Bangladesh Paradox: Exceptional Health Achievement Despite Economic Poverty. *The Lancet* 382 (9906): 1734–1745.

Devarajan, S. 2005. South Asian Surprises. *Economic and Political Weekly* 40: 4013–4015.

Di John, J., and J. Putzel. 2009. Political Settlements: Issues Paper. Discussion Paper. University of Birmingham, Birmingham, UK. Available at https://www.gsdrc.org/docs/open/EIRS7.pdf. Accessed 25 October 2020.

Hall, P., and D. Soskice. 2001. *Varieties of Capitalism: The Institutional Foundations of Comparative Advantage*. Oxford: Oxford University Press.

Khan, M. 1995. State Failure in Weak States: A Critique of New Institutionalist Explanations. In *The New Institutional Economics and Third World Development*, ed. J. Harriss, J. Hunter, and C. Lewis. London: Routledge.

Khan, M. 2000. Rent-Seeking as a Process: Inputs, Rent-Outcomes and Net Effects. In *Rents, Rent-Seeking and Economic Development*, ed. M. Khan and K.S. Jomo. Cambridge: Cambridge University Press.

Kohli, A. 2004. *State-Directed Development: Political Power and Industrialization in the Global Periphery*. Cambridge: Cambridge University Press.

Mahmud, W., S. Ahmed, and S. Mahajan. 2008. Economic Reforms, Growth, and Governance: The Political Economy Aspects of Bangladesh's Development Surprise. In *Leadership and Growth*, 227. Washington, DC: World Bank Publications.

Melling, J. 1991. Industrial Capitalism and the Welfare of the State: The Role of Employers in the Comparative Development of Welfare States. A Review of Recent Research. *Sociology* 25 (2) (May): 219–239.

Moore, B. 1966. *The Social Origins of Democracy and Dictatorship: Lord and Peasant in the Making of the Modern World*. Boston: Beacon Press.

Index

R. A. M. Titumir, *Numbers and Narratives in Bangladesh's Economic Development*,
https://doi.org/10.1007/978-981-16-0658-8

The manufacturer's authorised representative in the EU is Springer
Nature Customer Service Centre GmbH, Europaplatz 3, 69115 Heidelberg,
Germany. If you have any concerns regarding our products, please
contact ProductSafety@springernature.com

Printed and bound by CPI Group (UK) Ltd, Croydon, CR0 4YY
30/09/2026
02225326-0007